Form and content of company accounts

Fifth edition

Coopers & Lybrand

Form and content of company accounts

Fifth edition

Comprehensive coverage of disclosure requirements of the Companies Acts 1985 and 1989, FRSs, SSAPs and the Yellow Book

Croner Publications Ltd
Croner House
London Road
Kingston upon Thames
Surrey KT2 6SR
Tel: 081-574 3333

Fifth edition 1993

Published by
Croner Publications Ltd
Croner House
London Road
Kingston Upon Thames
Surrey KT2 6SR
Telephone: 081 547 3333

British Library Cataloguing in Publication Data

Form and content of company accounts: comprehensive
coverage of disclosure requirements of the Companies Act
1985, FRSs, SSAPs and the Yellow Book. - 5th ed.
1. Great Britain. Companies. Accounts. Law
I. Coopers & Lybrand. Firm

ISBN 1 85524 165 X

Printed in Great Britain by
Whitstable Litho Printers Ltd., Whitstable, Kent

Preface

Since the publication of the previous edition of this book, much change has taken place in the area of financial reporting in the UK. A new era of improved financial reporting was heralded by the establishment of an independent Accounting Standards Board (ASB) overseen by a Financial Reporting Council and backed up by a Review Panel. Since its inception in August 1990, the ASB has issued three Financial Reporting Standards of which FRS 3 'Reporting Financial Performance', which introduces a fourth primary statement, is by far the most radical in its application. Also, the ASB has issued discussion documents and exposure drafts of its Statement of Principles that will form the framework for issuing future accounting standards and provide a basis on which to exercise judgement in resolving accounting issues. Through its Urgent Issues Task Force (UITF), the ASB has also been active in providing timely and authoritative guidance on a number of new and emerging issues. To date, the UITF has published seven Abstracts. The Review Panel, the body set up to challenge accounts where there appears to be a departure from the specific requirements of the Companies Act 1985 and accounting standards which might lead to the accounts in question not giving a true and fair view, is also having a growing influence on the standard of financial reporting in this country.

This latest edition incorporates all the accounting pronouncements published by the ASB and the UITF as at 28 February 1993. Significant rulings made by the Review Panel are also explained. The book does not comment on the ASB's Statement of Principles, because not all of the individual chapters have been issued and those that have are only discussion documents or exposure drafts.

As in previous editions, the book is arranged to provide easy access to all the requirements of the Companies Act 1985*, various statutory instruments (including a new one on small and medium-sized companies), accounting standards and, for listed companies, the continuing obligations imposed by The International Stock Exchange's Yellow Book. The book follows the structure of accounts required by the Companies Act 1985, and draws on the enormous fund of experience of the authors, Coopers & Lybrand. It also covers other matters related to the preparation and publication of accounts, requirements for accounting and statutory records and certain of the Act's rules on capital and distribution of profits. This edition also contains a specimen annual report showing the style and the layout commonly adopted in the UK.

Form and content of company accounts has been written by National Accounting Support in Coopers & Lybrand. This edition has been revised by **Jyoti Ghosh**. Previous contributors are **Tony Bingham** and **David Pimm**.

* In the book a reference to the Companies Act 1985 followed by a reference to the Companies Act 1989 in brackets is to the relevant section or paragraph of the 1985 Act *as amended* by the 1989 Act. In many cases the 1989 Act replaces a section of the 1985 Act in its entirety.

Acknowledgement

Permission of Her Majesty's Stationary Office to reproduce the balance sheet and profit and loss account formats from the Companies Act 1985 is gratefully acknowledged.

List of chapters

Detailed contents

Page

Chapter 1 Introduction

Chapter 2 Directors' Report

Chapter 2 *continued*

Chapter 3 Format

Chapter 4 Accounting Principles and Policies

Chapter 5 Balance Sheet

Chapter 6 Profit and Loss Account

Chapter 6 *continued*

1 Introduction

General

1 This book summarises the statutory and other disclosure requirements for the accounts of both companies and groups. It covers the requirements of the Companies Acts 1985 and 1989, Statements of Standard Accounting Practice (SSAPs), Financial Reporting Standards (FRSs), Urgent Issues Task Force Abstracts (UITF Abstracts) and The International Stock Exchange's Yellow Book. Recommendations made by the Cadbury Committee in its report on 'The financial aspects of corporate governance' are also covered, where relevant. Further comment and explanation is provided by the author, Coopers & Lybrand, where there is uncertainty in interpreting the statutory requirements or where additional disclosure may be desirable. In cases of difficulty, reference should always be made to the relevant legislative or other accounting pronouncements. For this reason the statutory or other authority is indicated in the reference column wherever possible.

2 The prime requirement of company law is that the accounts of both companies and groups should give a true and fair view of the state of the company's or group's affairs and of its profit or loss for each financial year.

3 Company law also prescribes in detail the required form and content of the balance sheet, profit and loss account and notes to the accounts.

4 The overriding requirement to give a true and fair view means that:

(a) where compliance with the detailed requirements would not be sufficient to give a true and fair view, additional information must be given;

(b) where, in special circumstances, compliance with the detailed requirements would be inconsistent with the requirement to give a true and fair view, the accounts should depart from those requirements to the extent necessary. Details must be given of the departure indicating the reasons and the effect.

5 No definition of a true and fair view is provided in statute, but it is generally accepted that, to give such a view, accounts must:

(a) be prepared on the basis of the four fundamental accounting concepts (viz going concern, accruals, consistency, prudence); 1985 4 sch 10-13 SSAP 2:14

(b) determine separately each individual asset or liability that makes up a particular item; 1985 4 sch 14

(c) present an overall picture that is in accordance with the economic substance of the transaction rather than its legal form and is not in any way misleading or biased;

(d) employ appropriate accounting policies consistently applied;

(e) disclose all information material to a proper understanding of the accounts;

(f) describe the amounts in the accounts in such a way that their true nature is explained unambiguously; and

(g) strike a balance between completeness of disclosure and the summarisation necessary for clarity.

6 The Act permits, but does not require, directors to depart from any of the four generally accepted fundamental accounting concepts and the separate valuation rule for assets and liabilities in preparing the accounts if there are special reasons for doing so. In that situation, the facts must be explained, together with the reasons for the departure and the effects thereof (see Chapter 3). 1985 4 sch 15

Materiality

7 The detailed requirements set out in schedules 4 and 4A to the Companies Act 1985 and in accounting standards may be disregarded if the amounts involved are not material in the context of the particular requirement. Amounts may generally be regarded as immaterial if it is judged that they would be unlikely to affect a user's understanding of the accounts. 1985 4 sch 86

Sources of disclosure requirements

8 The Companies Act 1985 (as amended by the Companies Act 1989) lays down minimum statutory requirements for the preparation of accounts of companies and groups. These requirements are supplemented by:

(a) Financial Reporting Standards;

(b) Statements of Standard Accounting Practice;

(c) Urgent Issues Task Force Abstracts; and

(d) The Continuing Obligations in The International Stock Exchange's Yellow Book (for listed companies only).

9 In addition to summarising the disclosure requirements contained in the above, this book deals with certain legislative requirements in connection with a company's accounts which do not strictly relate to disclosure (e.g. the Companies Act regulations on the filing of accounts).

10 This edition includes requirements published up to 28 February 1993. The main new requirements since the previous edition are as follows:

(a) SSAP 4 (revised) - 'Accounting for government grants' - effective for accounting periods beginning on or after 1 July 1990;

(b) SSAP 15 (amended) - 'Accounting for deferred tax' - effective immediately;

(c) SSAP 25 - 'Segmental reporting' - effective for accounting periods beginning on or after 1 July 1990;

(d) FRS 1 - 'Cash flow statements' - effective for accounting periods ending on or after 23 March 1992;

(e) FRS 2 - 'Accounting for subsidiary undertakings' - effective for accounting periods ending on or after 23 December 1992;

(f) FRS 3 - 'Reporting financial performance' - effective for accounting periods ending on or after 22 June 1993;

(g) UITF Abstract 1 - 'Convertible bonds - supplemental interest/premium' - effective for accounting periods ending on or after 31 August 1991;

(h) UITF Abstract 2 - 'Restructuring costs' - withdrawn (superseded by FRS 3);

(i) UITF Abstract 3 - 'Treatment of goodwill on disposal of a business' - effective for accounting periods ending on or after 23 January 1992 (note: this abstract has been incorporated into FRS 2);

(j) UITF Abstract 4 - 'Presentation of long-term debtors in current assets' - effective for accounting periods ending on or after 23 August 1992;

(k) UITF Abstract 5 - 'Transfers from current assets to fixed assets' - effective for accounting periods ending on or after 23 December 1992;

(l) UITF Abstract 6 - 'Accounting for post-retirement benefits other than pensions' - effective for accounting periods ending on or after 23 December 1994 (23 December 1992 for disclosures);

(m) UITF Abstract 7 - 'True and fair override disclosures' - effective for accounting periods ending on or after 23 December 1992.

11 Reference is also made to exposure drafts (EDs) of SSAPs and financial reporting exposure drafts (FREDs) of FRSs where relevant. EDs and FREDs may be taken to be indicative of good practice but are not mandatory until or unless published and effective as FRSs. The following EDs and FREDs are in issue at the time of writing:

ED 46	Disclosure of related party transactions
ED 47	Accounting for goodwill
ED 48	Accounting for acquisitions and mergers
ED 51	Accounting for fixed assets and revaluations
ED 52	Accounting for intangible assets
ED 53	Fair value in the context of acquisition accounting
ED 55	Accounting for investments
FRED 3	Accounting for capital instruments
FRED 4	Reporting the substance of transactions

The Companies Acts 1985 and 1989

12 Prior to the introduction of the Companies Act 1989, the last major revision to company law was the consolidation, in 1985, of the Companies Acts 1948 to 1983. The purpose of consolidating the previous Acts into a single Companies Act 1985, which came into force on 1 July 1985, was, *inter-alia,* to present the legislation in a more logical manner and to avoid the need to cross-refer to other Acts and amending legislation. The accounting provisions were set out in Part VII of the 1985 Act and reflected the requirements of the EC Fourth Directive, dealing with individual company accounts.

13 The Companies Act 1989 was enacted in November 1989, bringing into UK legislation the provisions of the EC Seventh and Eighth Directives on group accounts and the regulation of auditors. The Companies Act 1985 remains the principal Act but the 1989 Act makes significant changes to its requirements by rewriting and amending the existing accounting provisions of the 1985 Act and by inserting new sections and schedules.

14 The changes to accounting and audit requirements brought about by the Companies Act 1989 are all by way of substitutions and amendments to the Companies Act 1985. Many of the provisions dealt with in this book are therefore to be found in the Companies Act 1989 although the statutory reference remains to the Companies Act 1985. For this reason also audit reports continue to refer only to accounts being properly prepared in accordance with the Companies Act 1985.

15 The main accounting and audit requirements are contained in Part VII of the 1985 Act which was completely rewritten as Part I of the 1989 Act. The detailed rules on the preparation and presentation of accounts are set out in the schedules to the 1985 Act (as amended) as follows:

(a) schedule 4 - form and content of company accounts (with minor amendments in schedule 1, Companies Act 1989);

(b) schedule 4A - form and content of group accounts (inserted by schedule 2, Companies Act 1989);

(c) schedule 5 - disclosure of information: related undertakings (substituted for old schedule 5 by schedule 3, Companies Act 1989). This schedule deals with disclosures in relation to subsidiaries, associated undertakings, significant shareholdings in other undertakings and identification of ultimate parent company;

(d) schedule 6 - disclosure of information: emoluments and other benefits of directors and others (amended by schedule 4, Companies Act 1989). All the disclosure requirements in relation to remuneration of, loans to and transactions favouring directors and officers are now contained in this schedule;

(e) schedule 7 - matters to be included in the directors' report (amended by schedule 5, Companies Act 1989);

(f) schedule 8 - exemptions for small and medium-sized companies (substituted for old schedule 8 by schedule 6, Companies Act 1989);

(g) schedule 9 - special provisions for banking and insurance companies and groups (amended by schedule 7, Companies Act 1989).

Statutory Instruments

16 Statutory Instruments are from time to time issued to modify or supplement existing statutes. References are made in the text to these Instruments where relevant.

Accounting standards

17 Prior to the establishment of the Accounting Standards Board, Statements of Standard Accounting Practice ('SSAPs') were prepared by the Accounting Standards Committee (ASC), and issued by the Councils of its governing accountancy bodies. They contain both accounting policy and disclosure requirements and apply to all accounts intended to give a true and fair view of the financial position and profit or loss. This book deals with SSAPs as they affect disclosure in accounts. The explanatory foreword to SSAPs requires that significant departures should be disclosed and their effect estimated wherever practicable.

18 The Companies Act 1989 established a framework for a new accounting standards regime following the recommendations of the Dearing Committee's Report - 'The making of accounting standards', issued in September 1988. Consequently, in August 1990, the Accounting Standards

Committee was stood down and an independent Accounting Standards Board (ASB), overseen by a Financial Reporting Council and backed up by a Review Panel, was established.

19 The ASB took over from the former ASC the role of issuing accounting standards applicable in the United Kingdom. The ASB, which has been authorised by the Secretary of State for the purpose, is independent and acts under its own authority, needing no external approval for its actions. The ASB has however made it clear that it intends to consult widely on its proposals. Accounting standards developed by the ASB are known as Financial Reporting Standards (FRSs). The ASB has adopted the 22 extant SSAPs issued by the ASC. Accounting standards developed by the former ASC and adopted by the ASB continue to be known as SSAPs.

20 FRSs issued and SSAPs adopted by the ASB are 'Accounting standards' for the purposes of the Companies Act 1985, which requires accounts, other than those prepared by small and medium-sized companies (as defined by the Act) to state whether they have been prepared in accordance with applicable accounting standards and to give particulars of any material departure from those standards and the reasons for it (see Chapter 4). 1985 s 256 (1989 s 19)

21 In July 1991, the ASB published an exposure draft of its 'Foreword to accounting standards'. The foreword explains the authority, scope and application of accounting standards issued by the ASB. The foreword also considers the procedure by which the ASB issues accounting standards and their relationship to International Accounting Standards, issued by the International Accounting Standards Committee.

ASB's Statement of Principles

22 FRSs issued by the ASB are based on the Statement of Principles for Financial Reporting being developed by the ASB, which addresses the concepts underlying the information presented in financial statements. The Statement of Principles will not itself be an accounting standard, but will provide a conceptual framework for the consistent and logical formulation of accounting standards. The framework will also provide a basis on which others can exercise judgement in resolving accounting issues.

23 The ASB's Statement of Principles when completed will comprise seven chapters addressing the following topics:

(a) the objective of financial statements;

(b) the qualitative characteristics of financial information that enable financial statements to achieve their purpose;

(c) the elements that make up the financial statements;

(d) the recognition of items in financial statements;

(e) the valuation bases to be applied to recognised items;

(f) the presentation of items in financial statements; and

(g) the principles underlying consolidation, equity accounting and proportional consolidation.

At the time of writing, the ASB has issued exposure drafts on (a), (b) and (f) above. Discussion documents have also been issued on (c) and (d). The ASB intends to issue an exposure draft covering all the topics in due course.

Financial reporting exposure drafts

24 Prior to the issuance of a financial reporting standard, an exposure draft of an FRS is issued by the ASB for public comment. Where the proposals in a financial reporting exposure draft conflict with the requirements of an existing SSAP, the ASB has stated that the provisions of an existing accounting standard must be followed until such time as the FRED is converted into an FRS. However, some companies may wish to provide additional information reflecting proposals contained in a FRED. In the ASB's views there are two ways in which this can be achieved:

(a) insofar as the information does not conflict with existing accounting standards, it could be incorporated in the accounts. It should be remembered, however, that the proposals may change before forming part of an accounting standard and the consequences of a change to the proposals should be considered;

(b) the information could be provided in supplementary form.

Urgent Issues Task Force

25 In March 1991, the ASB created the Urgent Issues Task Force (UITF). The main role of the UITF is to assist the ASB in areas where an accounting standard or Companies Act provision exists, but where unsatisfactory or conflicting interpretations have developed or seem likely to develop. In such circumstances, the Task Force will endeavour to reach a consensus on the desirable accounting treatment for the matter in question. Where such a consensus is achieved the intention is that it should be considered to be part of the corpus of practices forming the basis for what determines a true and fair view, and the expectation is that companies will comply with it. Pronouncements issued by the UITF are known as UITF Abstracts.

The Financial Reporting Review Panel

26 The Financial Reporting Review Panel (FRRP) is a new body in UK financial reporting. Its creation follows the introduction into the companies legislation of provisions for the revision of defective accounts (See Chapter 9). The FRRP has authority to examine departures from the accounting

requirements of the Companies Act 1985 and accounting standards where they result in the accounts in question not giving a true and fair view as required by the law. Where a company's accounts are defective the FRRP will, wherever possible, endeavour to secure revision by voluntary means; but if this approach fails it has the power to make an application to the court for an order compelling the revision. The FRRP's ambit covers public and large private companies, the Department of Trade and Industry dealing with all other cases.

The International Stock Exchange Admission of Securities to Listing and the Unlisted Securities Market

27 There are additional disclosure requirements for companies listed on The International Stock Exchange. These are set out in the Stock Exchange publication Admission of Securities to Listing, which is generally known as the Yellow Book. Section 5 sets out the continuing obligations accepted by listed companies by virtue of their application for and subsequent maintenance of listing. It should be noted that the Stock Exchange is currently revising the Yellow Book and a new version to be called 'The Listing Rules' is due to be issued sometime in 1993. Until the new rules come into effect, the provisions of the existing Yellow Book continue to apply.

28 Companies whose shares are dealt with on the Unlisted Securities Market ('USM') are similarly subject to the requirements set out in the Stock Exchange publication Unlisted Securities Market (the Green Book). The additional disclosures required by USM companies are very similar to those of the Admission of Securities to Listing. The requirements in this book referenced to the Admission of Securities to Listing should be taken to apply to USM companies, unless otherwise indicated. However, the Stock Exchange has proposed that no new admissions to the USM will be allowed after 30 June 1993. Existing USM companies will be expected to move to the main market by the end of 1995.

Accounting principles and rules

29 The Companies Act 1985 lays down several accounting principles and rules which a company must adopt in the preparation of its accounts. These rules are of two types - the 'historical cost accounting rules' and the 'alternative accounting rules'. The latter must be used if the main accounts are prepared on a current cost basis or, alternatively, to the extent that the main historical cost accounts incorporate the revaluation of any assets. The historical cost rules have been included in the disclosure requirements chapters, under relevant headings. The requirements set out in these chapters must be followed by companies in preparing their main accounts whether these are prepared on an historical cost or a current cost basis. The relevant additional requirements relating to the alternative accounting rules are set out in Chapter 4.

Banking and insurance companies

30 The basic legal regulation dealing with banks' and insurance companies' accounts is contained in the Companies Act 1985. However, the accounting and disclosure rules that are contained in schedule 4 to the Companies Act 1985 apply to companies generally and do not reflect the special nature of banking and insurance business. Therefore, banks and insurance companies are afforded special treatment under the Act. The special accounting and disclosure provisions that apply to the accounts of banking and insurance companies and groups are included in schedules 9 and 9A respectively to the Companies Act 1985.

31 It should be noted that the schedule 9 rules that apply to banking companies have been amended recently. This has become necessary in order to implement into UK law the requirements of the EC Bank Accounts Directive that adapted the provisions of the EC Fourth and the Seventh Company Law Directives to accounts prepared by banks. The amendments to the schedule 9 rules were made by a statutory instrument, the Companies Act 1985 (Bank Accounts) Regulations 1991 (SI 1991 No 2705) and the revised rules take effect for banks' financial years beginning on or after the 23 December 1992.

32 The regulations rewrite sections 255-255B and Parts I-III of schedule 9, amend section 255C, create a new schedule 9A, change the status of schedule 10, and make the necessary consequential amendments. Section 255D and Part IV of schedule 9 remain unaltered. They also lay down a transitional provision whose effect is to allow banks to adopt the new requirements early if they so wish.

33 Section 255 provides that the individual company accounts of a bank must be prepared according to the rules in Part I of schedule 9, instead of the rules in schedule 4 that apply to the generality of companies. Section 255A contains the corresponding provisions for group accounts. The accounts of a banking group are to be prepared in accordance with the provisions applying to companies generally, in particular the rules in schedule 4A, but with the modifications made by Part II of schedule 9. Whereas schedule 4 is disapplied in its entirety and Part I of schedule 9 takes its place, schedule 4A does apply to banks, albeit in modified form. Both the individual company accounts and the accounts of a banking group (if applicable) must contain a statement that they have been prepared in accordance with the special rules, and the provisions relating to a 'true and fair view' apply accordingly.

34 For completeness, it may be noted that the accounts of insurance companies are now to be prepared according to Part 1 of schedule 9A (or schedule 4 if the company prefers). Schedule 9A is essentially Part I and II of the 'old schedule 9', as it stands before the 1991 amendments, which applies to insurance companies. In due course, schedule 9A will need to be amended

in order to implement EC legislation on insurance companies accounts. The new legislation will supersede the rules currently set out in the 1985 Act that relate specifically to insurance companies and effectively bring them into line, in a manner appropriate for insurers, with those applicable to the generality of companies governed by the 1985 Act.

35 The following definitions apply:

(a) 'banking company' means a company which is authorised under the Banking Act 1987; 1985 s 744 (1989 10 sch 16)

(b) 'insurance company' means a company to which Part II of the Insurance Companies Act 1982 applies. In practice this can be taken to include all British insurance companies; 1985 s 744

(c) a 'banking group' is a group where either the parent company is a banking company or the parent company does not itself carry on any material business apart from the acquisition, management and disposal of interests in subsidiary undertakings and its principal subsidiary undertakings are wholly or mainly banking companies; 1985 s 255A(4) (1989 s 18) amended by SI 1991 No 2705

(d) an 'insurance group' is a group where either the parent company is an insurance company or the predominant activity of the group is insurance business and activities which are a direct extension of or ancillary to insurance business. 1985 s 255A(5) (1989 s 18) amended by SI 1991 No 2705

36 This book only deals with the Companies Act requirements applying to companies in general. The requirements in relation to banking and insurance companies and groups are not dealt with in this book and reference should be made to the Act.

Investment companies

37 Investment companies (as defined by section 266 of the 1985 Act) are outside the scope of this book. The special requirements for such companies are set out in Part V of schedule 4 and paragraph 1(3) of schedule 4A to the 1985 Act, and in sections 5 and 10 of the Admission of Securities to Listing.

Specimen annual report

38 This edition of the book contains a specimen annual report of a hypothetical listed company, GAAP UK plc group of companies (see Appendix 2). The report has been prepared for illustrative purposes only and shows the disclosures and formats that might be expected for a group of this size which prepares its accounts in accordance with schedule 4 and schedule 4A to the Companies Act 1985 as amended by the Companies Act 1989. The specimen report cannot of course illustrate the disclosure requirements for all situations and, therefore, it should not be used as a checklist.

Abbreviations and references

39 The following abbreviations are used throughout this book:

the Act/1985 Act	Companies Act 1985 (as amended by the Companies Act 1989)
the 1989 Act	Companies Act 1989
BNA 1985	Business Names Act 1985
s	Companies Acts, section reference
sch	Schedule reference to the Companies Acts
SI	Statutory Instrument
SSAP	Statement of Standard Accounting Practice
ED	Exposure draft of SSAP
FRS	Financial Reporting Standard
FRED	Financial Reporting Exposure Draft
ASL	Admission of Securities to Listing. Paragraph references are to Section 5 Chapter 2 of the Yellow Book
USM	The Unlisted Securities Market Green Book
UK	United Kingdom
EC	European Community
Author	Additional comments or suggested treatment in the absence of legal or similar requirements.

Unless otherwise stated all references to statute in this book are to the Companies Act 1985 as amended by the Companies Act 1989, e.g.:

(a) 1985 s 258(4) - section 258 subsection (4) of the Act; and

(b) 1985 4 sch 1(2) - schedule 4 to the Act, paragraph 1 sub-paragraph (2).

In many cases the 1989 Act amends or replaces a section of the 1985 Act and where this is so both references have been given.

Paragraphs dealing with specific items in the standard balance sheets have been referred to format 2 (see Appendix 1).

2 Directors' Report

General

1 A directors' report is one of the documents to be included with a company's annual accounts laid before the company in general meeting and delivered to the registrar. 1985 s 241,242 (1989 s 11)

2 Reference is made throughout this chapter to the directors' report accompanying group accounts. If a company has no subsidiary undertakings, references to the 'group' should be construed as applying to the company.

Principal activities

3 The principal activities of the group during the year, and significant changes in such activities during the year, must be disclosed. 1985 s 234(2) (1989 s 8)

Business review

4 The report must contain a fair review of the development of the business of the group during the year, and of its position at the year end. 1985 s 234(1)(a) (1989 s 8)

5 The Act gives no guidance as to what form the review should take, nor does it indicate the detail the directors must include in their review. This provision is expressed in broad terms only, so as to allow directors as much freedom as possible to decide how best the information should be presented. Consequently, in practice, both the format and content of this review vary considerably. Also many public companies do not include the review in their directors' report. Instead, they include the required information either in their chairman's statement or in a detailed review of operations. Provided that the directors' report refers to the place where the information appears, it still complies with the Act. Author

6 The ASB issued a discussion paper containing preliminary proposals for an Operating and Financial Review (OFR) to be included in the annual report of large companies. The ASB's proposals are intended to add to the usefulness of existing disclosures and to codify the style and content in a way that will be helpful to preparers of accounts. The discussion paper envisages that the OFR would contain three main areas:

(a) a commentary on operating results;

(b) a review of financial needs and resources; and

(c) a commentary on shareholders' return and value.

7 The paper makes clear that it does not seek to prescribe a particular format for the OFR. It is for directors to decide how the information should best be presented, as they are responsible for financial reporting. Where it is more radical, however, is in the range of subjects that it proposes should be discussed under each of the above topic headings. The ASB has indicated that the OFR would not become an accounting standard, so it is unclear how widely it would be adopted. It should be noted that the Cadbury Committee Report supports the ASB's proposals on the OFR.

Material differences from published forecasts

8 The directors' report for a listed company should contain an explanation in the event that the trading results shown by the accounts differ materially from any published forecast made by the (parent) company. ASL 21(b)

Future developments

9 An indication of likely future developments in the business of the group must be given. 1985 7 sch 6(b)

10 In interpreting this requirement, directors should consider for disclosure major changes in activities which are planned or clearly envisaged. The legal provision is not considered to be a requirement to produce a forecast. Author

11 In practice, many public companies include the business review and likely future developments either in the chairman's statement or in a detailed review of operations. Provided that the directors' report refers to the place where the information appears, it still complies with the Act. Author

Dividends

12 The dividends recommended by the directors, and any amounts proposed to be carried to reserves, must be disclosed. 1985 s 234(1)(b) (1989 s 8)

Significant changes in fixed assets

13 Particulars of significant changes in the fixed assets of the group during the year must be stated. 1985 7 sch 1(1)

Differences between market value and book value of land

14 Substantial differences between the market and book values of interests in land held as fixed assets by a group must be indicated as precisely as practicable if, in the opinion of the directors, they are of such significance 1985 7 sch 1(2)

as to require them to be drawn to the attention of the members or debenture holders. Interests in land include the buildings thereon.

15 It is recommended that where there are several interests in land, the aggregate market value and the aggregate book value should be compared to see if the difference is substantial. When it is considered that a substantial difference exists, the basis on which the market value has been arrived at should be stated. Consideration should be given to what reference, if any, should be made to taxation, including where appropriate capital gains tax, payable on sale at a price equal to the estimated market value. An independent professional valuation is not required if the directors are competent to arrive at the market value themselves, but the wording should make the position clear in this respect. Where property is situated overseas, especially in territories subject to political unrest or where the remittance of currencies is restricted, it may not always be practicable, and may be misleading, to give the information required. In such cases the wording should make this clear. Author

Post balance sheet events

16 Particulars of important events which have occurred between the end of the financial year and the date of approval of the accounts, and which affect the company or any of its subsidiaries, must be disclosed. This requirement gives rise to two potential conflicts between the law and SSAP 17: 1985 7 sch 6(a) Author

(a) SSAP 17 envisages disclosure only of non-adjusting events (and the reversal of window-dressing transactions), whereas the Act does not differentiate and thus must be construed as requiring disclosure of post balance sheet events whether adjusting or non-adjusting. SSAP 17:23

(b) The Act specifies disclosure in the directors' report whereas SSAP 17 requires disclosure in the accounts.

17 Regarding (a) above, the financial effect of adjusting post balance sheet events, if particularly significant by reason of size or nature, would be disclosed in the accounts as exceptional or extraordinary items (see Chapter 6) in accordance with the requirements of FRS 3. It is considered that such disclosure or its absence is a fair measure of whether the post balance sheet event is 'important' and thus falls to be disclosed in the directors' report. Author

18 Regarding (b), if companies wish to make the disclosure only once there should be a cross reference from either the directors' report or the accounts to where the full disclosure is given. Author

Research and development

19 An indication of the activities, if any, of the group in the field of research and development must be given. 1985 7 sch 6(c)

Contributions for political and charitable purposes

20 The separate total of contributions for political and charitable purposes made by the company (not being a wholly-owned subsidiary of a company incorporated in Great Britain) or by the group, if together they exceed £200, must be disclosed. The name of the recipient must be given in the case of individual political contributions exceeding £200. Donations for political or charitable purposes made to persons (or parties) outside the UK are exempt. 1985 7 sch 3-5

Disabled persons

21 If the average number of UK employees of the company during the year exceeded 250, the directors' report must state the company's policies for: 1985 7 sch 9

(a) the employment of disabled persons;

(b) the continued employment and training of persons who become disabled whilst employed by the company; and

(c) the training, career development and promotion of disabled persons.

Health and safety at work

22 The Secretary of State may require any class of company to disclose specified information in the directors' report relating to the health, safety and welfare at work of its employees. No orders have yet been made under this provision and therefore this provision does not yet apply. 1985 7 sch 10

Employee involvement

23 If the average number of UK employees employed under contract of service by the company in each week during the year exceeded 250, the directors' report must describe the action taken during the year to introduce, maintain or develop arrangements aimed at: 1985 7 sch 11

(a) providing employees systematically with information of concern to them as employees;

(b) consulting employees or their representatives on a regular basis so that the views of employees can be taken into account in making decisions that are likely to affect their interests;

(c) encouraging employee involvement in the company's performance through an employees' share scheme or by some other means; and

(d) achieving a common awareness on the part of employees of the financial and economic factors affecting the performance of the company.

Directors

24 The names of the persons who were directors of the (parent) company at any time during the financial year are to be disclosed. 1985 s 234(2) (1989 s 8)

Directors' service contracts

25 The directors' report for a listed company must further state the unexpired period of any service contract of any director proposed for re-election at the forthcoming annual general meeting. (This further provision does not apply to USM companies.) The Cadbury Committee Report recommends that directors' service contracts should not exceed three years without shareholders' approval. ASL 42(c) USM 8:4

Insurance effected for officers or auditors

26 If the company has effected insurance for any officers or auditors of the company against liability in relation to the company (e.g. for negligence or breach of duty), that fact must be stated. 1985 7 sch 5A (1989 s 137(2))

27 Where such insurance is purchased or maintained for a director of a company, a taxable benefit (e.g. a proportion of the premiums paid) may arise, in the hands of the director. In such circumstances, the value of the benefit should be included within the figure for directors' emoluments and the appropriate bandings. Author

Directors' interests

28 The following information must be given in the directors' report or in the notes to the accounts in respect of each person who was a director of the (parent) company at the end of the year: 1985 7 sch 2 (1989 5 sch)

(a) whether the director was, at the end of the year, interested in shares or debentures of the company or of any of its subsidiaries, holding companies or fellow subsidiaries; 1985 7 sch 2A (1989 5 sch)

(b) if so, the number of those shares or amount of those debentures, specifying in which company they were held;

(c) if the director was so interested at the end of the year, the information corresponding to that in (a) and (b) as at the beginning of the year or, if later, the date when the person first became a director;

(d) whether any right (e.g. an 'option') to subscribe for such shares or debentures was granted to, or exercised by, the director or a member of the director's immediate family during the year; and 1985 7 sch 2B (1989 5 sch)

(e) if so, the number of shares or amount of debentures in respect of which the right was granted or exercised, specifying to which company they relate.

An 'interest in shares or debentures' (sub-paragraph (a) above) includes a right to subscribe for shares or debentures already in issue. A right to subscribe for unissued shares or debentures is covered by (d) above.

29 The above details (there are no exceptions on grounds of immateriality), must be given for each director and where no shares are held by a director this fact must be stated. The information is to be taken from the register of directors' interests and must include the interests of spouses and infant children. These details need not be given: 1985 7 sch 2,2A,2B (1989 5 sch) 1985 s 328(1)

(a) in accounts of a wholly-owned subsidiary where a person is a director of both the subsidiary and its holding company, provided disclosure is made in the holding company directors' report; SI 1985 No 802

(b) in accounts of a wholly-owned subsidiary of a company incorporated outside Great Britain in respect of interests in that company;

(c) in relation to interests in a society registered under the Industrial and Provident Societies Act 1965;

(d) in respect of certain trustee shareholdings of a director, or those held by a company as trustee and over which a director has influence; and

(e) for shadow directors (but see paragraph 31 below).

30 For listed companies, directors' interests in shares and debentures of the company and each of its subsidiaries (as required to be disclosed by the Act), together with any options to subscribe for such capital, should be distinguished between beneficial and other interests. It should be noted that the distinction between beneficial and other interests applies equally to share options held. (It may be appropriate for all companies to adopt this disclosure.) Particulars should be given as at the balance sheet date, but changes between that date and a date not more than one month prior to the date of the notice of the general meeting held to consider the accounts are to be shown as a note. If there are no changes, that fact should be disclosed. ASL 21(h) Author ASL 21(h)

Shadow directors

31 A shadow director, meaning a person in accordance with whose directions or instructions the directors of a company are accustomed to act, is treated as a director for purposes of registration of directors' names and of directors' interests in shares or debentures, and in relation to inspection of directors' service contracts. The requirements referred to above to disclose certain details in respect of directors in the directors' report do not explicitly include shadow directors. However it is sensible to interpret the disclosure as applying to shadow directors and certainly one should not object to their inclusion. References elsewhere to accounts disclosure in respect of directors should normally be interpreted as including shadow directors, either because it is a specific requirement, or for the reason given. 1985 s 741(2) Author

Non-executive directors

32 Listed companies are required to disclose the identity of independent non-executive directors, together with a short biographical note on each. ASL 21(t)

Waivers of dividends

33 For listed companies, particulars of any arrangements under which any shareholder has waived or agreed to waive any dividends should be disclosed. ASL 21(o)

Substantial holdings

34 A statement should be given of persons (other than directors) holding or beneficially interested in any substantial part of the share capital of a listed company, disclosing the amounts of the holdings in question at a date not more than one month prior to the date of notice of the meeting. If appropriate, a negative statement is to be given. A substantial shareholding is one which amounts to three per cent or more of any class of capital having full voting rights. Holdings by different companies in a group are counted as one for this purpose. This requirement applies only to UK companies. ASL 21(i)

35 USM companies need only disclose the above information insofar as it is known to the directors. This information will, in practice, be available to the directors of USM companies by virtue of section 198 of the Act, which requires the holders of substantial interests in the equity capital of a public company to notify the company. USM 8:4

Corporate substantial shareholders

36 Listed companies are required to give particulars in the annual report and accounts of:

(a) any contract of significance between the company, or a subsidiary, and a corporate substantial shareholder; and ASL 21(l)

(b) any contract for the provision of services to the company or a subsidiary by a corporate substantial shareholder (except if the services provided are the shareholder's principal business and it is not a contract of significance). ASL 21(m)

A contract of significance means one per cent or more of the net assets (for capital transactions) or of total purchases, sales, payments or receipts (as appropriate). In a group of companies materiality is to be based on consolidated figures. Corporate substantial shareholder means any body corporate that controls 30 per cent or more of the voting power, or the composition of the board.

Company's interest in its own shares

37 Where shares in the company: 1985 7 sch 7

(a) are purchased by the company or acquired by forfeiture or by surrender in lieu of forfeiture; or

(b) are acquired by the company's nominee or any other person with financial assistance from the company and in a situation where the company has a beneficial interest in the shares; or

(c) are subject to a lien or other charge taken by the company;

the following information must be disclosed: 1985 7 sch 8

(a) the number and nominal value of the shares purchased during the year, the consideration given, and the reasons for their purchase;

(b) the number and nominal value of the shares so acquired or charged;

(c) the maximum number and nominal value of the shares acquired or charged, held during the year;

(d) the number and nominal value of the shares acquired or charged, which were disposed of or cancelled during the year;

(e) the percentages of the called up share capital represented by the shares disclosed in (a) to (d) above;

(f) the amount of the charge on any of the shares concerned; and

(g) the consideration for any such shares disposed of.

38 Listed companies are required to give particulars of any shareholders' authority for purchase by the company of its own shares existing at the year end. Also, for purchases or proposals to purchase during the year otherwise than through the market or by tender or partial offer to all shareholders, particulars of the sellers should be given. Finally, for purchases, options or contracts entered into since the year end, equivalent information is required to that listed in the preceding paragraph. This applies only to UK companies. ASL 21(p)

Close company status

39 For listed companies a statement should be made as to whether or not the close company provisions of the Income and Corporation Taxes Act 1988 apply to the (parent) company and whether there has been any change since the end of the financial year. Where there is doubt, the existence of the doubt and basis on which taxation provisions have been made is to be noted. ASL 21(j)

It is regarded as good practice for all companies to make this disclosure, whether listed or not. Author

Exemptions for small companies

40 Small companies and groups headed by a small company are exempt from disclosing certain information in their directors' report. The exemptions were brought into effect for accounting periods ending on or after 16 November 1992, by 'The Companies Act 1985 (Accounts of small and medium-sized enterprises and publication of accounts in ECUs) Regulations 1992'. The Regulations insert a new Part II in schedule 8 of the Act that provides exemptions with respect to the directors' report. SI 1992 No 2452

41 The directors' report of a small company or a group headed by a small company need not disclose the following information (the paragraph references refer to the paragraphs above which deal with these disclosures): 1985 8 sch part II (amended by SI 1992 No 2452)

(a) paragraph 4 (fair review of business);

(b) paragraph 9 (future developments);

(c) paragraph 12 (amounts to be paid as dividends and amounts to be carried to reserves);

(d) paragraph 13 (significant changes in fixed assets);

(e) paragraph 14 (differences between market value and book value of land);

(f) paragraph 16 (post balance sheet events);

(g) paragraph 19 (research and development);

(h) paragraph 22 (health and safety at work);

(i) paragraph 23 (employee involvement); and

(j) paragraph 26 (insurance effected for officers or auditors).

42 Where a small company has taken advantage of the exemptions in respect of the preparation of the directors' report, the directors must make a statement immediately above the signature on the directors' report that: 1985 s 246(1B) (amended by SI 1992 No 2452)

(a) advantage has been taken, in the preparation of the report, of the special exemptions as applicable to small companies; and

(b) where the company's balance sheet for that year does not contain a statement of the grounds on which a company is entitled to the exemptions, the grounds on which, in the directors' opinion, the company is entitled to the exemptions.

Small companies are further dealt with in Chapters 3 and 9.

Reappointment of auditors

43 It is customary to state at the end of the directors' report that a resolution will be put to the general meeting, regarding the appointment or reappointment of the auditors. Where a private company has elected to dispense with the requirement to appoint auditors annually such a statement will of course not be relevant, although companies may wish to include a statement indicating that in the absence of a notice proposing that the appointment be terminated, the auditors will be deemed to be re-appointed for the next financial year. Author

Auditors' responsibility

44 In preparing their report on the accounts, the auditors are required to consider whether in their opinion the information in the directors' report is consistent with the accounts, and if not they are required to say so. Auditors are not otherwise required to give an opinion on the directors' report. 1985 s 235(3) (1989 s 9)

Notice of meeting

45 For listed companies, whenever shareholders are sent notice of a meeting to transact non-routine business at or on the same day as an AGM, unless an explanatory circular accompanies the notice an explanation must be incorporated in the directors' report. ASL 31

Approval and signature

46 The directors' report must be approved by the board and signed on its behalf by a director or the secretary. There is no legal requirement to date the directors' report, but this is regarded as good practice. 1985 s 234A(1) (1989 s 8) Author

47 Every copy of the directors' report which is laid before the company in general meeting, or which is otherwise issued, must state the name of the person who signed it. The copy delivered to the registrar must be signed. 1985 s 234A(2),(3) (1989 s 8)

3 Format

Introduction

1 Section 226 of the Act contains the requirement for accounts to be prepared in a standard format. A choice of formats is permitted and these formats are set out in full in Appendix 1 to this book. 1985 s 226 (1989 s 4)

2 Two balance sheet formats are permitted. They generally specify the same main headings and differ principally in using in one case a vertical format and in the other a horizontal format. 1985 4 sch 1

3 Four profit and loss account formats are permitted. These consist of two alternative approaches, either of which may be adopted in a vertical or horizontal format. The principal difference between these approaches is in the classification of expense items. Formats 1 and 3 analyse expenses by function, and so disclose cost of sales, distribution costs and administrative expenses. Formats 2 and 4 analyse expenses by nature, showing raw materials purchased, staff costs, depreciation and other charges.

4 Generally, companies should adopt the format with which they are most easily able to comply, for example by using the type of format used internally for management account headings. It should be noted that the structure of the profit and loss account has been recently reformed following publication of FRS 3 (see paragraph 26 below). Author

5 The consolidated accounts of a group are required to comply with the standard formats as if the group were a single company. For this purpose the formats are adapted to include minority interests and associated undertakings, as explained in Appendix 1 to this book. 1985 4A sch 1(1) (1989 2 sch)

6 In addition to the profit and loss account and balance sheet, companies are required to prepare two other primary statements: a statement of total recognised gains and losses required by FRS 3 (see paragraph 27 below) and a statement of cash flows required by FRS 1 (see Chapter 7).

7 The standard balance sheet formats and the accounting requirements of the Act are further modified for small companies. These modifications apply not only to the individual accounts and directors' reports of small companies, but

also to the consolidated accounts where a small company prepares them. The modifications were brought in by The Companies Act 1985 (Accounts of Small and Medium-sized Enterprises and Publication of Accounts in ECUs) Regulations and these regulations are considered further in paragraphs 39 to 52 below. SI 1992 No 2452

Compliance with rules for formats

8 All items in the standard formats are prefixed with a letter, a Roman numeral or an Arabic numeral. These indicate respectively headings, subheadings and detail. The letters and numbers used for identification purposes in the formats need not be written into the accounts. 1985 4 sch 1(2)

9 Items listed in the standard formats and prefixed with a letter or a Roman numeral must be included in the accounts in the same order and under the same headings and subheadings as in the standard format chosen unless there are no amounts for the current and previous period. 1985 4 sch 1

10 Once a standard format has been chosen, it must be adopted consistently in future years unless, in the opinion of the directors, there are special reasons for a change, in which case details of the change and the reasons for it must be given in a note to the accounts (see paragraph 35 below). 1985 4 sch 2(1) 1985 4 sch 2(2)

11 Corresponding amounts for the previous financial year must be shown for every item in the balance sheet, profit and loss account, and notes to the accounts, except in those cases specifically mentioned in this book. 1985 4 sch 4(1)

12 Where a corresponding amount would not be comparable with the current year item, an adjusted corresponding amount must be shown. Particulars of the adjustment and the reasons for it must be included in a note. 1985 4 sch 4(2)

13 Netting off assets and liabilities or income and expenditure is not permitted. This does not preclude the aggregation of debtor and creditor balances with the same party, so as to arrive at a net indebtedness. The full amounts of bank loans and overdrafts should be shown unless there is a legal right of set off, in which case these amounts should be netted off and the resultant balance shown as item C IV or E 2 (format 2: C 2 as appropriate). 1985 4 sch 5 Author

Flexibility

14 There is flexibility in the format rules contained in the Act as explained below.

15 Any item to be shown in the chosen format may be shown in greater detail, for example, the wording of the heading or subheading may be expanded or the amounts may be subanalysed. 1985 4 sch 3(1)

16 Additional headings or subheadings may be included if not covered by an item in the standard formats. 1985 4 sch 3(2)

Format

17 The arrangement and headings and subheadings included in the formats in respect of items to which an Arabic numeral is assigned shall be adapted where the special nature of the company's business requires such adaptation. Potentially this allows considerable flexibility, particularly in the profit and loss account, since any format heading and/or its order may be changed if following strictly the formats contained in the Act would not be meaningful in view of the nature of the company's business. Care is required in judging the merits of changes and a common sense attitude should be taken against the background of complying with the spirit of the law. 1985 4 sch 3(3) Author

18 Items indicated by an Arabic numeral in the standard formats may be combined in the balance sheet or profit and loss account, provided the individual items are shown in the notes, if such combination aids comprehension of the accounts. This is a valuable provision in ensuring that only important detail is included on the face of the profit and loss account and balance sheet with the less important detail in the notes. 1985 4 sch 3(4) Author

19 A heading must be omitted from the specified formats where there is a nil balance for both the current and preceding financial years. 1985 4 sch 3(5),4(3)

20 The amount of any item indicated by an Arabic numeral, if immaterial, may be included under another heading within the format. In such circumstances, disclosure in the notes is not required. 1985 4 sch 3(4)(a) Author

21 The disclosure requirements of schedule 4 to the Act may be disregarded in respect of any amounts which are considered immaterial. This dispensation does not apply to disclosure requirements elsewhere in the Act, or introduced by other legislation. 1985 4 sch 86

22 Unless otherwise indicated in this book, the disclosures required in addition to those of the standard formats may be made either on the face of the accounts or in the notes. Author

Reporting financial performance

23 In October 1992, the ASB issued FRS 3 - 'Reporting Financial Performance'. FRS 3 applies to all undertakings issuing accounts intended to give a true and fair view except to the extent that these requirements are not permitted by any statutory framework under which such undertakings report. It should be adopted as soon as possible and becomes mandatory for accounting periods ending on or after 22 June 1993.

24 FRS 3 supersedes SSAP 6 - 'Extraordinary items and Prior Year Adjustments' and amends SSAP 3 - 'Earnings per share'. SSAP 6 was issued in 1974 and revised in 1986. Despite this revision, however, there remained significant problems with the interpretation of SSAP 6 in practice, Author

particularly in the classification of unusual items as exceptional or extraordinary. As a result, the value of earnings per share, which excluded extraordinary items, as a measure of financial performance also suffered.

25 The principal purpose of FRS 3 is to produce a set of rules for the presentation of statements of financial performance which will be more effective than those in SSAP 6. It achieves this purpose by adopting a twofold approach. Author

(a) First, it requires more detailed disclosure in the profit and loss account of information on the various elements of financial performance, such as continuing and discontinued operations. As part of this, it virtually abolishes extraordinary items and requires earnings per share to be calculated after extraordinary items (if any) thus reducing its importance as a measure of financial performance; and

(b) Secondly, it requires several statements of performance which taken together give an information set that includes all the elements of a company's performance including all gains or losses of the period, whether recognised in the profit and loss account or taken to reserves as required by law or accounting standards.

The aim of the approach is to enable a reader to make his own judgement about performance based on prominent disclosure of the various elements of performance coupled with greater analysis of key elements.

Changes to the profit and loss account format

26 In order to achieve the above objective, FRS 3 introduced several changes to the profit and loss account by adopting a layered format which is designed to highlight a number of important components of financial performance, viz: Author

(a) results of continuing operations (including the results of acquisitions);

(b) results of discontinued operations;

(c) profits or losses on the sale or termination of an operation, costs of a fundamental reorganisation or restructuring and profits or losses on the sale of fixed assets; and

(d) extraordinary items (which will be extremely rare).

The way in which the profit and loss account is affected by the above disclosures is considered further in Chapter 6.

Statement of total recognised gains and losses

27 Not all gains and losses will be recognised in the profit and loss account. There are other changes in net assets of a reporting entity arising from transactions and other events, other than those resulting from capital contributed by or repaid to shareholders, that are equally important in assessing the overall performance of a reporting entity. The standard, therefore, requires the presentation of a statement of total recognised gains and losses as a primary financial statement. Author FRS 3:27

28 The statement of total recognised gains and losses is a major innovation in UK accounting and is fundamental to the concept of 'performance' embraced by the ASB in FRS 3. When presenting this statement, the following requirements should be observed: Author FRS 3:27

(a) it should be presented as a primary financial statement with the same prominence as the other primary statements;

(b) it should show the total of recognised gains and losses in the period and its components, whether recognised in the profit and loss account or reserves, that are attributable to shareholders; and

(c) it should exclude any goodwill written off directly to reserves in the period.

Note of historical cost profits and losses

29 The standard requires a note of historical cost profits and losses whenever there is a material difference between the result as disclosed in the profit and loss account and the result on an unmodified historical cost basis. This applies for example, where the disclosed results include revaluations of assets. In presenting the note, the following requirements should be observed: FRS 3:26

(a) the note should include a reconciliation between the reported profit on ordinary activities before tax and the equivalent historical cost amount;

(b) the note should show the retained profit for the period on a historical cost basis; and

(c) the note should appear immediately after the profit and loss account or the statement of total recognised gains and losses.

Where the full historical cost information is unavailable or cannot be obtained without undue expense or delay, the earliest available values should be used.

Reconciliation of movements in shareholders' funds

30 The statement of total recognised gains and losses does not include movements between reserves. These will continue to be shown in a reserves note as required by schedule 4 and discussed in Chapter 5 of this book. However, the standard does require a new note or primary statement that reconciles the opening and closing totals of shareholders' funds of the period. If included as a primary statement, the reconciliation should be shown separately from the statement of total recognised gains and losses. Consequently, considerable flexibility is allowed as to where the reconciliation appears and thus to the prominence or lack of prominence given to the statement. Author FRS 3:28 FRS 3:59

The reconciliation would normally include the following: Author

(a) the components of total recognised gains and losses of the year;

(b) dividends as a deduction from profit for the financial year rather than from total recognised gains and losses;

(c) goodwill written off immediately to reserves on acquisitions made during the year;

(d) goodwill previously written off now included in profit for the financial year;

(e) share capital subscribed or repaid; and

(f) amounts written off against share premium account where permitted by law.

31 It should be noted that the reconciliation does not differentiate between the different types of reserve or capital that make up the total of shareholders' funds. For this reason it is not a substitute for the notes required by law relating to share capital, share premium account and other reserves, which must still be given in the accounts.

Comparative figures

32 Comparative figures should be given for all items in the primary statements and such notes as are required by the standard, that is, the profit and loss account, the statement of total recognised gains and losses, the note of historical cost profits and losses and the reconciliation of movements in shareholders' funds. In the profit and loss account, comparative figures should include in the continuing operations category only the results of those operations that are included in the current period's continuing operations. This means that the prior year's results of operations that have been discontinued during the current year will need to be restated and shown under the discontinued operations category (see Chapter 6). FRS 3:30

Investment companies

33 Investment companies as defined in section 266 of the Act are afforded special treatment under the standard. For such companies, the profit and loss account should only include profits available for distribution. All other gains and losses of a capital nature should be shown in the statement of total recognised gains and losses. FRS 3:31,66

True and fair override

34 There is the overriding consideration that a true and fair view must be given in the accounts. Directors are therefore required to: 1985 s 226(2) (1989 s 4)

(a) provide additional information, either in the accounts or in a note, where compliance with the standard formats and disclosure rules would not be sufficient to give a true and fair view; and 1985 s 226(4) (1989 s 4)

(b) depart from the standard formats or disclosure rules where, owing to special circumstances, compliance would be inconsistent with the requirement to give a true and fair view. 1985 s 226(5) (1989 s 4)

35 If the directors apply sub-paragraph (b) above, then they have to give the particulars of, reasons for, and the effects of such departures. As the Act gives no further elaboration of this requirement, the UITF has issued an Abstract that provides the following guidance on how the statutory disclosure requirements should be interpreted:

(a) particulars of departure should include a statement of the treatment which the Act would normally require in the circumstances and a description of the treatment actually adopted; UITF Abstract 7

(b) reasons for the departure should include a statement as to why the treatment prescribed would not give a true and fair view; and

(c) the effect of the departure should include a description of how the position shown in the accounts is different as a result of the departure, normally with quantification, except:

(i) where quantification is already evident in the accounts themselves (an example of which might be a presentation rather than a measurement matter, such as an adaptation of the headings in the Act's format requirements not covered by paragraph 17 above); or

(ii) where the effect cannot be quantified, in which case the directors should explain the circumstances.

36 Where the departure in sub-paragraph 34(b) above occurred in a previous year and still continues, the disclosures required by paragraph 35 should be made in all subsequent accounts, and should include corresponding amounts for the previous year. UITF Abstract 7

37 Where the departure affects only the corresponding amounts, the disclosures required by paragraph 35 should be given for those corresponding amounts. UITF Abstract 7

38 The disclosure required by paragraph 35 above should either be included, or cross referenced, in the note that includes a statement as to whether the accounts have been prepared in accordance with 'applicable accounting standards' in accordance with paragraph 36A of schedule 4 to the Act (see Chapter 4).

Format for small companies

39 As stated in paragraph 7 above, The Companies Act 1985 (Accounts of Small and Medium-sized Enterprises and Publication of Accounts in ECUs) Regulations modifies the balance sheet formats and introduces new exemptions from the disclosure requirements of schedule 4 for small companies and groups. The modified formats and the available exemptions (but not compulsory) apply to annual accounts (i.e. shareholders' accounts) and directors' report of small companies and groups for accounting periods ending on or after 16 November 1992. SI 1992 No 2452

40 The Regulations introduces new Parts I and II into schedule 8 to the Act that deal with the preparation of annual accounts and the directors' report respectively. The old Parts I and II of schedule 8 that deal with the filing of abbreviated accounts for small and medium-sized companies and which continue to apply are now renumbered as sections A and B respectively of Part III of schedule 8 (see Chapter 9).

Balance sheet formats

41 In preparing its balance sheet according to the balance sheet formats specified in schedule 4 to the Act, a small company may claim any or all of the available exemptions. The exemptions allow a small company to combine many of the headings preceded by Arabic numerals in the schedule 4 balance sheet formats into new headings. The general headings and the items preceded by Roman numerals remain unchanged. The balance sheet formats as adapted for small companies are shown in Appendix 1. 1985 8 sch 2(1) (amended by SI 1992 No 2452)

42 Where any of the above modifications are applied by a small company, schedule 4 should be read as if the balance sheet formats were the formats as modified and references to the formats and the items in them should be construed accordingly. 1985 8 sch 2(2) (amended by SI 1992 No 2452)

Notes to the balance sheet formats

43 The notes to the balance sheet formats in schedule 4 continue to apply to items that have been renumbered or combined. However a small company:

(a) in the case of both formats 1 and 2, need not comply with the requirements to show amounts falling due after more than one year separately for each item included under debtors (Note 5 of Notes on the 1985 8 sch 5(a) (amended by SI 1992 No 2452) balance sheet formats) if it discloses in the notes to the accounts the aggregate amount included under 'Debtors' (items C II 1 to 6) falling due after more than one year; and

(b) in the case of Format 2, need not comply with the requirements to show separately the amounts falling due within one year and after one year for each of the items C 1 to 9 (Note 13 of Notes to the balance sheet formats), if it discloses in the notes to the accounts the aggregate amount included under 'Creditors' (item C under liabilities) falling due within one year and the aggregate amount falling due after one year. 1985 8 sch 5(b) (amended by SI 1992 No 2452)

Notes to the balance sheet

44 A small company need *not* give any of the information supplementing the balance sheet required by the following paragraphs of schedule 4: 1985 8 sch 6 (amended by SI 1992 No 2452)

(a) paragraph 40 - particulars of any contingent right to the allotment of shares (see Chapter 5, paragraph 124);

(b) paragraph 41 - information regarding issue and redemption of debentures (see Chapter 5, paragraph 175);

(c) paragraph 44 - details of the company's freehold and leasehold properties (see Chapter 5, paragraph 29);

(d) paragraph 47 - the amount of any provision for deferred and other taxation (see Chapter 5, paragraph 149);

(e) paragraph 48(2) - the terms of repayment and interest rates for debts (see Chapter 5, paragraph 166);

(f) paragraph 48(4)(b) - the nature of securities given for debts (see Chapter 5, paragraph 167);

(g) paragraph 51(2) - the aggregate amount of loans provided by way of financial assistance for the purchase of own shares (see Chapter 5, paragraph 119); and

(h) paragraph 51(3) - the amount recommended for distribution by way of dividend (see Chapter 5, paragraph 181).

45 Further exemptions and modifications that are permitted in respect of balance sheet information are as follows:

(a) Where the value of stocks and fungible assets included in the accounts differs materially from their relevant alternative amount (i.e. the replacement cost or most recent purchase or production cost), the amount of the difference need not be disclosed (see Chapter 5, paragraph 86); 1985 8 sch 7 (amended by SI 1992 No 2452)

(b) Disclosure of debts repayable in more than five years by instalments or otherwise by instalments need not be given for each item included in 'Creditors' if the required information is given in aggregate for all items (see Chapter 5, paragraph 165); — 1985 8 sch 8 (amended by SI 1992 No 2452)

(c) Disclosure of dealings with or interests in group undertakings (required where amounts attributable to such dealings are shown in the company's balance sheet) need not be given (see chapter 5, paragraph 2); — 1985 8 sch 10 (amended by SI 1992 No 2452)

(d) Disclosure of the financial year of any subsidiary undertaking that did not end with that of the parent company and the reasons for adopting a different year end need not be given (see Chapter 5, paragraph 58); and — 1985 8 sch 11 (amended by SI 1992 No 2452)

(e) Where consolidated accounts are not prepared, the aggregate amount of the total investment in shares of subsidiary undertakings calculated under the equity method of valuation need not be given (see Chapter 5, paragraph 60). — 1985 8 sch 11 (amended by SI 1992 No 2452)

46 *Notes to the profit and loss account*

A small company need *not* give any of the information supplementing the profit and loss account required by the following paragraphs of schedule 4: — 1985 8 sch 6 (amended by SI 1992 No 2452)

(a) paragraph 53(2) - details of interest payable or similar charges (see Chapter 6, paragraph 95);

(b) paragraph 53(3) - amounts set aside for redemption of share capital and loans (see Chapter 6, paragraph 113);

(c) paragraph 53(4) - the amount of income from listed investments (see Chapter 6, paragraph 57);

(d) paragraph 53(5) - the amount of rentals from land (see Chapter 6, paragraph 55(b));

(e) paragraph 53(6) - amounts payable in respect of hire of plant and machinery (see Chapter 6, paragraph 98);

(f) paragraph 54 - particulars of tax (see Chapter 6, paragraphs 101, 104 and 108);

(g) paragraph 55 - particulars of turnover (see Chapter 6, paragraphs 37 to 40). If, however, the company has supplied geographical markets outside the UK, the notes must state the percentage of turnover attributable to those markets. In giving this information, the directors must consider the manner in which the company's activities are analysed (see Chapter 6, paragraph 39); and — 1985 8 sch 9 (amended by SI 1992 No 2452)

(h) paragraph 56 - particulars of staff numbers and costs (see Chapter 6, paragraphs 76 and 77).

47 The following information regarding directors' emoluments need not be given: 1985 8 sch 12 (amended by SI 1992 No 2452)

(a) The breakdown of the aggregate amount of directors' emoluments for services as directors of the company or its subsidiaries and otherwise in connection with the management of the affairs of the company or its subsidiaries (see Chapter 6, paragraph 66(a));

(b) details of chairman's and directors' emoluments (see Chapter 6, paragraph 71); and

(c) details of pensions of directors and past directors (see Chapter 6, paragraph 66(b)).

Information must still be given of the aggregate amount of directors' emoluments (without the breakdown mentioned in (a) above), directors' emoluments waived, compensation for loss of office and sums paid to third parties for making available the services of directors.

Consolidated accounts

48 Where a parent company of a small group is exempt from preparing consolidated accounts under section 248 (see Chapter 9, paragraph 22) but nevertheless chooses to do so, it may take the same exemptions as explained in paragraphs 41 to 47 above that are available in preparing of the individual accounts, suitably modified for consolidated accounts. The modifications relate to the group balance sheet formats which are explained in the notes to Appendix 1 to this book. 1985 8 sch 13(1) (amended by SI 1992 No 2452)

49 Where a small company or a parent company of a small group prepares its individual accounts or consolidated accounts by taking advantage of any or all of the exemptions provided by Part I of schedule 8, the directors must make a statement, immediately above the signature on the company's balance sheet required by section 233, that: 1985 s 246(1A) (inserted by SI 1992 No 2452)

(a) advantage has been taken, in the preparation of the accounts, of special exemptions as applicable to small companies; and

(b) a statement of the grounds on which, in the directors' opinion, the company is entitled to the exemptions.

50 As stated in Chapter 2, small companies are also given exemptions from disclosing certain information in the directors' report.

51	Where a small company has taken advantage of the exemptions allowed in preparing its annual accounts, those accounts shall not be deemed, by reason only of the fact that advantage has been taken of any exemptions set out in Part I of schedule 8, not to give a true and fair view as required by the Act.	1985 8 sch 14(2) (amended by SI 1992 No 2452)
52	Where the company is entitled to, and has taken advantage of, any exemptions set out in Part I of schedule 8, the auditors need only state in their report whether in their opinion the annual accounts have been properly prepared in accordance with the provisions of the Act applicable to small companies.	1985 8 sch 14(3) (amended by SI 1992 No 2452)

4 Accounting Principles and Policies

General

1 The Act sets out accounting principles which must be followed in the statutory accounts, whether these are prepared on an historical or current cost basis. The accounting principles follow closely the fundamental accounting concepts mentioned in SSAP 2. 1985 4 sch 9

Accounting principles

2 The Act and SSAP 2 specify four fundamental accounting principles which must be applied. They are as follows:

(a) the company shall be presumed to be carrying on its business as a going concern; 1985 4 sch 10 SSAP 2:14(a)

(b) accounting policies must be applied consistently to like items within the same accounts and from one financial year to the next; 1985 4 sch 11 (1989 1 sch 5) SSAP 2:14(c)

(c) all items must be determined on a prudent basis, and in particular: 1985 4 sch 12 SSAP 2:14(d)

(i) revenue and profits must not be anticipated, but should be recognised by inclusion in the profit and loss account only when realised in the form of cash or of other assets the ultimate realisation of which can be assessed with reasonable certainty; and

(ii) all liabilities and losses which have arisen or are likely to arise in respect of the financial year to which the accounts relate or a previous financial year must be taken into account, including those which only become apparent between the balance sheet date and the date on which the balance sheet is signed; and SSAP 17:19,22

(d) all income and charges relating to the financial year covered by the accounts must be taken into account without regard to the date of receipt or payment. This is commonly referred to as the accruals concept.

1985 4 sch 13
SSAP 2:14(b)

3 In determining the aggregate amount of any item in a company's balance sheet or profit and loss account, the amount of each individual asset or liability included in that amount shall be determined separately. For example, in calculating the amount at which stocks are to be stated, the test 'lower of cost and net realisable value' is to be applied to each individual stock line, rather than to the total stock holding.

1985 4 sch 14
Author

4 If the directors consider that there are special reasons for departing from any of the principles set out above they may do so, provided that particulars of the departure, the reasons for it, and its effect are stated in a note to the accounts. The way in which such departures should be reported in the accounts is discussed in Chapter 3.

1984 sch 15
SSAP 2:17

Accounting rules

5 There are two sets of accounting rules, known respectively as the historical cost accounting rules and the alternative accounting rules (see paragraphs 22 to 56 below). Whichever set of accounting rules is adopted, the accounting principles set out above remain of general application. Companies normally choose to adopt the historical cost accounting rules for the majority of their assets, but often adopt the alternative accounting rules for certain assets such as land and buildings or investments.

1985 4 sch 16-34
1985 4 sch 9
Author

Accounting policies

6 The accounting policies adopted in determining the amounts to be included in respect of all material items shown in the balance sheet and in determining the profit or loss must be stated in a note to the accounts. In particular the Act requires the policies followed in respect of the following matters to be explained:

1985 4 sch 36
SSAP 2:18

(a) foreign currency translation and in particular the method used in the translation of the accounts of foreign enterprises and the treatment accorded to exchange differences; and

1985 4 sch 58
SSAP 20:59

(b) depreciation and diminution in value of assets.

1985 4 sch 36
SSAP 12:25

7 Additionally, various accounting standards require the adoption and disclosure of accounting policies in respect of certain other items not specifically covered by the Act. These are dealt with in this book under the relevant headings.

Compliance with accounting standards

8 The notes to the accounts must include a statement as to whether the accounts have been prepared in accordance with 'applicable accounting standards'. Particulars must be given of any material departure from those standards and the reasons for the departure. This disclosure need not be given by small and medium-sized companies.

1985 4 sch 36A
(1989 7 sch)
1985 s 246(1)
(1989 s 13)

9 'Applicable accounting standards' are statements of standard accounting practice that are:

1985 s 256
(1989 s 19)

(a) issued by such body or bodies as may be prescribed by regulations; and

(b) relevant, in accordance with the terms of the standard, to the company's circumstances and to the accounts.

As stated in Chapter 1, the ASB has taken over the role of issuing accounting standards applicable in the UK. It is prescribed as the standard setting body with effect from 20 August 1990 by the Accounting Standards (Prescribed Body) Regulations 1990 (SI 1990 No 1667).

10 The FRRP has ruled that a statement that the accounts have been prepared in accordance with applicable accounting standards (the 'compliance statement') as required by paragraph 36A of schedule 4 (see paragraph 8 above) does not exempt companies from the requirements to state their main accounting policies as required by paragraph 36 of schedule 4 (see paragraph 6 above). The Panel has taken legal advice that confirms that the requirements of the two paragraphs are separate and distinct. This is so both with respect to a policy which a company chooses to adopt and with respect to a policy that a company is compelled to adopt by virtue of the application of an accounting standard.

11 Paragraph 2 of the Explanatory Foreword to Statements of Standard Accounting Practice, and paragraph 21(a) of the continuing obligations for listed companies in the Stock Exchange's Yellow Book (applicable to UK companies only), already require that significant departures from SSAPs are adequately disclosed and explained in the accounts.

12 In July 1991, the ASB issued an ED of a Foreword to Accounting Standards which envisages that only in exceptional circumstances will departure from the requirements of an accounting standard be necessary in order for the accounts to give a true and fair view. In such circumstances, informed and unbiased judgement should be used to devise an appropriate alternative treatment, which should be consistent with the economic and commercial characteristics of the circumstances concerned. Particulars and reasons for any material departure from an accounting standard should be disclosed. The financial effects of the departure should also be given unless such disclosure

Exposure Draft

would be impracticable or misleading in the context of giving a true and fair view.

13 The Review Panel has also ruled that where there is a departure from accounting standards the particulars of and clear reasons for the departures should be included either as part of the compliance statement itself or by that statement containing a specific cross-reference to the Note in which the particulars and reasons for the departures are given. These requirements are also contained in UITF Abstract 7 which is discussed in Chapter 3.

Accounting for substance

14 FRED 4 'Reporting the substance of transactions' was issued in February 1993. It supersedes proposals issued by the ASC which took the form of two exposure drafts, ED 42 and its subsequent revision by ED 49. Like its predecessors, FRED 4 states unequivocally that accounts should reflect the substance of a transaction. The FRED sets out the principles to be followed in determining the substance of transactions and arrangements, whether any resulting assets and liabilities should be recognised in the balance sheet, and what disclosures should be made. Like ED 49, it provides application notes to clarify the application of its principles to a range of transactions and arrangements. The principal proposals of the FRED are summarised below.

15 In determining the substance of a transaction, it is necessary to consider:

(a) whether or not the transaction has given rise to new assets or liabilities FRED 4:13
and whether or not it has increased or decreased the assets or liabilities (actual or contingent) of the reporting entity; and

(b) all aspects and implications of the transaction, including options, FRED 4:12,15
guarantees or conditional provisions, giving greater weight to those likely to have a commercial effect in practice. A series of linked transactions should be viewed as a whole. Where an option exits, but FRED 4:16
there is no genuine commercial possibility that it will be exercised, it should be ignored. However, where there is no commercial possibility that an option will not be exercised, its exercise should be assumed.

16 Once it has been determined whether an asset or liability has been identified, it is necessary to consider whether it qualifies for recognition. An asset or liability will qualify for recognition if it meets the definition of an asset or liability and satisfies the two general recognition criteria that follow the definitions given below:

(a) assets are defined as rights or other access to future economic benefits FRED 4:2
controlled by an entity as a result of past transactions or events;

(b) liabilities are defined as an entity's obligations to transfer economic FRED 4:4
benefits as a result of past transactions or events;

(c) the general recognition tests are: FRED 4:17

(i) there is sufficient evidence of the item including, where appropriate, evidence that a future inflow or outflow of benefit will occur; and

(ii) the asset or liability can be measured at a monetary amount with sufficient reliability.

17 An asset (or part of an asset) should cease to be recognised only if: FRED 4:19

(a) the entity retains no significant or other access to material economic benefits relating to the asset (or part); and

(b) any risk retained relating to the asset (or part) is immaterial in relation to the variation in benefits likely to occur in practice.

18 Assets and liabilities qualifying for recognition on the balance sheet should not be offset. However, debit and credit balances should only be aggregated into a single net item (i.e. offset) where they do not constitute separate assets and liabilities. FRED 4:24

19 Sufficient information should be disclosed in the accounts whether or not the transactions result in assets or liabilities being recognised on the balance sheet. In addition, where a transaction has resulted in the recognition of assets or liabilities whose nature differs from that expected of an item included under the relevant heading, the difference should be explained. FRED 4:25,26

20 The ASB has introduced in the FRED a linked presentation for certain types of non-recourse finance arrangements. In such arrangements, the finance relating to a particular asset (or group of assets) should be deducted from the related asset (or group of assets) on the face of the balance sheet where: FRED 4:20,21

(a) the finance will be repaid only from proceeds generated by the specific item it finances (or by transfer of the item itself) and there is no possibility whatsoever of a claim on the entity being established other than against funds generated by that item (or the item itself); and

(b) there is no provision whereby the entity may either keep the item on repayment of the finance or reacquire it at any time.

The situations when a linked presentation can be used are strictly controlled by a number of detailed tests that are specified in paragraph 21 of the exposure draft. Such a presentation does not constitute an offset (see paragraph 18 above), but it is additional information about a (net) asset, necessary in order to give a true and fair view.

21 In some situations, a group may conduct its business through entities that it directly or indirectly controls, but which do not fall within the legal FRED 4:30,32

definition of a subsidiary undertaking. Such entities are normally referred to as 'quasi subsidiaries'. The FRED proposes that the assets, liabilities, profits,losses and cash flows of a quasi subsidiary should be included in the consolidated accounts of the group in the same way as if it were a subsidiary. However, where such a subsidiary holds a single item or a single portfolio of similar items and where the criteria for linked presentation are met, the quasi subsidiary should be included in the consolidated accounts using the linked presentation (see Chapter 8).

Historical cost accounting rules

Fixed assets

22 The following accounting policies apply to all items described in the balance sheet as fixed assets and therefore relate to intangibles, tangibles and also fixed asset investments.

Cost

23 Subject to any provision for depreciation, the amount to be included in respect of any fixed asset must be its purchase price or production cost. Such purchase price or production cost must be determined according to the following rules: 1985 4 sch 17

(a) purchase price must include the incidental costs of acquisition; 1985 4 sch 26(1)

(b) production cost must include the purchase price of raw materials and consumables used, together with other costs incurred which are directly attributable to the production of the asset; 1985 4 sch 26(2)

(c) production cost may include a reasonable proportion of the costs incurred by the company which are only indirectly attributable to the production of that asset, but only to the extent that they relate to the period of production; and 1985 4 sch 26(3)(a)

(d) production cost may include interest on capital borrowed to finance the production of that asset, to the extent that it accrues in respect of the period of production. Interest so included is to be disclosed in a note to the accounts. 1985 4 sch 26(3)(b)

24 Where no record of the purchase price or production cost of an asset exists, or such record cannot be obtained without unreasonable expense or delay, the purchase price or production cost shall be the value of the asset according to the earliest available record of its value. Where advantage is taken of this rule for the first time, particulars must be given in a note to the accounts. 1985 4 sch 28; 1985 4 sch 51(1)

25 Where the amount repayable on a debt exceeds the value of consideration received (e.g. redemption of a loan issued at a discount), the difference may be treated as an 'asset', which must be written off by reasonable amounts 1985 4 sch 24

each year, and be completely written off prior to repayment of the debt. If the unamortised amount is not shown in the balance sheet as a separate item, it must be disclosed in a note to the accounts. However, this provision of the Act has little effect in practice and will be superseded once FRED 3 becomes an accounting standard. Under FRED 3 the difference between the net proceeds and the total payments made in respect of the debt represents finance costs which should be allocated to periods over the term of the debt. The difference cannot be treated as an asset. — Author; FRED 3:25

Depreciation

26 Fixed assets having a limited useful economic life are to be depreciated to their residual values, if any, systematically over such life. However, it should be noted that SSAP 19 states that certain investment properties should not be depreciated in this way. The consequences of this recommendation are discussed in paragraphs 54 to 56 below. — 1985 4 sch 18; SSAP 12:14-15; SSAP 19:10

27 The depreciation charge in the profit and loss account should be based on the carrying amount of the asset in the balance sheet, whether historical cost or revalued amount. The whole of the depreciation charge should be reflected in the profit and loss account and no part of the depreciation charge should be set directly against reserves. Supplementary depreciation should not be charged in the profit and loss account. — SSAP 12:16

28 Normally the net book amount of fixed assets should be written off over the remaining useful life where there is either:

(a) a revision of the estimated useful life; or — SSAP 12:18

(b) a change in the method of depreciation. — SSAP 12:21

Where, however, in following the accounting treatment in (a) the future results or financial position will be distorted, the adjustment to accumulated depreciation should be recognised in the accounts in accordance with FRS 3. This means that such an adjustment will usually be dealt with in arriving at the profit on ordinary activities. The nature and amount of the adjustment should be disclosed.

29 Any fixed asset (including an investment) whose value is considered to have diminished permanently must be written down to its estimated recoverable amount, which if necessary should then be amortised over its remaining useful life. If at any time the reasons for making such a provision cease to apply, the provision should be written back to the extent that it is no longer necessary. In the case of an asset that has not been revalued, provisions for permanent diminution in value of an asset (and any reversals) should be charged (credited) in the profit and loss account of the period. — 1985 4 sch 19(2); SSAP 12:19; 1985 4 sch 19(3); SSAP 12:20

30 Fixed asset investments may, however, be written down where there has been a diminution in value even if that diminution is not considered to be — 1985 4 sch 19(1)

permanent. The law is permissive rather than prescriptive on this point. Such a write down may be prudent, but would not be regarded as normal practice. Author

Government grants

31 Government grants should be recognised in the profit and loss account so as to match them with the expenditure towards which they are intended to contribute. Where grants are given for immediate financial support or assistance, they should be recognised in the profit and loss account of the period in which they became receivable. A government grant should not be recognised in the profit and loss account until the conditions for its receipt have been complied with and there is reasonable evidence that the grant will be received. Where the recognition in the profit and loss account of part or all of the grant that has been received is deferred, the amount so deferred should be treated as deferred income. SSAP 4:23 SSAP 4:24

32 Prior to the revision of SSAP 4 in July 1990, government grants, unless treated as a deferred credit, could be deducted from the cost of the fixed assets to which the grants relate. Following Counsel's opinion, SSAP 4 (revised) has removed the option for schedule 4 companies to deduct government grants from the purchase price or production cost of assets. Banking companies are similarly restricted under the new schedule 9 rules. The option, however, remains available to unincorporated entities and insurance companies preparing accounts under Part I of schedule 9A to the Act. SSAP 4:25 Author

33 Government grants sometimes become repayable because certain conditions are not fulfilled. The enterprise should therefore consider regularly whether there is a likelihood of a breach of the conditions on which the grant is made. If such a breach has occurred, or appears likely to occur, the potential liability to repay the grant should be provided to the extent that its repayment is probable. Author SSAP 4:29

Current assets

34 Subject to the provisos in the following two paragraphs, the amount to be included in respect of any current asset must be its purchase price or production cost determined in the same way as for a fixed asset. These concepts will normally only be relevant to stocks and investments. 1985 4 sch 22 Author

35 Where the net realisable value of any current asset is lower than the purchase price or production cost, it must be included at net realisable value. 1985 4 sch 23(1)

36 It will not normally be appropriate to include interest payable on borrowings as part of the production cost of work in progress, unless sums borrowed can be identified as financing specific long-term contracts. SSAP 9: Appendix 1:21 Author

37 Where a current asset has been written down to net realisable value in accordance with the preceding paragraph, the asset must be restored (wholly

or partly as appropriate) to its original value if the reasons for writing it down cease to apply. 1985 4 sch 23(2)

38 Distribution costs must not be included in production cost for any current asset. 1985 4 sch 26(4)

39 The purchase price or production cost of any stocks or fungible assets (see below) may be determined by any one of the following methods: 1985 4 sch 27(1),(2)

(a) FIFO (first in, first out);

(b) LIFO (last in, first out);

(c) weighted average; and

(d) other methods similar to (a), (b) or (c).

40 Although the law allows the adoption of LIFO, SSAP 9 points out that its use can result in the reporting of current assets at amounts that bear little relationship to recent costs. This may result in not only a significant misstatement of balance sheet amounts but also a potential distortion of current and future results. In any case the method of determining cost must be one which appears to the directors to be appropriate in the circumstances of the company. 1985 4 sch 27(1),(2) SSAP 9:39

41 Fungible assets are assets which are substantially indistinguishable from other assets included in the same category. These will include investments (see Chapter 5). 1985 4 sch 27(6)

Transfers from current assets to fixed assets

42 Where assets are transferred from current assets to fixed assets because the asset is to be retained for use on a continuing basis, the transfer should be made at the lower of cost or net realisable value. Where the transfer is made at net realisable value at the date of transfer (which is the date of management's change of intent) and if this amount is less than its previous carrying value the diminution should be charged in the profit and loss account, reflecting the loss to the company while the asset was held as a current asset. UITF Abstract 5

43 Where assets are transferred at cost or at net realisable value in accordance with the above paragraph, fixed asset accounting rules will apply to the assets subsequent to the date of transfer. In cases where the transfer is at net realisable value, the asset should be accounted for as a fixed asset at a valuation (under the alternative accounting rules) as at the date of transfer. At subsequent balance sheet dates it may or may not be revalued, but in either event the disclosure requirements appropriate to a valuation should be given. UITF Abstract 5

Alternative accounting rules

44 The general intent of the alternative accounting rules is to give statutory support to the concept of providing current cost information in accounts, and to permit the inclusion of certain assets at a valuation in accounts that are in other respects prepared under the historical cost convention.

45 The accounts which a company must prepare to comply with legislation, i.e. its main accounts, may take one of the three following forms:

(a) pure historical cost accounts;

(b) historical cost accounts incorporating certain asset revaluations; and

(c) current cost accounts.

Any of those three forms may use either the nominal pound or a unit of constant purchasing power (CPP) as the unit of measurement. The former is almost always adopted.

46 In addition, companies may attach supplementary accounts, prepared under the current or historical cost conventions, as appropriate. In most cases such companies will prepare their main accounts under the historical cost convention (with or without asset revaluations), with supplementary current cost accounts. The statutory provisions regarding main accounts do not apply to such supplementary accounts; however, they should have the same general structure as the main accounts in order to aid comparison.

47 Detailed guidance on accounting for the effects of changing prices, including current cost asset valuation, is contained in 'Accounting for the effects of changing prices: a Handbook' issued in 1986 by the Accounting Standards Committee. Reference should be made to that book if current cost information is presented as the main accounts or as supplementary accounts.

48 If the main accounts are prepared on anything other than a pure historical cost basis, the alternative accounting rules set out in the Act must be followed. These are summarised below. 1985 4 sch 29-34

49 Assets may be valued according to the following rules:

(a) intangible fixed assets, other than goodwill, at current cost; 1985 4 sch 31(1)

(b) tangible fixed assets at market value at the date of their last valuation, or at current cost; 1985 4 sch 31(2)

(c) stocks at current cost; 1985 4 sch 31(5)

(d) fixed asset investments either: 1985 4 sch 31(3)

(i) at market value at the date of their last valuation; or

(ii) on a basis considered by the directors to be appropriate in the company's circumstances, provided that the basis of valuation and the reasons for its adoption are stated;

(e) current asset investments at current cost; and

(f) current assets not covered in (a) to (e) above, on an historical cost basis.

50 The notes must describe the valuation bases and methods adopted. 1985 4 sch 33(2)

51 Neither the Act nor SSAP 22 permits the writing up of goodwill above historical cost. 1985 4 sch 31(1) SSAP 22:41(a)

52 All surpluses (or deficits) arising on restating assets on a basis set out in paragraph 49 above are included in the statement of total recognised gains and losses (see Chapter 3) and are credited (or debited) to a 'revaluation reserve' (see Chapter 5) although it need not be called by that name. 1985 4 sch 34(1)(2) FRS 3:8,27

53 The taxation treatments of items charged or credited to the revaluation reserve must be stated. In practice, this will mean stating whether or not any provision for deferred tax has been established in relation to revaluation surpluses. 1985 4 sch 34(4) Author

54 The historical cost accounting rules set out above in respect of depreciation and other diminutions in value are also to be applied to assets valued according to the alternative accounting rules. For example, stocks are to be included in the balance sheet at net realisable value if this is lower than current cost. The current cost or market value of fixed assets must be reduced by deprecation calculated to write off that amount systematically over the asset's useful economic life. 1985 4 sch 32 Author

55 Where the balance sheet includes any items on a basis other than historical cost (i.e. at a revalued amount) the following information must be given, either on the face of the balance sheet or in a note to the accounts, in respect of each such balance sheet item (except stocks):

(a) the corresponding historical cost amount and, if relevant, accumulated depreciation; or 1985 sch 33(3),(4)

(b) the difference between the historical cost amount(s) and the amount(s) included in the balance sheet; 1985 4 sch 33(3)(b)

(c) except in the case of listed investments, the years in which the assets were severally valued and the several values; and 1985 4 sch 43(a)

(c) in the case of assets valued during the year, the names of the valuers or particulars of their qualifications, and the bases of valuation used. 1985 4 sch 43(b)

56 Where the main accounts are modified historical cost accounts (including asset revaluations) or current cost accounts, the company may show historical cost depreciation on the face of its profit and loss account, provided that the difference between historical cost depreciation and that based on the valuation of the asset is shown separately, either by note or on the face of the profit and loss account. In fact, FRS 3 requires a separate note of historical cost profits and losses for the period, in those instances where there is a material difference between the result as disclosed in the profit and loss account and the result on an unmodified historical cost basis (see chapter 3). This will aid comparability among companies that prepare accounts on a different basis. 1985 4 sch 32(3) Author

Investment properties

57 Compliance with SSAP 19 requires investment properties to be carried in the balance sheet at market value and brings the company within the scope of the alternative accounting rules. These rules require revalued fixed assets to be depreciated, and a conflict therefore arises between the rules and SSAP 19 (which states that the depreciation provisions of SSAP 12 should not be followed in respect of freehold investment properties). SSAP 19:11 1985 4 sch 32

58 Non-depreciation of investment properties as required by SSAP 19 is a departure from the Act only in certain circumstances. For example, the residual value of a company's investment properties might be such that any resulting depreciation would be immaterial. In this circumstance, following SSAP 19 does not constitute a departure from the depreciation rules in the Act. However, where the circumstances are such that the Act would require depreciation whereas SSAP 19 does not, it is necessary to depart from the otherwise specific requirement of the law in order to comply with the overriding requirement for the accounts to give a true and fair view. Where the true and fair override is invoked, the directors must give, in a note to the accounts, particulars of the departure, the reasons for it, and its effect (see Chapter 3). Author SSAP 19:17,18

Investment companies

59 Investment companies are exempted from some of the applications of the alternative accounting rules. Details are given in part V of schedule 4 to the Act. 1985 4 sch 71(1)

5 Balance Sheet

Format

1 The rules governing the selection and adaptation of the alternative formats are set out in Chapter 3 of this book. In the following paragraphs, items are dealt with in the order in which they arise in balance sheet format 2, and references to 'item ....' in the following paragraphs are to that format.

Group companies

2 If a company is a member of a group, for every item where the balance sheet formats require the disclosure of the balance attributable to group undertakings (viz investments, debtors and creditors) there must be a further analysis between: 1985 4 sch 59 (1989 1 sch 11(2))

(a) amounts attributable to any parent undertaking or fellow subsidiary undertaking; and

(b) amounts attributable to the company's subsidiaries.

There is an equivalent provision, in relation to consolidated accounts, with respect to balances attributable (a) to parent and fellow subsidiary undertakings of the parent company and (b) to unconsolidated subsidiaries. 1985 4A sch 1(2) (1989 2 sch 1)

Abbreviated accounts

3 Companies preparing 'abbreviated accounts' should refer to Chapter 9, which explains how the rules set out in this chapter are to be applied to the abbreviated accounts which may be filed by small and medium-sized companies.

Fixed Assets (Item B)

Definition

4 Fixed assets are assets intended for use on a continuing basis in the company's activities. Current assets are defined as those not intended for such use. 1985 s 262(1) (1989 s 22)

General

5 Fixed assets must be shown subdivided into three groups: 1985 4 sch formats

(a) Intangible assets.

(b) Tangible assets.

(c) Investments.

6 In respect of each item shown as a fixed asset in the standard format there must be stated: 1985 4 sch 42(1),(2)

(a) the amount of that item stated at cost (or, where the alternative accounting rules are used, at a revaluation or current cost) at the beginning and end of the financial year; and

(b) the effect on that item of:

(i) acquisitions during the year;

(ii) disposals during the year;

(iii) transfers of assets of the company to and from that item during the year; and

(iv) any revision of the amount of that item during the year as a result of that item being valued on an acceptable accounting basis other than cost.

7 In respect of each item shown above, there must also be stated the amounts of: 1985 4 sch 42(3)

(a) the accumulated depreciation at the beginning and end of the financial year;

(b) any provisions for depreciation or diminution in value made in the financial year;

(c) any adjustments to such provisions resulting from the disposal of any assets during the financial year; and

(d) any other adjustments made to such provisions during the year.

8 Corresponding amounts for the previous year are not required for the reconciliations in the preceding two paragraphs. 1985 4 sch 58(3)

9 In addition SSAP 12 requires, for all fixed assets subject to depreciation, the disclosure of: SSAP 12:25

(a) the depreciation method(s) used;

(b) the useful economic lives or the depreciation rates used; and

(c) the effect, if material, on depreciation in the year of:

(i) a change in the method of depreciation and the reason for the change; and — SSAP 12:26

(ii) a revaluation of fixed assets. — SSAP 12:27

10 Where any fixed assets are valued on a basis other than cost, the alternative accounting rules, which require additional disclosures, apply (see Chapter 4). In particular, these rules apply to historical cost accounts including land and buildings at a revalued amount. — 1985 4 sch 29-34

11 Where interest on capital borrowed to finance the production of an asset has been included in the production cost of that asset, that fact must be disclosed together with the amount of interest so included. Such interest may only be included to the extent that it accrues in respect of the period of production. — 1985 4 sch 26(3)(b)

12 It is not clear whether the amount of such interest should be disclosed only in the year in which it is first capitalised, or in all subsequent years in which the asset is carried in the accounts. The Act requires disclosure of 'the amount of interest so included'. This presumably means that the cumulative amount of capitalised interest rather than the amount capitalised during the year should be disclosed. Consequently for fixed assets the disclosure ought to continue beyond the production period. However, listed companies should state the amount of interest capitalised *during the year* and treatment of any related tax relief. Interest may be capitalised either gross or net of tax relief. — Author; ASL 21(g)

13 In May 1990, the ASC issued ED 51 - 'Accounting for fixed assets and revaluations'. The major changes to existing accounting practice that are proposed in the ED concern the treatment of permanent diminutions in value of revalued assets and a new requirement to keep valuations up to date. The ASB is currently developing revised proposals that may in due course require regular revaluations of selected fixed assets. — Author

Intangible fixed assets (item B I)

14 *Development costs (item B I 1)*

Although pure and applied research expenditure must be written off as incurred, development costs may be included in a company's balance sheet in special circumstances. In such cases there must be stated in a note to the accounts: — 1985 4 sch 3(2)(c); SSAP 13:24,25; 1985 4 sch 20

(a) the reasons for capitalising the expenditure; and

(b) the period over which the costs are being written off.

SSAP 13 sets out the criteria for determining such 'special circumstances'. Expenditure incurred in locating and exploiting mineral deposits in the extractive industries is excluded from the scope of the standard. SSAP 13:25 SSAP 13:18

15 All companies must disclose movements on deferred development expenditure and the amounts carried forward at the beginning and end of the period, under intangible fixed assets in the balance sheet. Certain companies must disclose the details of research and development expenditure charged in the profit and loss account (see Chapter 6). SSAP 13:31,32

16 The accounting policy followed for research and development expenditure should be clearly explained. SSAP 13:30

17 Development expenses are to be treated as a realised loss in computing distributable profits, even if carried forward, unless the directors consider that there are special circumstances (see above) for not so treating them. Such reason must be disclosed in a note to the accounts together with the fact that the development expenses are not to be treated as a realised loss. 1985 s 269

Concessions, patents, licences, trade marks and similar assets (item B I 2)

18 Trade marks, patents and similar rights and assets must not be included in a balance sheet unless: 1985 4 sch format, note 2

(a) the assets were acquired for valuable consideration, and are not required to be shown as goodwill; or

(b) the assets in question were created by the company itself.

Goodwill (item B I 3)

19 SSAP 22 'Accounting for goodwill' sets out rules that apply both to goodwill in the individual accounts of a company and to goodwill arising on consolidation. In February 1990, the ASC published ED 47 which proposed important changes to SSAP 22. It proposed to remove the existing preferred option set out in paragraph 22 below of eliminating goodwill immediately against reserves. Instead, it proposed that purchased goodwill should be carried in the balance sheet and amortised over its useful economic life. Accounting for goodwill attracted a large volume of comments in response to the ASC's proposals. The ASB has inherited ED 47 from the ASC but is expected to develop its own proposals on the subject in due course. The requirements set out below are as stated in the existing standard. Author

20 The accounting policy followed in respect of goodwill should be explained in the notes to the accounts. SSAP 22:43

21 Amounts representing goodwill can only be included to the extent that the goodwill was acquired for valuable consideration. No amount should be attributed to non-purchased goodwill in the balance sheet and goodwill should not be revalued upwards. 1985 4 sch format, note 3 SSAP 22:35,41(a) 1985 4 sch 31(1)

22 Purchased goodwill should not be carried in the balance sheet as a SSAP 22:38-40
permanent item. Purchased goodwill (other than negative goodwill) should 1985 4 sch 21(1)-(3)
normally be eliminated from the accounts immediately on acquisition against
a suitable reserve. Negative consolidation difference ('negative goodwill')
should be credited directly to reserves.

23 Goodwill arising on consolidation appears only in consolidated accounts. Author
Where it is eliminated immediately it may be written off directly against the
consolidated profit and loss account reserve or some other reserve, such as
a merger reserve, if one exists in the consolidated accounts. It may not be 1985 4 sch 34(3)
written off against revaluation reserve. (1989 1 sch)

24 Where goodwill arises in the accounts of an individual company and is Author
written off directly against reserves, the question arises as to whether it
should be deducted from realised reserves. Where goodwill is written off as SSAP 22: Appendix 2
a matter of accounting policy rather than because of an actual diminution in
value, realised reserves need not be reduced immediately and goodwill may
be charged initially to a suitable unrealised reserve, if one exists. A suitable
unrealised reserve might be a merger reserve (arising from the use of
acquisition accounting where merger relief is available) or a reserve arising
from crediting negative goodwill to reserves. Revaluation reserve may not 1985 4 sch 34(3)
be used to write off goodwill. Goodwill written off against unrealised (1989 1 sch)
reserves should however be treated as a realised loss on a systematic basis SSAP 22: Appendix 2:2
in the same way as if the goodwill had been amortised. Negative goodwill SSAP 22: Appendix 2:3
should initially be credited to an unrealised reserve, from which it may be
transferred to realised reserves in line with the depreciation or realisation of
the assets acquired in the acquisition giving rise to the negative goodwill.

25 Purchased goodwill may alternatively be eliminated by amortisation through SSAP 22:41
the profit and loss account on a systematic basis over its useful economic
life. When purchased goodwill is eliminated by amortisation:

(a) it should be shown as a separate item under intangible fixed assets until SSAP 22:45
fully written off;

(b) the movement on the goodwill account during the year has to be 1985 4 sch 42
disclosed, showing the cost, accumulated amortisation and net book SSAP 22:45(a)
value at the beginning and end of the year and the amount of goodwill
amortised through the profit and loss account during the year; and

(c) the reason for choosing the period over which the goodwill is written 1985 4 sch 21
off and the period chosen for each major acquisition must be disclosed SSAP 22:45(b)
in a note to the accounts.

26 There shall also be stated in a note to the accounts the cumulative amount of 1985 4A sch 14
goodwill resulting from acquisitions in the current and earlier years which (1989 2 sch)
has been written off (either by immediate write off or by amortisation), after

deducting any goodwill attributable to subsidiary undertakings disposed of prior to the balance sheet date.

27 The amount of goodwill recognised as a result of any acquisitions during the year should be shown separately for each acquisition where material. Disclosure should indicate the method of dealing with goodwill arising, including whether it has been carried forward or written off and, in the latter case, against which reserve it has been written off. The treatment of goodwill arising on disposals is explained in Chapter 6. SSAP 22:44,47

Tangible fixed assets (item B II)

28 Tangible fixed assets include land and buildings, plant and machinery, fixtures, fittings, tools and equipment, payments on account and fixed assets under construction. The general rules regarding fixed assets have been set out above. Certain specific rules are set out below.

Land and buildings (items B II 1)

29 In relation to any amount which is shown in respect of the item 'land and buildings' in the company's balance sheet: 1985 4 sch 44

(a) the amounts included as freehold and leasehold land must be disclosed separately; and

(b) leasehold land must be analysed between long and short leases.

30 Long leases are those for which the unexpired term at the balance sheet date is not less than 50 years, and short leases are all other leases. 1985 4 sch 83

Investment properties

31 An investment property is defined as an interest in land and/or buildings: SSAP 19:7

(a) in respect of which construction and development have been completed; and

(b) which is held for its investment potential, with any rental income being negotiated at arm's length.

However, a property owned by a company and either occupied by it for its own purposes, or let to another group company, is not to be treated as an investment property. SSAP 19:8

32 Investment properties should be carried in the balance sheet at open market value, and that carrying value should be prominently displayed. This requirement will be satisfied by showing investment properties separately in the analysis of fixed assets given in the notes. Carrying investment properties at market value will automatically bring the company within the scope of the alternative accounting rules (see Chapter 4, which also refers to the non-depreciation of investment properties). SSAP 19:11,15 Author

33 Changes in the value of investment properties during the year should be recognised in the statement of total recognised gains and losses and disclosed as a movement on an investment revaluation reserve. If a deficit on revaluation exceeds the balance on the investment revaluation reserve, the excess should be charged to the profit and loss account and the reversal of the previously recognised surplus shown in the statement of total recognised gains and losses for the year. SSAP 19:13

34 The names of the valuers, or particulars of their qualifications, must be disclosed together with the bases of valuation used by them. If a valuer is an employee or officer of the company or group, that fact should also be stated. 1985 4 sch 43; SSAP 19:12

Other tangible fixed assets

35 Tangible fixed assets of a kind which are constantly being replaced (e.g. moulds and dies or hotel furnishings) may be included at a fixed quantity and value where their overall value is not material to assessing the company's state of affairs, and their quantity, value and composition are not subject to material variation. 1985 4 sch 25(1)(2)

Assets held under finance leases

36 Disclosure should be made of the accounting policy for finance leases. A finance lease is a lease, or equivalent hire purchase contract, that transfers substantially all the risks and rewards of ownership of an asset to the lessee. This should be presumed if at the inception of a lease the present value of the minimum lease payments (calculated by using the interest rate implicit in the lease), including any initial payment, amounts to substantially all (normally 90 per cent or more) of the fair value of the leased asset. Any other lease is an operating lease. SSAP 21:17; SSAP 21:15,31; SSAP 21:17

37 The presumption may be rebutted, notwithstanding this fact, if it can be clearly demonstrated that the lease in question does not transfer substantially all the risks and rewards of ownership (other than legal title) to the lessee. Similarly, the presumption that a lease whose discounted minimum lease payments do not exceed 90 per cent of the fair value of the asset is an operating lease may be rebutted if it can be clearly demonstrated that such a transfer of risks and rewards does occur. SSAP 21:16

38 A finance lease should be recorded in the balance sheet of a lessee as a tangible fixed asset and as an obligation to pay future rentals (paragraphs 168 to 170). At the inception of the lease the amounts to be recorded are based on the present value referred to above. SSAP 21:32

39 For assets capitalised under finance leases and shown separately either on the face of the balance sheet or in the notes to the accounts, the following must be disclosed, analysed by each major class of leased asset: SSAP 21:49

(a) gross amount;

(b) accumulated depreciation; and

(c) depreciation allocated for the period.

The depreciation allocation should be based on the shorter of the lease term and the asset's useful life. The lease term includes the optional secondary rental period where it is reasonable to assume that the lessee will exercise the option. SSAP 21:36 SSAP 21:19

40 Alternatively, the information required in the preceding paragraph may be included within the totals disclosed for each major class of owned tangible fixed asset. In this case the notes to the accounts must show in respect of assets held under finance leases: SSAP 21:50

(a) net amount of leased assets included in overall totals for each class; and

(b) total amount of depreciation allocated for the period in respect of leased assets.

The treatment adopted should normally depend on the materiality of the amounts involved. Author

Assets held for leasing or hire purchase

41 An asset held for use in operating leases by a lessor should be recorded as a fixed asset and depreciated over its useful life. SSAP 21:42 The gross amounts of assets held for use in operating leases, including equivalent hire purchase contracts, and the related accumulated depreciation charges, should be disclosed. SSAP 21:59

42 Where assets are leased either under a finance lease or under an equivalent hire purchase agreement, the lessor should record the amount due from the lessee as a debtor at the amount equal to the lessor's net investment in the lease after making provision for bad and doubtful rentals receivable. SSAP 21:38 The net investments in each of finance leases and equivalent hire purchase contracts at the balance sheet date should be disclosed. SSAP 21:58 As with other debtors the amounts falling due after more than one year from the balance sheet date must be shown separately (see paragraph 91). Author

43 There should additionally be disclosed:

(a) the cost of assets acquired, whether by purchase or finance lease (including equivalent hire purchase), for the purpose of letting under finance leases, or equivalent hire purchase contracts; and SSAP 21:60(c)

(b) the accounting policy adopted by lessors for accounting for finance leases and operating leases, including equivalent hire purchase contracts respectively. SSAP 21:60(a)

Investments (item B III or C III)

General

44 Investments may be included in the balance sheet as either fixed or current assets. Investments in the nature of trade investments or other investments

held on a long-term basis should normally be treated as fixed, and investments of a temporary nature (e.g. investments representing the employment outside the business of temporarily surplus funds) should be treated as current assets.

45 Listed investments are those which have been granted a listing either on a 'recognised investment exchange' other than an overseas investment exchange within the meaning of the Financial Services Act 1986 or on any stock exchange of repute outside Great Britain. A 'recognised investment exchange' means any body of persons that is a recognised investment exchange for the purposes of the Financial Services Act 1986. Currently, the only body designated in Great Britain as a recognised investment exchange is The International Stock Exchange. For guidance as to whether or not a stock exchange outside Great Britain is 'reputable', The International Stock Exchange should be consulted. In practice this would include most stock exchanges. Shares dealt in on the USM are not listed. 1985 4 sch 84 Author

46 For each item listed in the standard formats under investments (whether fixed or current) there must be stated the amount attributable to listed investments, and an analysis given differentiating between investments listed on a recognised stock exchange and those which have been granted a listing on other stock exchanges of repute. 1985 4 sch 45(1)

47 For listed investments there must also be stated: 1985 4 sch 45(2)

(a) the aggregate market value of those investments, where it differs from the amount at which they are included in the balance sheet; and

(b) the market value and the stock exchange value, if for accounts purposes the former is taken as higher than the latter.

These provisions apply for example to a holding company having a listed subsidiary. In such circumstances the stock exchange price may be an unrealistic measure of market value, since it will not contemplate a holding affording a controlling interest. If the directors consider that the market value exceeds the stock exchange value, disclosure must be made under (b) above, and it is desirable for the notes to include an explanation of the reasons for the differing valuations. Author

Fungible assets

48 Assets of any description are regarded as fungible if they are indistinguishable one from another. Such assets will normally only include stocks and investments. The following rules will usually only be relevant to investments because there are equivalent provisions (set out elsewhere in this chapter) which apply to all stocks, whether fungible or not. Shares of a particular class which confer identical rights on the holder should be regarded as fungible, even though they are individually distinguishable by numbers. 1985 4 sch 27(6) Author

49 The cost of any fixed or current asset which is considered to be fungible may be determined by either the FIFO, LIFO, weighted average or any other similar method which matches sales with original cost on an estimated basis. 1985 4 sch 27(1),(2)

50 If there is a material difference between the value for accounts purposes of any fungible assets, whose cost is determined by one of the above methods, and its value at replacement cost or most recent purchase price or production cost (whichever the directors consider the more appropriate comparison) the amount of the difference must be stated in a note to the accounts. 1985 4 sch 27(3)-(5)

Own shares (item B III 7 or C III 2)

51 The nominal value of any of its own shares held by a company and disclosed under one of the above headings must be shown separately. 1985 4 sch format, Note 4

Subsidiary undertakings

52 The definition of subsidiary undertaking is given in Chapter 8. This section explains the disclosures required for all subsidiary undertakings which apply whether or not consolidated accounts are prepared. Also set out below are those disclosures required only by companies not required to prepare consolidated accounts. The requirements for consolidated accounts are explained in Chapter 8.

53 If the disclosures required by schedule 5 to the Act and set out in paragraphs 55 to 68 below would, in the opinion of the directors, result in information of excessive length, the information need only be given in respect of: 1985 s 231(5),(6) (1989 s 6)

(a) those undertakings whose results or financial position principally affect the figures shown in the accounts; and

(b) any material subsidiaries excluded from consolidation.

If advantage is taken of this provision, that fact must be stated in the accounts and full particulars annexed to the next annual return.

54 With the consent of the Secretary of State, the information required by schedule 5 to the Act and set out in paragraphs 55 to 68 below need not be given in respect of undertakings established or carrying on business outside the UK, if in the opinion of the directors this would be seriously prejudicial to the business of the company, that subsidiary or any other subsidiary of the parent company. This exemption does not apply to paragraphs 60 and 64 below. Where advantage is taken of this exemption, that fact must be stated in the accounts. 1985 s 231(3),(4) (1989 s 6)

55 If, at the end of its financial year, a company has subsidiaries but is not required to prepare consolidated accounts, the reason why it is not required to do so must be stated. The company's individual accounts should state that its accounts present information about it as an individual undertaking and not about its group. This statement should include or refer to a note giving the 1985 5 sch 1 (1989 3 sch) FRS 2:22

grounds on which the parent company is exempt from preparing consolidated accounts. If the reason is that all of its subsidiaries fall within the exclusions provided for in section 229 of the Act (see paragraph 31 of Chapter 8) then it shall be stated with respect to each subsidiary which of those exclusions applies. Companies required to prepare consolidated accounts must disclose in respect of any subsidiaries excluded from the consolidation, the reasons for their exclusion (see Chapter 8). 1985 5 sch 15(4) (1989 3 sch)

56 Where at the end of the financial year the company has subsidiary undertakings, the following information must be given in respect of each subsidiary: 1985 5 sch 1-3,15-17 (1989 3 sch)

(a) the subsidiary's name;

(b) the country of incorporation (if other than Great Britain), the country of registration (England and Wales or Scotland) if incorporated in Great Britain, or the address of its principal place of business if unincorporated;

(c) a description of each class of shares held and the proportion of the nominal value of the allotted shares of that class represented by those shares (distinguishing between shares held by or on behalf of the parent company and those held by subsidiaries). The corresponding amount for the previous year need not be stated; 1985 4 sch 58(3) (1989 1 sch 10)

(d) the aggregate capital and reserves at the subsidiary's most recent financial year end;

(e) the profit or loss for that year;

(f) the nature of its business (if a principal subsidiary); and

(g) in the case of a listed holding company, the principal country of operations of active material subsidiaries. ASL 21(d)

57 The information in (d) and (e) of the preceding paragraph is not required if: 1985 5 sch 3,17 (1989 3 sch)

(a) the company is exempt from the requirement to prepare consolidated accounts by virtue of section 228 of the Act (being included in the accounts of a larger group, see Chapter 8); or

(b) the company is required to prepare consolidated accounts and:

(i) the accounts of the subsidiary are included in the consolidation; or

(ii) the investment in the subsidiary is included in the accounts by way of the equity method of valuation; or

(c) the company holds less than half of the nominal value of the allotted share capital of the subsidiary, and the subsidiary is not required by the Companies Act to file its balance sheet for its most recent financial year with the registrar and does not otherwise publish that balance sheet in Great Britain or elsewhere; or

(d) the information is not material.

58 Where the accounting period of any subsidiary (whether or not dealt with in the consolidated accounts) does not end with that of the parent company, the accounts must explain for each such subsidiary the reasons why the directors consider that its financial year should not end with that of the parent company, and give either the dates of the ends of each such subsidiaries' financial years ending last before that of the parent company, or the earliest and latest of those year end dates. Additionally, the names of the principal subsidiaries concerned should be stated. Where the accounting period of a principal subsidiary is of a different length from that of the parent company, the accounting period of the subsidiary should be stated. 1985 5 sch 4,19 (1989 3 sch) FRS 2:44

59 In respect of each subsidiary not included in consolidated accounts the following must be disclosed: 1985 5 sch 5,18 (1989 3 sch)

(a) any qualifications in the auditors' report on the subsidiary's accounts for financial years ending with or during the financial year of the company; and

(b) any note or saving in the subsidiary's accounts to call attention to a matter which, apart from the note or saving, would properly have been referred to in such a qualification,

insofar as the subject matter of the qualification or note is not covered by the company's own accounts and is material from the point of view of its members.

60 Companies not required to prepare consolidated accounts must state the aggregate amount of their total investment in shares of subsidiary undertakings, calculated using the equity method of valuation. This disclosure need not be made by a company which is exempt from the requirement to prepare consolidated accounts because it is included in the accounts of a larger group (see Chapter 8), provided the directors include a statement that in their opinion the aggregate value of the company's investment in subsidiaries is not less than the aggregate of the amounts at which that investment is stated in its balance sheet. Investment here includes shares in and amounts owing from subsidiaries. 1985 5 sch 5(2) (1989 3 sch)

61 Insofar as information required by the preceding two paragraphs is not obtainable, a statement to that effect must be included instead. 1985 5 sch 5,18 (1989 3 sch)

Shares in own parent

62 With certain exceptions, a subsidiary company cannot hold shares in its holding company. Any allotment or transfer of shares in a holding company to its subsidiary is void. ('Holding company' here means all companies of which the company in question is a subsidiary, including intermediate holding companies. The definition of subsidiary for this purpose is given in section 736 of the Act, as substituted by section 144 of the 1989 Act.) 1985 s 23 (1989 s 129)

63 The only exceptions to this rule are where: 1985 s 23 (1989 s 129)

(a) the subsidiary is concerned only as personal representative or trustee, unless the holding company is a beneficiary;

(b) the subsidiary is concerned only as a market maker; or

(c) the subsidiary became a holder of shares:

  (i) before 1 July 1948;

  (ii) before commencement of section 129 of the 1989 Act in circumstances not previously prohibited; or

  (iii) in circumstances in which the holding of those shares was not then prohibited, e.g. it was not then a subsidiary, but becomes prohibited, e.g. by becoming a subsidiary.

In the circumstances set out in sub-paragraph (c) the subsidiary may continue to hold those shares, but has no right to vote on those shares.

64 If a subsidiary holds, either directly or through nominees, shares in or debentures of its holding company, the holding company must disclose in a note to its accounts the number, description and amount of shares or debentures so held. However, disclosure is not required if the shares or debentures are held either: 1985 5 sch 6,20 (1989 3 sch)

(a) as personal representative; or

(b) as trustee, and neither the company nor any subsidiary is beneficially interested under the trust, otherwise than by way of security for transactions entered into in the ordinary course of business.

Significant holdings in the other undertakings

65 The information specified in paragraphs 66 and 67 below must be given in respect of each undertaking, other than subsidiary undertakings, in which the company has a significant holding. Where a parent company is required to prepare consolidated accounts this information must be given both in respect of undertakings in which the parent company has a significant holding and undertakings in which the group has a significant holding, unless that undertaking is a subsidiary, a joint venture or an associated undertaking. For 1985 5 sch 7 (1989 3 sch) 1985 5 sch 23,26 (1989 3 sch)

this purpose a holding is significant if:

(a) it amounts to 10 per cent or more of the nominal value of the allotted shares of any class in the undertaking; or

(b) the amount of the holding (as stated in the company's or the group's accounts) exceeds 10 per cent of the company's or group's total assets.

66 The information to be disclosed in respect of significant holdings in other undertakings is as follows: 1985 5 sch 8,24,27 (1989 3 sch)

(a) the undertaking's name;

(b) the country of incorporation (if other than Great Britain), the country of registration (England and Wales or Scotland) if incorporated in Great Britain or the address of its principal place of business if unincorporated; and

(c) a description of each class of shares held and the proportion of the nominal value of the allotted shares of that class represented by those shares. The corresponding amount for the previous year need not be stated. 1985 4 sch 58(3) (1989 1 sch 9)

67 Where the company or the group has a significant holding in an undertaking amounting to 20 per cent or more of the nominal value of the allotted shares in the undertaking, there shall also be stated in respect of each such undertaking: 1985 5 sch 9,25,28 (1989 3 sch)

(a) the aggregate capital and reserves at the undertaking's most recent financial year end; and

(b) the profit or loss for that year.

That information is not required if:

(i) the company is exempt from the requirement to prepare consolidated accounts by virtue of section 228 of the Act (being included in the accounts of a larger group, see Chapter 8) and the company's investment in all such undertakings is shown in aggregate in the notes to the accounts by way of the equity method of valuation; or

(ii) the company holds less than 50 per cent of the nominal value of the allotted share capital of the undertaking, and the undertaking is not required by the Companies Act to file its balance sheet for its most recent financial year with the registrar and does not otherwise publish that balance sheet anywhere in the world; or

(iii) the information is not material.

68 In the accounts of a listed company (or group) the following information should be disclosed in respect of each company (not being a subsidiary) in which the investment exceeds 20 per cent of the equity capital: ASL 21(e)

(a) its principal country of operation;

(b) particulars of its issued capital and debt securities; and

(c) the percentage of each class of debt securities attributed to the company's interest.

Where the number of such companies is large, particulars with regard to those of less importance can be omitted.

69 The disclosures required by schedule 5 to the Act and set out in paragraphs 55 to 68 above are subject to the exceptions set out in paragraphs 53 and 54 above (information of excessive length or seriously prejudicial to the business). 1985 s 231 (1989 s 6)

Participating interests

70 The 1989 Act introduce a new term 'participating interest' which replaces all references to 'shares in related companies'. Participating interest is defined as an interest in the shares of another undertaking held on a long-term basis for the purpose of securing a contribution to its activities by the exercise of control or influence arising from that interest. A holding of 20% or more of the shares of an undertaking is presumed to be a participating interest unless the contrary is shown (see Chapter 8). 1985 s 260 (1989 s 22)

71 The amounts to be included under investments in the balance sheet headings 'participating interest' and 'loans to undertakings in which the company has a participating interest' exclude group undertakings. It will include interests defined in the Act as 'associated undertakings', the definition of which is very similar to the definition of an associated company in SSAP 1. In the investing company's own balance sheet participating interests are normally stated at cost less provision for any permanent diminution in value. The disclosure requirements discussed in paragraphs 66 to 68 above apply to participating interests. Author

Associated undertakings

72 The Act defines associated undertakings only in relation to the consolidated accounts of a group. The definition of associated undertaking and the treatment in consolidated accounts is dealt with in Chapter 8. Set out below are the accounting treatment and disclosures specified by SSAP 1 for associated undertakings in the accounts of an investing company which does not prepare consolidated accounts.

73 In the investing company's own balance sheet interests in associated undertakings, like other investments, should be stated either at cost less any amounts written off or at a valuation. SSAP 1:25

74 Except where it is a wholly-owned subsidiary, an investing company which does not prepare consolidated accounts should show the information required by SSAP 1 in the notes to the accounts by preparing a separate profit and loss account and balance sheet or by adding supplementary information to its own accounts. The information required is discussed in Chapter 8 and includes: SSAP 1:24,35

(a) the investing company's or group's interest in associated undertakings shown by way of the equity method of valuation;

(b) the total of the investing company's or group's share of associated undertakings' profit less losses, taxation, extraordinary items (if any) and net profits retained;

(c) loans to and from associated undertakings;

(d) trading balances; and

(e) accumulated reserves.

The equity method of valuation is a method that arrives at the same balance sheet amount as would be shown by the equity method of accounting, but with changes in the year being passed through revaluation reserve rather than the profit and loss account. Author

Meaning of 'shares held'

75 References to shares held by the company or the group include any shares held by a person acting on behalf of the company or the group respectively. Shares shall be treated as not held if they are held by the company or group on behalf of another person or as security in connection with the granting of loans as part of normal business activities if the rights attached to them are exercisable only in the interests of the person providing the security. 1985 5 sch 13,32 (1989 3 sch)

Debentures of the company

76 The nominal amount and book value of any debentures of the company held by a nominee or trustee for the company must be shown. Such debentures could conveniently be shown as other investments under item C III 3, and the details disclosed by note. 1985 4 sch 41(3) Author

Tax certificates of deposit

77 Tax certificates of deposit should be shown separately in the balance sheet, and will normally be treated as current assets and included as item C III 3. Author

Current Assets (Item C)

Stocks (item C I)

78 Total stocks should be stated in the balance sheet in accordance with the valuation rules at the lower of cost and net realisable value, and subclassified 1985 4 sch 23(1) SSAP 9:26,27

so as to indicate the amounts held in each of the main categories in the balance sheet formats.

79 Where differing bases have been adopted for valuing different types of stocks and work in progress, the amount included in the accounts under each basis should be stated. SSAP 9:14

80 A suitable description of the amount at which stocks (excluding long-term contract balances) are stated in financial statements would be 'at the lower of cost and net realisable value'. In the case of long-term contract balances classified as stocks a suitable description would be 'at net cost, less foreseeable losses and payments on account'. The method used to ascertain turnover and attributable profit on long-term contracts should be stated. SSAP 9:12 SSAP 9:13 SSAP 9:32

81 The purchase price or production cost of stocks may be determined by whichever of the following bases appears appropriate to the directors: 1985 4 sch 27(1),(2)

(a) FIFO (first in, first out);

(b) LIFO (last in, first out);

(c) Weighted average method;

(d) Other methods similar to (a), (b) or (c).

However, regardless of the basis adopted, purchase price or production cost is to be determined in the same way as for all assets. These rules are set out in Chapter 4. 1985 4 sch 26

82 In selecting the methods referred to in the preceding paragraph, management should ensure that the valuation method adopted provides the fairest approximation to actual cost, which LIFO is unlikely to do. Accordingly, although permitted by law, LIFO is not used in practice. SSAP 9: Appendix 1:12

83 In describing the basis of valuation of stocks, 'market value' is only an appropriate phrase where a genuine market, e.g. The London Metal Exchange, exists. Where no such market exists, the term 'net realisable value' should be used. Author

84 Where a significant proportion of stocks held is subject to suppliers' reservation of title, it may be appropriate to disclose the facts and amounts involved. Author

85 Items included as 'raw materials and consumables' which are constantly being replaced may be included at a fixed quantity and value, provided that: 1985 4 sch 25

(a) their overall value is not material; and

(b) their quantity, value and composition are not subject to material variation.

86 If there is a material difference between the value of stocks as included in the accounts and the value of stocks at replacement cost or most recent purchase or production cost (whichever the directors consider the more appropriate comparison), the amount of the difference must be stated in a note to the accounts. 1985 4 sch 27(3)-(5)

Long-term contracts

87 A long-term contract is a contract where the contract activity falls into different accounting periods, usually, but not necessarily, extending for a period exceeding one year. SSAP 9:22

88 Long-term contracts should be assessed on a contract by contract basis and reflected in the profit and loss account by recording turnover and related costs as contract activity progresses. Turnover is ascertained in a manner appropriate to the stage of completion of the contract, the business and the industry in which it operates. SSAP 9:28

89 Where it is considered that the outcome of a long-term contract can be assessed with reasonable certainty before its conclusion, the prudently calculated attributable profit should be recognised in the profit and loss account as the difference between the reported turnover and related costs for that contract. SSAP 9:29

90 Long-term contracts should be disclosed in the balance sheet as follows: SSAP 9:30

(a) the amount by which recorded turnover is in excess of payments on account should be classified as 'amounts recoverable on contracts' and separately disclosed within debtors;

(b) the cost of long-term contracts, net of amounts transferred to cost of sales, should be classified as 'long-term contract balances' separately disclosed within the balance sheet heading 'stocks', after deducting foreseeable losses and payments on account not matched with turnover. The balance sheet note should disclose separately the balances of:

    (i) net cost less foreseeable losses; and

    (ii) applicable payments on account;

(c) if provisions or accruals for foreseeable losses exceed costs incurred (after transfers to cost of sales) that excess should be included within either provisions for liabilities and charges or creditors as appropriate; and

(d) the balance of payments on account (in excess of amounts (i) matched with turnover; and (ii) offset against long-term contract balances) should be classified as payments on account and separately disclosed within creditors.

Debtors (item C II)

91 *General*

The amount falling due after more than one year must be shown separately for each item included under debtors (see also paragraph 94 below). — 1985 4 sch format, note 5

92 The amount by which recorded turnover on long-term contracts is in excess of payments on account should be classified as 'amounts recoverable on contracts' and separately disclosed within debtors. Further detail regarding long-term contracts is to be found in paragraphs 87 to 90 above. — SSAP 9:30

93 Prepayments and accrued income may be shown in either of the two positions (item C II 6 or D) indicated in the standard formats. — 1985 4 sch format, note 6

Presentation of long-term debtors in current assets

94 As stated in paragraph 91 above in most cases it will be satisfactory to disclose the size of debtors due after more than one year in the notes to the accounts. However, there may be instances where the amount is so material in the context of the total net current assets that in the absence of disclosure of debtors due after more than one year on the face of the balance sheet readers may misinterpret the accounts. Consequently, in such circumstances, the amount should be disclosed on the face of the balance sheet. — UITF Abstract 4

Loans to and other transactions favouring directors

95 The provisions of this part of the Act are complex. It is recommended that reference should be made to the Act itself and, in cases of doubt, legal advice should be sought. In general a company is, with certain specific exemptions, prohibited from making loans to or providing security for loans to directors. Nevertheless, details of any such transactions together with details of substantial contracts with directors must be disclosed, but corresponding figures for the previous year are not required. Where the company fails to make adequate disclosure the auditors must include the relevant information in their report. — Author; 1985 s 330; 1985 6 sch 15,16 (1989 4 sch 4); 1985 4 sch 58(3)(c) (1989 1 sch 9); 1985 s 237(4) (1989 s 9)

96 In addition to the legal requirements set out below, the ASC has published an exposure draft 'Disclosure of related party transactions'. The proposals are explained in paragraphs 112 to 118 below. — ED 46

97 Subject to certain specific exemptions below, the requirements to disclose apply to all transactions or arrangements whether or not: — 1985 6 sch 19 (1989 4 sch 4)

(a) they were unlawful;

(b) the director with whom they were made was a director or connected person at the time the transactions were made; and

(c) a company was a subsidiary of a company other than its current holding company when the transactions were made.

98	The transactions or arrangements concerned include principally:	1985 s 330
	(a) loans;	
	(b) quasi-loans;	
	(c) credit transactions;	
	(d) guarantees or provision of security in connection with (a), (b) or (c) above; and	
	(e) any other transaction or arrangement with a person who was a director at any time during the period, and who had, either directly or indirectly, a material interest in that transaction.	1985 6 sch 15(c),16(c) (1989 4 sch 4)
99	The transactions or arrangements to be disclosed include those between the company, or its subsidiary, and a director or connected person, of the company or of its holding company.	1985 6 sch 15,16 (1989 4 sch 4)
100	Transactions and arrangements are deemed to include an agreement to make any such transaction or arrangement.	1985 6 sch 15(b),16(b) (1989 4 sch 4)
101	A 'director' for the purposes of paragraphs 95 to 108 includes a 'shadow director', defined as a person in accordance with whose instructions the directors are accustomed to act, unless such instruction represents merely advice given in a professional capacity.	1985 6 sch 27(2) (1989 4 sch 5) 1985 s 741(2)
102	A 'connected person' is a spouse, child under 18 years of age, body corporate with which the director is associated, a trustee of a trust of which the director is a beneficiary, or partner of either the director or any person connected with the director.	1985 s 346
103	A 'quasi-loan' is defined as a transaction under which one party (the 'creditor') defrays or agrees to defray the expenditure of another (the 'borrower') either:	1985 s 331(3)
	(a) on terms that the borrower will reimburse the creditor; or	
	(b) in circumstances where the borrower becomes liable to reimburse the creditor.	
104	A 'credit transaction' is a transaction under which one party (the 'creditor'):	1985 s 331(7)
	(a) supplies any goods or sells any land under a hire purchase agreement or conditional sale agreement; or	
	(b) leases or hires any land or goods in return for periodical payments; or	
	(c) otherwise disposes of land or supplies goods or services on the understanding that payment (whether in a lump sum or instalments or by way of periodical payments or otherwise) is to be deferred.	

105	The following particulars must be given in the notes to the accounts (by all companies other than banking companies or their holding companies) for any transaction, arrangement or agreement required to be disclosed in respect of items referred to above:	1985 6 sch 22(1) (1989 4 sch 4) 1985 9 sch IV 2 (1989 7 sch)
	(a) a statement that it was made or subsisted during the year;	1985 6 sch 22(2)(a) (1989 4 sch 4)
	(b) names of directors (and, where relevant, connected persons) concerned and, for transactions referred to in paragraph 98(e) above, the nature of the directors' interests;	1985 6 sch 22(2)(b),(c) (1989 4 sch 4)
	(c) principal terms (including those relating to repayment, interest and security);	1985 6 sch 22(1) (1989 4 sch 4) Author
	(d) for loans, or agreements for or arrangements relating to loans:	1985 6 sch 22(2)(d) (1989 4 sch 4)
	(i) the amount of the liability (principal and interest) at the beginning and end of the year;	
	(ii) the maximum amount of the liability during the year;	
	(iii) the amount of any arrears of interest;	
	(iv) any provision against non-repayment of the whole or any part of the principal or interest;	
	although loans by a company (and its subsidiaries) totalling a maximum of £5,000 and made to one of its directors (or to a holding company director) are legal, full disclosure must still be made;	1985 s 334 (1989 s 128)
	(e) for guarantees or the provision of security, or agreements or arrangements relating thereto:	1985 6 sch 22(2)(e) (1989 4 sch 4)
	(i) the amounts for which the company (or its subsidiary) was liable at the beginning and end of the year;	
	(ii) the maximum amount for which the company (or its subsidiary) may become so liable;	
	(iii) any amount or liability incurred in fulfilling the guarantee or discharging the security; and	
	(f) for any other transactions, arrangements or agreements, the value of the transaction or arrangement. For a quasi-loan value is the maximum amount liable to be repaid, and for a credit transaction value is the arm's length value of the goods or services concerned. Although credit	1985 6 sch 22(2)(f) (1989 4 sch 4) 1985 s 340 1985 s 335(1)

transactions totalling a maximum of £10,000 for a director are legal, full disclosure must still be made.

106 Where loans, quasi-loans or agreements to make such loans are made by a reporting company to or for: 1985 6 sch 23 (1989 4 sch 4)

(a) its parent company when the reporting company is wholly-owned; or

(b) a fellow subsidiary when both are wholly-owned; or

(c) its wholly-owned subsidiary;

and disclosure would not be required by the reporting company if the other companies had not been associated with the director, then the disclosure in the preceding paragraph is confined to (a) and (b) and the disclosure under (c) to (f) is not required.

107 The following are exempted from the disclosure requirements set out above:

(a) transactions, arrangements or agreements between two companies where a director is interested only by virtue of being a director of both companies; 1985 6 sch 18(a) (1989 4 sch 4)

(b) service contracts between a company and its directors or directors of its holding company; 1985 6 sch 18(b)

(c) transactions, arrangements or agreements which were not entered into during the financial year and which did not subsist at any time during the financial year; 1985 6 sch 18(c)

(d) transactions, arrangements or agreements with a director which, in aggregate, did not exceed £5,000 and which are credit transactions or related to credit transactions; and 1985 6 sch 24(1),(2)

(e) transactions or arrangements (of the types envisaged by paragraphs 15(c) and 16(c) of schedule 6 to the Act, see paragraph 98(e) above) in which the director has a material interest if:

(i) (A) each party to the transaction or arrangement which is a member of the same group of companies (meaning a holding company and subsidiary) as the company, enters into the transaction or arrangement in the ordinary course of business; and 1985 6 sch 20(a)

(B) the terms of the transaction or arrangement are not less favourable to any such party than it would be reasonable to expect if the material interest had not been an interest of a person who was a director of the company or of its holding company; 1985 6 sch 20(b)

(ii) (A) the company is a member of a group of companies (meaning a holding company and its subsidiaries); and 1985 6 sch 21(a)

(B) either the company is a wholly-owned subsidiary or no body corporate (other than the reporting company or its subsidiary) which is a member of the group of companies which includes the reporting company's ultimate holding company was a party to the transaction or arrangement; and 1985 6 sch 21(b)

(C) the director in question was at some time during the relevant period associated with the company; and 1985 6 sch 21(c)

(D) the material interest of the director in question in the transaction or arrangement would not have arisen if he had not been associated with the company at any time during the relevant period; or 1985 6 sch 21(d)

(iii) the value of each transaction did not at any time in the year exceed in the aggregate: 1985 6 sch 25 (1989 4 sch 4)

(A) £1,000; or, if greater than £1,000;

(B) the lower of £5,000 and 1 per cent of the company's net assets at the year end.

108 Consolidated accounts are required to show the above information only for holding company directors. The disclosure must, however, include transactions and arrangements between those directors and any subsidiaries (see paragraph 99). 1985 6 sch 15 (1989 4 sch 4)

Transactions favouring officers other than directors

109 In respect of each of the following categories (which include related guarantees, securities, arrangements and agreements to enter into such transactions): 1985 6 sch 28,29 (1989 4 sch 6(2))

(a) loans;

(b) quasi-loans; and

(c) credit transactions;

made between the company (and, in the case of a holding company, its subsidiaries) and persons who were officers of the company (other than directors or shadow directors) at any time during the year, there must be shown: 1985 6 sch 29

(i) the aggregate amounts outstanding at the end of the year;

(ii) the numbers of officers with whom such transactions or agreements were made;

however:

(iii) no corresponding amounts need be shown for the previous year; and — 1985 4 sch 58(3) (1989 1 sch 9)

(iv) consolidated accounts need only include the information relating to holding company officers. — 1985 6 sch 29(1) (1989 4 sch 6(3))

Where the aggregate amount due to the company (or group) from an officer at the year end under all transactions of the types mentioned above is less than £2,500, the information relating to that officer is not required to be included in the totals disclosed. — 1985 6 sch 29(2)

110 There is no precise legal definition of an 'officer', although it has been established that the term includes company secretaries and general managers. [1985 s 744] It appears that an officer is a person acting in a decision making capacity, rather than one who merely implements the decisions of others. All persons named in the accounts as officers should be regarded as officers for the purpose of these disclosures. [Author]

111 There are special rules, outside the scope of this guidance, dealing with the disclosures of arrangements by banking companies for their officers or their holding companies' officers. — 1985 9 sch IV 3 (1989 7 sch)

Related party transactions

112 The ASC published ED 46 'Disclosure of related party transactions' which proposes extending the disclosure requirements for related party transactions. It also proposes extending the definition of related parties to those where, for all or part of the financial period: — ED 46:22

(a) one party is able to exercise either direct or indirect control, or significant influence, over the other party or over the assets or resources of the other party; or

(b) such parties are subject either to common control or significant influence from the same source.

Until such time as the exposure draft is finally approved the disclosures set out below are considered to be good practice. The ASB is expected to come out with its own proposals, which may differ in detail from the exposure draft.

113 The ED requires disclosure only of *abnormal* transactions, although this in particular is likely to be changed. A normal transaction is defined as one undertaken by the reporting enterprise in the ordinary course of business on normal commercial terms except where it is so material that it has a significant impact on the financial statements. An abnormal transaction is any transaction other than a normal transaction. — ED 46:27,29

114 It is proposed that the following information will be required for each abnormal transaction with, on behalf of, or for the benefit of, a related party: ED 46:32

(a) the name of the related party;

(b) the relationship between the parties;

(c) the extent of any ownership interest (in percentage terms) in the related party or by it in the reporting enterprise;

(d) the nature of the transaction;

(e) the amounts involved, either in percentage or in monetary terms;

(f) the amount due to or from the related party at balance sheet date;

(g) the basis on which the transaction price has been determined; and

(h) any other information necessary for an understanding of the commercial substance of the transaction and of its effects on the financial statements.

115 Transactions with an individual related party may be aggregated unless separate disclosure is necessary for an understanding of the impact on the accounts or is otherwise required by statute or The International Stock Exchange. ED 46:33

116 Disclosure of intra-group transactions will not be required: ED 46:34

(a) in consolidated accounts, if the item has been eliminated on consolidation;

(b) in a parent company's accounts where consolidated accounts are presented at the same time; or

(c) in the accounts of wholly-owned subsidiaries if the identity of the ultimate parent company is disclosed.

117 It is proposed that the existence and nature of controlling related party relationships, and the name of the controlling enterprise, should be disclosed whether or not any transactions between the parties have taken place. ED 46:35

118 Where transactions or other facts arising from a relationship with another party have a pervasive influence on the reporting enterprise, it is proposed that the identity of that party and a general indication of the nature and extent of any dependence should be disclosed. ED 46:36

Financial assistance for acquisition of shares

119 In cases where a company is permitted to give financial assistance for the acquisition of its own shares or shares in its holding company (see Chapter 11), there must be stated the aggregate amount of loans made in each of the following cases: — 1985 4 sch 51(2) (1989 1 sch 9) 1985 s 153(4)

(a) loans made for the purposes of an employees' share scheme; — 1985 s 153(4)(b) (1989 s 132)

(b) provisions of financial assistance to enable or facilitate transactions in the company's shares by employees, former employees or their families; — 1985 s 153(4)(bb)

(c) loans made to employees, other than directors, to enable those persons to acquire fully paid shares in the company or its holding company; and — 1985 s 153(4)(c)

(d) permissible loans made by private companies. — 1985 s 155

Called up share capital not paid (item A or C II 5)

120 Called up share capital not paid may be shown in either of the two positions indicated in the standard balance sheet formats. — 1985 4 sch format, note 1

Expenditure not to be deferred

121 The following items of expenditure must not be treated as assets in any company's balance sheet and accordingly must be written off in the year in which they are incurred: — 1985 4 sch 3(2)

(a) preliminary expenses;

(b) expenses of and commission on any issue of shares or debentures;

(c) costs of research.

The disclosure requirements for development expenditure carried forward are set out under 'intangible fixed assets' above.

Called up share capital (item A I)

122 The amount of allotted share capital and the amount of called up share capital which has been paid up must each be shown separately. — 1985 4 sch format, note 12

123 The authorised share capital and, where shares of more than one class have been allotted, the number and aggregate nominal value of shares of each class allotted must be shown. — 1985 4 sch 38(1)

Options on unissued shares

124 Where any option to subscribe or any other right (including conversion rights) to require the allotment of shares exist, the number, description and amount of shares, together with the option price and period in which it is — 1985 4 sch 40

exercisable must be shown. The disclosure requirements for directors' share options are explained in Chapter 2.

Preference shares

125 Where the title of a class of preference shares (or participating preference or preferred ordinary shares) issued before 6 April 1973 includes a fixed rate of dividend, the rate of dividend appropriate after that date, i.e. adjusted to take account of the imputation basis of taxation, should be incorporated in the description of the shares in the balance sheet. SSAP 8:28

Redeemable shares

126 Where redeemable shares have been issued, there must be disclosed: 1985 4 sch 38(2)

(a) the earliest and latest dates of redemption;

(b) whether redemption is mandatory or at the option of the company or shareholder; and

(c) the premium, if any, payable on redemption.

Arrears of dividend

127 The amount of arrears of fixed cumulative dividend (excluding related ACT) for each class of shares and the period over which the arrears have accumulated must be disclosed. 1985 4 sch 49

Allotment of shares

128 For each class of share allotted during the year there must be shown the number of shares, aggregate nominal value, consideration received and reason for making the allotment. 1985 4 sch 39

129 For listed companies making an issue for cash of securities having an equity element not made to the company's existing equity shareholders in proportion to their existing holdings, there should be disclosed: ASL 21(q)

(a) the names of allottees if less than six in number, otherwise a brief generic description; and

(b) the market price at the date of fixing the terms of issue.

130 If the company has allotted shares during the year in consideration for shares in another company, and by virtue of section 131 of the Act (merger relief), any premium was not required to be transferred to the share premium account, there must be disclosed: 1985 5 sch 10,29 (1989 3 sch)

(a) the name of the acquired company;

(b) the number, nominal value and class of shares allotted;

(c) the number, nominal value and class of shares in the acquired company issued, transferred or cancelled; and

(d) particulars of the accounting treatment adopted, including that in the consolidated accounts if any.

Further disclosures are explained in paragraphs 24 and 25 of Chapter 6.

Share premium account (item A II)

131 Where a company issues shares at a value that exceeds their nominal value, a sum equal to the difference between the issue value and the nominal value must be transferred to a share premium account. The share premium account must be disclosed separately on the face of the balance sheet. Movements must be disclosed in the notes (see paragraph 139 below). 1985 s 130(1)

132 The share premium account can only be used for the following specific purposes to: 1985 s 130(2)

(a) pay up fully paid bonus shares;

(b) write off preliminary expenses;

(c) write off expenses of any issue of shares or debentures;

(d) write off commission paid or discount allowed on any issue of shares or debentures; and

(e) provide for the premium on any redemption of debentures.

133 In certain circumstances, the Act provides relief from the need to set up a share premium account. The relief, known as 'merger relief' is discussed in Chapter 8.

Reserves (items A III, IV, V)

134 Reserves should not include any amount which falls within the definition of a provision as set out below. Reserves are not defined in law (except in the case of companies covered by schedule 9A to the Act) but may be taken to be that part of shareholders' funds not accounted for by the nominal value of issued share capital or by the share premium account. Author

135 Accounts should preferably distinguish between non-distributable and distributable reserves, although this is not a statutory requirement. All reserves other than the profit and loss account will usually be non-distributable. Therefore, normally the notes to the accounts need only give details of reserves which the company does not regard as distributable where this is not apparent from the account heading. It should be noted that the illustrative examples in FRS 3 show separately distributable and non-distributable profits in the statement of recognised gains and losses, although the specific requirement to show them separately is not contained in the main body of the standard. Author

136 Reserves not set aside for a specific purpose should normally be combined with the balance on the profit and loss account, insofar as they are properly regarded as distributable, and included as item A V.

137 Any other non-distributable reserves not specifically mentioned in the formats (e.g. reserves arising on consolidation) might fall to be included under item A IV 4.

138 Contributions to a company's reserves that are capital in nature should normally be credited to 'other reserves', with full disclosure of the source where the amount is material. Unless the terms of the transaction specify otherwise such a receipt may qualify to be regarded as a realised amount. However, in the particular circumstances of a payment by a holding company to a subsidiary, it will normally be the intention of the payer for the amount to be treated as an additional contribution to the permanent capital of the subsidiary. In this case it will often be appropriate for the directors to state that they do not regard the amount in question as distributable.

139 All movements on those reserves listed in either of the standard formats must be shown, giving a reconciliation between the opening and closing balances with explanations of transfers to or from the reserve. Corresponding figures for the previous year are not required for this reconciliation. 1985 4 sch 46; 1985 4 sch 58(3) (1989 1 sch 10)

140 The net movement on reserves arising from foreign exchange differences should be disclosed. In addition the net amount of exchange gains or losses on foreign currency borrowings less deposits should be disclosed, identifying separately: SSAP 20:60

(a) the amount offset in reserves, as permitted by SSAP 20; and

(b) the net amount charged/credited to profit and loss account.

141 Material prior period adjustments should be accounted for by restating the comparative figures for the preceding period in the primary statements and notes and adjusting the opening balance of reserves for the cumulative effect. The cumulative effect of the adjustments should also be noted at the foot of the statement of total recognised gains and losses of the current period. The effect of the prior period adjustments on the results for the preceding period should be disclosed where practicable. With that exception, all profits and losses should be accounted for in the profit and loss account unless this conflicts with legislation or standard accounting practice. Examples of adjustments to reserves which are not profits or losses and which, by their nature, are not included in the determination of profit for the year are referred to in paragraphs 140 and 143. FRS 3:29

Revaluation reserve

142 The revaluation reserve must be reduced to the extent that the amounts transferred to it are no longer necessary for the purposes of the valuation method used (e.g if major fixed assets are disposed of or if for any reason current cost or market value declines, perhaps as a result of technological advance). However, an amount may only be transferred from the revaluation reserve:

1985 4 sch 34(3) (1989 1 sch 6) Author

1985 4 sch 34(3) (1989 1 sch 6)

(a) to the profit and loss account if the amount was previously charged to that account or if it represents a realised profit; or

(b) on capitalisation, i.e. applying it in wholly or partly paying up unissued shares in the company to be allotted to members as fully or partly paid shares.

The revaluation reserve may not be used for any other purpose. In particular, goodwill may not be written off against it (although goodwill arising on consolidation written off against revaluation reserve prior to commencement of the 1989 Act need not be written back).

Investment revaluation reserve

143 Changes in the value of investment properties should not be reflected in the profit and loss account, but should be transferred to an investment revaluation reserve. The reserve should be prominently displayed in the balance sheet. It will normally be appropriate to include the investment revaluation reserve within item A III. Any deficit arising on the investment revaluation reserve should be charged in the profit and loss account (see paragraph 33).

SSAP 19:13,15

Author

Provisions for Liabilities and Charges (Item B)

Definition

144 A provision for liabilities and charges is defined as an amount retained as reasonably necessary for the purpose of providing for any liability or loss which is either likely to be incurred, or certain to be incurred but uncertain as to amount or as to the date on which it will arise.

1985 4 sch 89

Movements on provision accounts

145 Where any amount is transferred to any of those provisions for liabilities or charges listed in either of the standard formats, or is transferred from any such provision otherwise than for the purpose for which it was created, a reconciliation must be given between the opening and closing balances on the provision with explanations of transfers to or from the provision. Corresponding figures for the previous year are not required for this reconciliation.

1985 4 sch 46

1985 4 sch 58(3) (1989 1 sch 10)

146 Movements on provisions related to acquisitions should be disclosed and analysed between the amounts used and the amounts released unused or

SSAP 22:49

applied for another purpose. Sufficient details should be given to identify the extent to which the provisions have proved unnecessary.

147 Particulars of each material provision included in the item 'other provisions' must be disclosed. This will normally be given in the notes to the accounts.

1985 4 sch 46(3)
Author

Taxation provisions

148 Tax effects should be shown in accounts separately from the items or transactions to which they relate.

SSAP 15:16

149 Deferred tax provisions must be stated separately from provisions for other taxation. Deferred tax provisions should be included in the formats under item B 2, and tax payable under item C 8. However, item B 2 must also include any provisions for taxation other than deferred taxation, (e.g. for items disputed with the Inland Revenue), and the amounts provided must be stated. Tax payable falling due within, or after more than, one year must be shown separately under item C 8 in the balance sheet (paragraph 183 below); there is no requirement to analyse deferred tax provisions in this manner.

1985 4 sch 47
(1989 1 sch 8)
SSAP 15:47,48

1985 4 sch format,
notes 9,13

150 In December 1992, the ASB issued an amendment to SSAP 15 that relaxes the existing requirements of the standard in accounting for the deferred tax effects of pensions and other post-retirement benefits accounted for in accordance with SSAP 24 and UITF Abstract 6 respectively. Under SSAP 24 and UITF Abstract 6 these long-term obligations are accounted for on a full provision basis, even though in many cases it is likely that they will continually roll over (i.e. as one obligation is settled another will arise). However, SSAP 15 would not allow the related deferred tax asset to be recognised because the reversing provision is replaced by a new one.

151 The amendment removes this inconsistency between SSAP 24 and SSAP 15 that use different criteria for the recognition of profit and loss account charges and related assets and liabilities. Companies are now permitted, where they consider it appropriate in their particular circumstances, to use the same recognition criteria for the tax implications of pensions and other post-retirement benefits as in accounting for the obligations to provide those benefits. This means that either the full provision basis or the partial provision basis may be used in accounting for the deferred tax implications of pensions and other post-retirement benefits.

SSAP 15:12A
(as amended)

SSAP 15:32A
(as amended)

152 Where a company changes its accounting policy to account for the deferred tax effects of pensions and other post-retirement benefits on a full provision basis, the effects of this change in the basis of taxation should be included in the tax charge or credit for the period and separately disclosed on the face of the profit and loss account in accordance with FRS 3. The new policy should also be disclosed.

SSAP 15 (as amended)
FRS 3:23

SSAP 15:32A

153	Where a company recognises a deferred tax asset in respect of a provision for pensions or other post-retirement benefits in accordance with paragraph 151 above, the normal rules regarding the recoverability of assets are applicable.	SSAP 15:12B (as amended)
154	Deferred tax carried forward as an asset should be included in the formats within 'current assets - debtors' under item C II 6, if it is current, or separately under main heading D. In the former case, any amount falling due after more than one year should be shown separately (see paragraph 91 above).	SSAP 15:50 1985 4 sch format, note 5
155	In determining the aggregate amount of deferred tax, deferred tax debit balances should be matched with deferred tax liabilities against which they will be able to be offset, because they are both elements of any aggregate deferred tax asset or liability and are not separate items.	SSAP 15:51
156	Transfers to and from deferred tax should be disclosed in a note.	SSAP 15:38
157	The deferred tax balance, and its major components, should be disclosed in the balance sheet or notes to the accounts. The total amount of any unprovided deferred tax should also be disclosed in a note, analysed into its major components.	SSAP 15:37 SSAP 15:40
158	The amount of deferred tax not provided should be based on reasonable assumptions. The accounts should contain sufficient information to indicate to the reader what assumptions have been used by management without going so far as to prejudice commercial confidentiality or to provide a quantified forecast.	SSAP 15:27 Author
159	Where amounts of deferred tax arise which relate to movements on reserves (e.g. resulting from the expected disposal of revalued assets) the amounts transferred to or from the deferred tax account should be shown separately as part of such movements. The tax treatment of amounts credited or debited to the revaluation reserve has to be disclosed.	SSAP 15:39 1985 4 sch 34(4)
160	Where the value of an asset is shown in a note (or in the directors' report) because it differs materially from its book amount, the note should also show, if material, the tax effects, if any, that would arise if the asset were realised at the balance sheet date at the noted value.	SSAP 15:42
161	Where the potential amount of deferred tax on a revalued asset is not shown because its disposal would not result in a tax liability, in which case the revaluation does not constitute a timing difference, the fact that it does not constitute a timing difference and that tax has therefore not been quantified should be stated.	SSAP 15:20,41
162	Where a company is a member of a group, any contingent deferred tax liability on behalf of other members of the group has to be shown separately in the accounts of any company which has undertaken the	1985 4 sch 59A (1989 1 sch 11) SSAP 15:43,54

commitment, analysed between amounts in respect of any subsidiary and amounts in respect of any parent undertaking or fellow subsidiary.

163 The extent to which deferred tax has been accounted for in respect of future remittances of the accumulated reserves of overseas subsidiary undertakings should be disclosed. Where deferred tax has not been provided in respect of all the accumulated reserves of overseas subsidiary undertakings, the reason for not fully providing should be disclosed in the notes to the accounts. FRS 2:54

Creditors (Item C)

General

164 Where balance sheet format 2 is adopted, each item included under creditors (liabilities, item C) must be split between the amounts payable within one year and after one year, and separate totals are to be shown. Format 1 provides for this analysis to be given on the face of the balance sheet. 1985 4 sch format, note 13

165 For each item shown under creditors (whichever balance sheet format is adopted) there must be disclosed separately the aggregate amount of debts falling into each of the following categories: 1985 4 sch 48(1)

(a) payable otherwise than by instalments and falling due for payment after the end of the five year period following the end of the financial year; or

(b) payable by instalments any of which fall due for payment after that period;

and, in the case of (b), the aggregate amount falling due after the five year period must also be shown.

166 Terms of repayment and interest rates for each debt covered by the disclosure under the preceding paragraph must be shown. If such a statement would be, in the view of the directors, excessively long, a general indication of repayment terms and interest rates will be sufficient. 1985 4 sch 48(2),(3)

167 For each item under creditors for which security has been given, an indication of the nature of the security given and the aggregate amount of debts included under that item covered by security must be stated. In giving 'an indication of the nature of the security', it will probably be acceptable to describe the charge in general terms, referring, for example, to 'mortgages on freehold land and buildings' rather than specifying the particular properties involved. Where a significant proportion of creditors relates to stocks held which are subject to suppliers' reservation of title, it may be appropriate to disclose the facts and amounts involved. 1985 4 sch 48(4) Author

Obligations under finance leases

168 The liabilities for obligations under finance leases (net of finance charges allocated to future periods) should be disclosed separately from other obligations and liabilities. SSAP 21:51

169 The lessee can show obligations under finance leases as a separate item on the balance sheet under 'creditors', or separately under this heading in the notes, or combine them within the total of another liability under the same heading, e.g. as 'bank loans, overdrafts and obligations under finance leases' or as part of 'creditors and accruals', with analysis in the notes to the accounts. The treatment should normally depend on the materiality of the amounts concerned. Author

170 The liabilities must be analysed between amounts payable: SSAP 21:52

(a) in the next year;

(b) in the second to fifth years inclusive; and

(c) in aggregate after five years, from the balance sheet date.

This analysis may be presented either:

(i) separately for obligations under finance leases, in which case as an alternative gross obligations may be shown with future finance charges being separately deducted from the total; or

(ii) by combining the lease obligations with other obligations and liabilities on the face of the balance sheet, in which case an equivalent analysis of the total in which it is included must be given in a note.

As with creditors generally the form of disclosure will depend on the chosen format (see paragraph 164). Author

Maturity analysis of debt

171 Listed companies are required to state in respect of bank loans and overdrafts and other borrowings of the company (or group), including obligations under finance leases, the aggregate amounts repayable: ASL 21(f)

(a) in one year or less, or on demand;

(b) between one and two years;

(c) between two and five years; and

(d) in five years or more.

172 FRED 3 - 'Accounting for capital instruments' proposes to extend the above analysis of the maturity of debts to all companies. For this purpose, FRED 3:29-31

the maturity of debt should be assessed according to the earliest date on which the lender could demand repayment, taking account of facilities granted by the same lender which may permit the refinancing of the debt (see paragraph 180(c)).

Borrowing powers

173 If limits are imposed upon the company's borrowing powers by its articles or debenture trust deeds, and those limits are exceeded at the year end, the facts and amounts involved together with a statement as to what is being done to rectify the situation should be disclosed in a note to the accounts. Author

Debentures (item C I)

174 There is no precise definition of a debenture, either in law or practice. It is essentially a formal acknowledgement of a debt, although the term is often applied to the debt itself. Debentures are usually, but need not be, secured. There may or may not be a trust deed to set out the respective rights of the company and the debenture holders. Author

175 If the company has issued any debentures during the financial year there must be stated: 1985 4 sch 41(1)

(a) the reason for making the issue;

(b) the classes of debentures issued; and

(c) for each class, the amount issued and the consideration received for the issue.

176 The number, description and amount of any debenture of the company held beneficially by its subsidiaries, or their nominees, must be shown in a note to the accounts. 1985 5 sch 6,20 (1989 3 sch)

177 The amount of any convertible loans must be shown separately. In addition, FRED 3 proposes disclosure of the date of redemption, the amount payable on redemption, the number and class of shares that may be issued on conversion and the date at, or period within, which the conversion takes place. It should also be stated whether conversion is at the option of the company or the holder. 1985 4 sch format, note 7

Redeemed debentures

178 Particulars must be given of redeemed debentures which the company has the power to reissue. Redeemed debentures may be reissued unless: 1985 4 sch 41(2) 1985 s 194(1)

(a) a provision to the contrary is contained in the articles, or in a contract; or

(b) the company has passed a resolution to the effect that they shall be cancelled.

Complex capital instruments

179 During the 1980's there was an explosive growth in a wide range of instruments available for raising finance. As investors and issuers became more sophisticated, the instruments became ever more legally and operationally complex with the result that accounting for such instruments failed to keep pace with the development of the instruments themselves. Although Technical Release TR 677 issued by the Technical Committee of the Institute of Chartered Accountants in England and Wales sets down the general principles which it is recommended should be applied when accounting for any form of complex capital issue, the accounting for some of the new instruments, particulary those that have debt and equity features, has not been uniform. Author

180 In view of the lack of authoritative guidance in this area, the ASB decided to undertake a project on accounting for capital instruments and published FRED 3 'Accounting for capital instruments' in December 1992. The principal proposals of the FRED are summarised below:

(a) capital instruments (other than shares and warrants) should be classified as liabilities if they contain an obligation to transfer cash or other resources; FRED 3:21

(b) convertible debt should be separately disclosed on the face of the balance sheet. It should be included in liabilities until such time as it is actually converted: conversion should not be anticipated. If the holder has to redeem at a premium, that premium should be accrued over the period to the earliest date at which the option can be exercised; FRED 3:22

(c) debts should be classified as current or non-current according to their strict contractual maturity, except where the same lender is committed to refinance the debt on the same terms; FRED 3:28,31

(d) debts should initially be recognised in the balance sheet at the amount received, less any issue costs. The finance cost which is the difference between net proceeds and the total repayments should be allocated to accounting periods so as to achieve a constant rate on the amount outstanding; FRED 3:24,25

(e) the aggregate amount of shareholders' funds should be analysed between amounts attributable to equity and non-equity interests. The amount of shareholders' funds attributable to non-equity interests is the aggregate amount (including attributable reserves) relating to all classes of non-equity shares and warrants. The balance is attributable to equity interests; and FRED 3:34

(f) minority interests in subsidiaries should be analysed between equity and non-equity interests. FRED 3:44

The FRED's proposals, if adopted as a future accounting standard, will have a significant effect on the way companies disclose their shareholders' funds and both long-term and short-term finance. It may also have an adverse effect on gearing ratios. Author

Dividends

181 The provision for the recommended dividend must be separately stated. Since the standard formats do not contain a separate heading for dividends payable, the recommended dividend will normally be included as a current liability, under item C 8, but disclosed in the notes to the accounts. It is not necessary to state separately the amount of any dividends already declared but unpaid at the balance sheet date. 1985 4 sch 51(3) Author

182 ACT on recommended dividends should not be included in the figures given in the above paragraph, but should be included as a current tax liability. SSAP 8:26

Tax liabilities

183 Liabilities, as opposed to provisions, for taxation must be included in the balance sheet under C 8 'other creditors including taxation and social security', with the liability for taxation and social security being shown separately from 'other creditors'. For most companies the balance sheet should contain one liability for mainstream corporation tax, being that on the profits of the year. If a company has two liabilities, being that on the profits of the previous year and on the profits of the current year, these liabilities may need to be separately disclosed, as a consequence of the requirement to analyse creditors between amounts due within one year and after one year. 1985 4 sch format, note 9 SSAP 8:14 1985 4 sch format, note 13

184 ACT on dividends paid before the year end, if it is regarded as recoverable, should be deducted from the full corporation tax charge on the profit of the year in arriving at the mainstream corporation tax liability shown in the balance sheet. SSAP 8:15

185 If the ACT on proposed dividends is regarded as recoverable, it should be deducted from the deferred tax account, if such an account is available for this purpose. In the absence of a deferred taxation account if the ACT is regarded as recoverable it may be put into the balance sheet formats as a prepayment, with disclosure if realisation is more than one year hence. SSAP 8:27 Author

186 Realisation may be less than one year from the balance sheet date where substantial amounts of franked investment income are regularly received, for example by an investment trust company.

187 The ACT payable on proposed dividends (whether recoverable or irrecoverable) should be included under creditors (item C 8) as a current taxation liability. The tax credit in respect of surplus franked investment income should be deducted from the current liability for ACT. SSAP 8:26

188 The net amount due to (or from) the Customs and Excise in respect of VAT should be included as part of creditors (or debtors) and will not normally require separate disclosure. SSAP 5:5

Payments received on account (item C 3)

189 Payments received on account, insofar as they are not shown as deductions from stocks, must be disclosed separately. This will normally only give rise to a creditor where the payments are in excess of both amounts matched with turnover and the amount at which the relevant stock or work in progress is stated. The amount by which the provision or accrual for foreseeable losses on long-term contracts exceeds the costs incurred, after transfers to cost of sales, should be included within either provisions for liabilities and charges (item B 3) or creditors (item C 9 or D) as appropriate. 1985 4 sch format, note 8 SSAP 9:30

Accruals and deferred income (item C 9 or D)

190 Accruals and deferred income may be included within the general heading 'creditors' or shown on the balance sheet as a separate heading outside net current assets. Accruals should always be included within the heading 'creditors - amounts falling due within one year'. However, deferred income, e.g. the deferred credit on government grants, should if material be shown as a separate heading on the face of the balance sheet. In these circumstances the heading 'accruals and deferred income' will have to be shown both as part of creditors and as a separate heading. 1985 4 sch format, note 10 Author

191 The liability for items such as goods or services received but uninvoiced at the balance sheet date should be treated as a trade creditor (item C 4), rather than as an accrual.

192 Where the recognition in the profit and loss account of part or all of a government grant that has been received is deferred, the amount so deferred should be disclosed as deferred income (liabilities, item D in balance sheet format 2), not as a reserve. SSAP 4:25

193 Where a government grant becomes repayable because certain conditions are not fulfilled, the repayment should be accounted for by setting off the repayment against any unamortised deferred income relating to the grant. Any excess should be charged immediately to the profit and loss account. SSAP 4:27

Net current assets/liabilities

194 Where format 1 is adopted any amounts shown under 'prepayments and accrued income' must be taken into account when calculating net current assets, whether such prepayments are shown as format item C II 6 or D. 1985 4 sch format, note 11

Pension funds and pension commitments

195 Details must be given of any pension provisions or prepayments in the company's balance sheet, and also of any such commitments for which no provision has been made. Particulars of pension commitments to past directors of the company must be disclosed separately. 1985 4 sch 50(4) SSAP 24:86

196 The following disclosures should be made in respect of a defined contribution pension scheme: SSAP 24:87

(a) the nature of the scheme (i.e. defined contribution);

(b) the accounting policy;

(c) the pension cost charge for the period (see Chapter 6 regarding the basis of calculation); and

(d) any outstanding or prepaid contributions at the balance sheet date.

197 The following disclosures should be made in respect of a defined benefit scheme: SSAP 24:88

(a) the nature of the scheme (i.e. defined benefit);

(b) whether it is funded or unfunded;

(c) the accounting policy and, if different, the funding policy;

(d) whether the pension cost and provision (or asset) are assessed in accordance with the advice of a professionally qualified actuary and, if so, the date of the most recent formal actuarial valuation or later formal review used for this purpose. If the actuary is an employee or officer of the reporting company, or the group of which it is a member, this fact should be disclosed;

(e) the pension cost charge for the period (see Chapter 6 regarding the basis of calculation) together with explanations of significant changes in the charge compared to that in the previous accounting period;

(f) any provisions or prepayments in the balance sheet resulting from a difference between the amounts recognised as cost and the amounts funded or paid directly;

(g) the amount of any deficiency on a current funding level basis, indicating the action, if any, being taken to deal with it in the current and future accounting periods;

(h) an outline of the results of the most recent formal actuarial valuation or later formal review of the scheme on an ongoing basis.

This should include disclosure of:

(i) the actuarial method used and a brief description of the main actuarial assumptions;

(ii) the market value of scheme assets at the date of their valuation or review;

(iii) the level of funding expressed in percentage terms; and

(iv) comments on any material actuarial surplus or deficiency indicated by (iii) above;

(i) any commitment to make additional payments over a limited number of years;

(j) the accounting treatment adopted in respect of a refund that is subject to deduction of tax under the UK Finance Act 1986 or equivalent legislation, where a credit appears in the financial statements in relation to it; and

(k) details of the expected effects on future costs of any material changes in the group's and/or company's pension arrangements;

198 Where a company or group has more than one pension scheme, disclosure should be given on a combined basis, unless disclosure of information about individual schemes is necessary for a proper understanding of the accounts. For the purposes of the disclosure required by item (g) above, a current funding level basis deficiency in one scheme should not be set off against a surplus in another. SSAP 24:89

199 A subsidiary company which is a member of a group scheme should disclose this fact in its financial statements and disclose the nature of the group scheme indicating, where appropriate, that the contributions are based on pension costs across the group as a whole. Such a company is exempt from the disclosure requirements of (g) and (h) above and should instead state the name of the holding company in whose financial statements particulars of the actuarial valuation of the group scheme are contained. This exemption only applies if the holding company is registered in the UK or the Republic of Ireland. SSAP 24:90

Post-retirement benefits other than pensions

200 Where companies have adopted a SSAP 24 basis of accounting for post-retirement benefits other than pensions (which, as indicated in paragraph 88 of Chapter 6, includes a FAS 106 basis), they should make disclosures in relation to them equivalent to those required in respect of pension schemes under SSAP 24 as outlined in paragraph 197 above. The information required to be disclosed includes details of any important UITF Abstract 6

assumptions which are specific to the measurement of such benefits, such as the assumed rate of inflation in the cost of providing the benefits.

201 Companies that have not yet provided for their post-retirement benefits other than pension obligations should under the transitional provisions of UITF Abstract 6 (recognition as a liability is mandatory for accounting periods ending on or after 23 December 1994) give the following disclosures: UITF Abstract 6

(a) a general description of the nature of the benefits to which employees are entitled and the approximate number of employees eligible to receive them;

(b) an estimate of the liability (i.e. the provision that would appear in the balance sheet if the obligation was recognised) or a statement why no reliable estimate can be made;

(c) a statement as to whether or not the employer expects the costs of meeting the liability to attract taxation relief when they are paid and if so an estimate of the amount of such relief, where practicable;

(d) the amount of expense recognised in the period in relation to these benefits. On a pay as you go basis this may be substantially less than the amount which would be recognised on an accruals basis, and if the difference is likely to be material this fact should be indicated; and

(e) the accounting policy applied in relation to such benefits.

Guarantees and other financial commitments

202 Particulars of charges on assets to secure the liabilities of any other person with, where practicable, the amount secured must be stated. 1985 4 sch 50(1)

203 The following information must be given in respect of any contingent liability (other than those above) insofar as it has not been provided and the possibility of loss is not remote: 1985 4 sch 50(2) SSAP 18:16,18,19

(a) the estimated amount of the liability not provided in the accounts;

(b) its legal nature;

(c) whether any security has been given and, if so, what;

(d) the factors affecting the likelihood of the liability crystallising; and SSAP 18:18

(e) if an estimate of the financial effect cannot be made, a statement to that effect.

204 The estimated financial effect of contingencies should be disclosed before taxation, the taxation implications if the contingencies crystallise being explained separately.

SSAP 18:20

205 Contingent gains should not be accrued, and should only be disclosed if the realisation of the gain is probable. If disclosure is made the information set out above should be given (with the exception of details regarding security).

SSAP 18:17

206 The aggregate amount of contracted capital expenditure not provided, and the amount authorised by directors but not contracted, must be shown where practicable. Capital commitments should include the amount of any irrecoverable VAT.

1985 4 sch 50(3)

SSAP 5:6,9

207 Details of any other financial commitments for which provision has not been made and which are relevant to assessing the company's state of affairs must be shown. This requirement is very widely drawn, and might include, for example, unmatched forward foreign exchange contracts.

1985 4 sch 50(5)

Author

208 The following lease commitments must be disclosed:

(a) the amount of any commitments in respect of finance leases which have been entered into before the balance sheet date but whose inception occurs after the year end and in respect of which the obligations have not been included in the accounts;

SSAP 21:54

(b) the payments which are committed to be made during the next year in respect of operating leases. These payments must be analysed between those in respect of leases where the commitment expires within that year, in the second to fifth years inclusive and over five years from the balance sheet date; and

SSAP 21:56

(c) the commitments in (b) in respect of operating leases of land and buildings must be disclosed separately from other operating leases.

Commitments in respect of hire purchase contracts should be included above where they have similar characteristics to the types of lease specified.

209 Financial commitments are unlikely to include the company's normal sales and purchases order books, its liability to continue to pay wages, or matched forward foreign exchange commitments.

Author

210 The disclosure above in respect of guarantees, commitments and pension funds must include separately details of commitments on behalf of, or for the benefit of:

1985 4 sch 59A
(1989 1 sch 11(3))

(a) any parent undertaking or fellow subsidiary undertaking of the company; and

(b) any subsidiary undertaking of the company.

211 An example of a circumstance which might involve disclosure under the above paragraph is the existence of cross-guarantees under a group banking scheme. Author

Post balance sheet events

212 SSAP 17 requires the following post balance sheet events to be disclosed in the accounts: SSAP 17:23

(a) non-adjusting events of such materiality that non-disclosure would affect the ability of accounts users to reach a proper understanding of the financial position; and

(b) the reversal or maturity of a transaction the substance of which was primarily to alter the appearance of the balance sheet ('window dressing'), regardless of whether it was treated as an adjusting or a non-adjusting event.

213 The following information should be given in respect of events disclosed under the preceding paragraph: SSAP 17:24,25

(a) the nature of the event;

(b) an estimate, before taking account of taxation, of its financial effect, or a statement that such an estimate is impracticable; and

(c) its taxation implications.

Identity of ultimate parent company and other parent undertakings

214 Every subsidiary undertaking and a parent undertaking that is itself a subsidiary undertaking must disclose the following information with respect to the company (if any) regarded by the directors as its ultimate parent company: 1985 5 sch 12,31 (1989 3 sch)

(a) the parent company's name; and

(b) if known, the country of incorporation (if other than Great Britain) or the country of registration (England and Wales or Scotland) if incorporated in Great Britain.

'Company' includes any body corporate. A body corporate includes a company incorporated elsewhere than in Great Britain. 1985 s 740

215 Every subsidiary undertaking must disclose certain information with respect to the parent undertakings of both: 1985 5 sch 11,30 (1989 3 sch)

(a) the largest group of which it is a member and for which consolidated accounts are drawn up (normally the ultimate parent undertaking); and

(b) the smallest group of which it is a member and for which consolidated accounts are drawn up (the immediate parent undertaking if it prepares consolidated accounts).

The information to be disclosed with respect to those parent undertakings is:

(a) their names;

(b) their countries of incorporation (if other than Great Britain), their countries of registration (England and Wales or Scotland) if incorporated in Great Britain or the addresses of their principal places of business if unincorporated; and

(c) if copies of the consolidated accounts are available to the public, the addresses from which copies can be obtained.

216 The disclosures set out in the preceding two paragraphs are subject to the exceptions set out in paragraphs 53 and 54 above (information of excessive length or seriously prejudicial to the business). 1985 s 231 (1989 s 6)

Date of approval of accounts by directors

217 The date on which the accounts were approved by the board of directors should be disclosed in the accounts. SSAP 17:26

6 Profit and Loss Account

Definition

1 The term profit and loss account includes, in the case of an undertaking not trading for profit, an income and expenditure account. 1985 s 262(2) (1989 s 22)

Groups

2 A parent company need not publish its individual profit and loss account where: 1985 s 230 (1989 s 5(4))

(a) it prepares consolidated accounts in accordance with the Act;

(b) the company's profit or loss for the financial year determined in accordance with the Act is disclosed in the notes to the company's individual balance sheet; and

(c) a note in the company's annual accounts states that the exemption applies.

Format

3 Four different formats are permitted for the profit and loss account, and the rules governing their modification are set out in Chapter 3 of this book. All the items listed in the standard profit and loss account formats are assigned Arabic numerals and accordingly may, under certain circumstances, be combined together on the face of the profit and loss account. In the interest of clear presentation, it is undesirable for immaterial items to be shown. Advantage may also be taken of the format rules for combination of material items, which should then be disclosed separately in the notes to the accounts. 1985 4 sch 1 1985 4 sch 3(4)

4 As stated in Chapter 3, FRS 3 represents a fundamental change in the way the profit and loss account is presented. It requires separate disclosure of results from continuing, discontinued and newly acquired operations. The way in which such disclosures should be made is dealt with in this Chapter. FRS 3 also requires a new note disclosing pure historical cost profit - profit as it would have been had there been no asset valuations. This requirement is set out in Chapter 3.

Abbreviated accounts

5 Small and medium-sized companies preparing abbreviated accounts should refer to Chapter 9, which explains how the rules set out in this chapter are to be modified in their circumstances.

General

6 In addition to the items required by the standard formats and FRS 3, every profit and loss account must show:

(a) profit or loss on ordinary activities before taxation; 1985 4 sch 3(6)

(b) any amount transferred or proposed to be transferred to or from reserves; and 1985 4 sch 3(7)(a)

(c) the aggregate amount of dividends paid or proposed excluding both the related ACT or attributable tax credit. 1985 4 sch 3(7)(b) SSAP 8:24

7 If either format 1 or format 3 is adopted, 'cost of sales', 'distribution costs' and 'administrative expenses' must be stated after taking account of provisions for depreciation or diminution in value of assets. 1985 4 sch format, note 14

Discontinued operations

8 The results of discontinued operations must be shown separately from the results of continuing operations and acquisitions (as a component of continuing operations). Discontinued operations are operations that are sold or terminated and that satisfy all of the following conditions: FRS 3:14 FRS 3:4

(a) the sale or termination is completed either in the period or before the earlier of three months after the commencement of the subsequent period and the date on which the accounts are approved;

(b) if a termination, the former activities have ceased permanently;

(c) the sale or termination has a material effect on the nature and focus of the reporting entity's operations and represents a material reduction in its operating facilities resulting either from its withdrawal from a particular market (whether class of business or geographical) or from a material reduction in turnover in the reporting entity's continuing markets; and

(d) the assets, liabilities, results of operations and activities are clearly distinguishable, physically, operationally and for financial reporting purposes.

Operations not satisfying all the above conditions are classified as continuing.

9 It can be seen that there are many parts to the definition of discontinued operations and care should be exercised in identifying those operations that have been discontinued during the year. Where the operations are in the process of discontinuing, the results of those operations should not be included in the discontinued category, although in some circumstances it may be appropriate to show the results as a subdivision of continuing operations in the notes. Author

10 Where an operation is closed or terminated during the year, its results up to the date of closure or termination should appear under the heading of discontinued operations. Any profit or loss arising on the discontinuance should be separately disclosed after operating profit and before interest and should also be described as 'discontinued operations'. Any reorganisation or restructuring of continued operations resulting from the closure or termination should be treated as a part of continuing operations (see further paragraph 14 below). FRS 3:17

Exceptional items

11 Exceptional items are defined as material items which derive from events or transactions that fall within the ordinary activities of the reporting entity and which individually or, if of a similar type, in aggregate, need to be disclosed by virtue of their size or incidence if the accounts are to give a true and fair view. FRS 3:5

12 The definition is very similar to that contained in SSAP 6 (withdrawn) but it is the standard's new definition of ordinary activities that brings within the scope of exceptional items all those items which under SSAP 6 would have been extraordinary. Ordinary activities include the effects on the reporting entity of any event in the various environments in which it operates, including political, regulatory, economic and geographical environments, irrespective of the frequency or unusual nature of the events. Consequently, almost any conceivable activity or event that occurs in a company's life will be included in ordinary activities. Such events and activities will only fall to be disclosed as exceptional if non-disclosure, because of their size or incidence, would mean that the accounts did not give a true and fair view. Examples of such exceptional items include losses arising from the expropriation of foreign assets (political), a natural disaster (geographical), currency devaluation (economic) or a fundamental change in the basis of taxation (regulatory). In relation to the last of these examples, see paragraph 110 below. Author FRS 3:2 Author

13 All exceptional items, other than those included in the items listed in paragraph 14 below, should be credited or charged in arriving at the profit or loss on ordinary activities. They should be included under the statutory formats to which they relate and classified under continuing or discontinued operations as appropriate. The amount of each exceptional item, either individually or in aggregate for items of a similar type, should be disclosed 1985 4 sch 57(3) FRS 3:19

in the notes or on the face of the profit and loss account if that is necessary to give a true and fair view. Each exceptional item should be suitably described to enable its nature to be understood.

14 The following items should be disclosed separately on the face of the profit and loss account after operating profit and before interest, classified under continuing or discontinued operations as appropriate: FRS 3:20

(a) profits or losses on the sale or termination of an operation (formerly shown as extraordinary under SSAP 6);

(b) costs of a fundamental reorganisation or restructuring having a material effect on the nature or focus of the company's operations. (UITF Abstract 2 that dealt with this issue is now withdrawn.); and

(c) profits or losses on the sale of fixed assets.

In calculating the profit or loss in respect of the above items consideration should be given to revenue and costs that are directly related to the items in question.

15 Provisions made in respect of the above items should also be included. Where the net amount of item (a) or (b) of the preceding paragraph is not material, but the gross profits or losses are material the relevant heading should still appear on the face of the profit and loss account with a reference to a related note analysing the profits and losses. FRS 3:20

Provisions for sale or termination of operations

16 Where a binding legal agreement for the sale of an operation has been signed, or where approval has been given to a detailed formal plan to terminate an operation from which the enterprise cannot realistically withdraw, provision should be made for: FRS 3:18

(a) the direct costs of the sale or termination; and

(b) any operating losses of the operation up to the date of sale or termination;

in both cases, to the extent not covered by expected future profits of the operation or disposal of its assets.

17 It should be noted that where a decision to sell an operation has been made but no legally binding sale agreement exists, no provision in respect of items (a) and (b) of the preceding paragraph is required, although any permanent diminution in asset values should be recognised. This contrasts with the standard's rules on providing for items (a) and (b) where a detailed formal plan for closure from which the enterprise cannot realistically withdraw is adopted. Furthermore, the standard states that an obligation arises when a reporting entity becomes demonstrably committed to the sale (e.g. public FRS 3:45

pronouncements of the sale, the commencement of implementation or other circumstances are indicative of the commitment to complete the sale). This would imply that there may be circumstances where provision could be made even if no legally binding sale agreement exists. The standard is, therefore, not entirely clear in this respect and it may well be that in some cases, provision should be made on the grounds of prudence even though not strictly required by the standard.

Author

18 The provisions for losses on sale or termination should be disclosed separately on the profit and loss account after operating profit and should be included under the continuing category unless the operation qualifies as a discontinued operation in the period under review.

FRS 3:18

19 In the subsequent period when the sale or termination has been completed and the operation qualifies as discontinued, the following disclosures apply:

FRS 3:18

(a) the results of the operation disposed of should be disclosed under each of the statutory profit and loss account headings and described as discontinued operations;

(b) any loss on disposal should be calculated and disclosed after operating profit and before interest under the discontinued heading;

(c) the provisions made in the previous year should be separately highlighted as an offset against the appropriate headings in sub-paragraph (a) above in arriving at the operating profit or loss disclosed for the discontinued operation; and

(d) any balance of the provision relating to items in sub-paragraph (b) above should be similarly highlighted as an offset against the loss on disposal of the discontinued operation.

Extraordinary items

20 Extraordinary items are not defined in the Act, but are defined in FRS 3 as those material items possessing a high degree of abnormality which arise from events or transactions that fall outside the ordinary activities of the reporting entity and which are expected not to recur.

1985 4 Sch 54(3)
FRS 3:6

21 Because the definition of ordinary activities as discussed in paragraph 12 above is so widely drawn, the incidence of extraordinary items will in future be extremely rare. In those rare situations, any extraordinary items should be shown separately on the face of the profit and loss account, after the profit or loss on ordinary activities after taxation and, in the case of consolidated financial statements, after minority interest but before deducting appropriations such as dividends. An adequate description of each extraordinary item should be given to enable its nature to be understood.

Author

FRS 3:22
1985 4 sch 57(2)

Profit or loss on disposal of assets

22 The profit or loss on disposal of assets should be accounted for in the period in which the disposal occurs as the difference between the net sale proceeds and the net carrying amount of the asset, whether carried at historical cost (less any provisions made) or at a valuation. FRS 3:21

23 The above requirement is new in UK accounting because up until now it has been quite acceptable to calculate the profit or loss on a previously revalued asset either on the above basis or by reference to the asset's depreciated historical cost. The difference between the two bases is that under the latter the previous revaluation surplus is passed through the profit and loss account on disposal whereas under the former basis it is not. The requirement introduced by the standard applies to all assets and not just to fixed assets. Author

Merger relief

24 This paragraph applies where a company has during the year, or during the two preceding years, allotted shares in consideration for shares in another company in circumstances in which merger relief was available. That is by virtue of section 131 of the Act any premium was not required to be transferred to the share premium account. There must be disclosed the amount of any profit or loss arising on, together with an explanation of, the following transactions: 1985 5 sch 10,29 (1989 3 sch)

(a) a disposal by the company or, in the case of consolidated accounts, by the group of any fixed assets of, or shares in, the acquired company or any of its subsidiaries; and

(b) if the company was already a subsidiary, the date on which the shares were allotted.

For the purpose of this section the Act provides that time of allotment will be defined as:

(a) the date on which the company became a subsidiary, or on which conditions were fulfilled making the allotment binding; or

(b) if the company was already a subsidiary, the date on which the shares were allotted.

25 The information set out in the preceding paragraph need not be given in respect of undertakings established or carrying on business outside the UK if, in the opinion of the directors, and with the consent of the Secretary of State, it would be seriously prejudicial to the business of the company, that subsidiary or any other subsidiary of the parent company. 1985 s 231(3) (1989 s 6)

Prior period adjustments

26 Material adjustments applicable to prior periods arising from changes in accounting policies and from the correction of fundamental errors should be accounted for by restating the corresponding primary statements and notes and the opening balance of reserves for the cumulative effect. The cumulative effect of the adjustments should also be noted at the foot of the statement of total recognised gains and losses of the current period. The effect of prior period adjustments on the results for the preceding period should be disclosed where practicable. FRS 3:7,29

27 Where any material amount relating to any preceding year is included in any item in the profit and loss account, the effect must be stated. Items relating to prior years arising mainly from the corrections and adjustments of accounting estimates should be included in the result for the year before tax and extraordinary items, and their effects stated where material. 1985 4 sch 57(1)

Information supplementing the profit and loss account

28 The further information set out below is required to supplement the profit and loss account and must, unless stated otherwise, be given either in the profit and loss account or in the notes. 1985 4 sch 3

Analysis of turnover

29 Turnover is defined as the amounts derived from the provision of goods and services falling within the company's ordinary activities, after deduction of trade discounts, value added tax and any other taxes based on the amounts so derived. 1985 s 262(1) (1989 s 22) SSAP 5:8

30 Turnover on long-term contracts is required by SSAP 9 to be ascertained 'in a manner appropriate to the stage of completion of the contract, the business and the industry in which it operates'. This requirement is intended to be flexible, and in particular to permit turnover to be determined either by reference to the cost of work carried out to date (the 'cost based' approach) or by reference to the sales value of work carried out (the 'revenue based' approach). SSAP 9:28 SSAP 9:Appendix 1:23

31 Turnover should be disclosed on the face of the profit and loss account so as to show separately turnover attributable to: FRS 3:14

(a) continuing operations;

(b) acquisitions as a component of continuing operations;

(c) discontinued operations; and

(d) total turnover.

Analysis of operating profit or loss

32 Operating profit or loss should be disclosed on the face of the profit and loss account so as to show separately operating profit or loss attributable to: FRS 3:14

(a) continuing operations;

(b) acquisitions as a component of continuing operations;

(c) discontinued operations; and

(d) total operating profit or loss;

33 Operating profit or loss, which does not appear in the statutory profit and loss account formats, should be disclosed before income from shares in group undertakings. This will be the normal position for non-financial companies although there may be cases where operating profit or loss is disclosed after income from associated undertakings or from other participating interests. FRS 3:14,39

Expenditure

34 For each of the statutory format headings between turnover and operating profit, an analysis must be given in the notes or on the face of the profit and loss account showing separately the amounts attributable to: FRS 3:14

(a) continuing operations;

(b) acquisitions as a component of continuing operations;

(c) discontinued operations; and

(d) the total for each statutory heading.

35 For companies that have adopted format 1, the relevant headings between turnover and operating profit are cost of sales; gross profit or loss; distribution costs; administrative expenses; and other operating income. Illustrations of the new profit and loss account formats are given in FRS 3. Those examples have been prepared using profit and loss account Format 1, but equivalent information should be shown if any of the other statutory formats are used.

36 The analysis in respect of continuing operations, acquisitions and discontinued operations is required only to the profit before interest level. In those circumstances where a company wishes to allocate interest or tax between continuing and discontinued operations, an explanation of the method and the underlying assumptions used in making the allocations should be disclosed. FRS 3:14

Segmental reporting of turnover and profits

37 For each class of business which in the opinion of the directors is substantially different from other business carried on there must be disclosed: 1985 4 sch 55(1)

(a) the amount of turnover attributable to that class; and

(b) the profit or loss before taxation attributable, in the opinion of the directors, to that class.

38 For each geographical market, being an individual country or group of countries which, in the opinion of the directors, is substantially different, the turnover attributable to that market must be shown. 1985 4 sch 55(2)

39 In deciding what constitutes a different class of business or market, the directors must consider the manner in which the company's activities are organised. Class of business and geographical segments are defined in SSAP 25 'Segmental reporting'. In identifying reportable segments the directors should have regard to the overall purpose of presenting segmental information. Guidance is given in SSAP 25 on the circumstances that are relevant to a user's understanding of the accounts and which can be communicated by means of segmental information. 1985 4 sch 55(3) SSAP 25:30,31

40 Classes of business or markets which, in the opinion of the directors, do not differ substantially are to be treated as one class or market, and any immaterial amounts attributable to one class of business or market may be included in the amount stated in respect of another class or market. The standard sets out size criteria for determining whether a segment is significant enough to be separately identified and reported. A segment should normally be regarded as significant if it accounts for ten per cent or more of any of the following: 1985 4 sch 55(4) SSAP 25:9

(a) total third party turnover of the entity;

(b) the combined result of all segments in profit or of all segments in loss, whichever combined result is greater; and

(c) total net assets of the entity.

41 SSAP 25 requires the following additional segmental disclosures by both class of business and geographical market for public limited companies (or their holding companies), banking and insurance companies or groups and entities exceeding the size criteria, multiplied in each case by ten, specified in Chapter 9 for medium-sized companies: SSAP 25:4

(a) turnover analysed between turnover derived from external customers and turnover derived from other segments. The geographical analysis should be made on the origin and destination basis unless there is no SSAP 25:34

material difference between them, in which case, the disclosure of turnover to third parties by origin is required;

(b) result before accounting for taxation, minority interest and extraordinary items (already required for classes of business, sub-paragraph 37(b) above); and

(c) net assets.

42 In sub-paragraph 37(b) above, segment results may be given before or after accounting for interest as appropriate. Where the nature of the business is such that interest income and/or expense are central to the business, the segment result should be shown after interest. In the majority of companies, however, segments will be financed by a mixture of debt and equity. In such cases, segment results should be disclosed before interest with interest shown separately. SSAP 25:22,34

43 The disclosure of segment result before interest is not strictly in accordance with the requirements of the Act, which requires disclosure of the profit or loss before taxation. However, for the reasons stated above, disclosure of the result before interest will normally be more meaningful. The standard suggests that in most cases the disclosure of results by segment should be based on the areas from which products or services are supplied (origin basis). Author SSAP 25:21

44 In determining segment results, head office or similar expenses which are common to more than one segment should be allocated among segments in a way that directors consider appropriate. SSAP 25 suggests that it will generally be appropriate to follow the allocation principles adopted for internal reporting purposes. Some companies may, however, not wish to apportion common costs, as any such apportionment may in many cases be on an arbitrary basis and therefore misleading. In such circumstances, the common costs should be deducted from the total of the segment results. SSAP 25:23

45 In most cases, net assets in sub-paragraph 41(c) above will be the non-interest bearing operating assets less non-interest bearing operating liabilities. However, where the segment results are disclosed after accounting for interest, the corresponding interest bearing operating assets and liabilities should be included in net assets. Additional guidance is given in the standard on the allocation of assets and liabilities to segments. SSAP 25:24,34

46 A segment's assets and liabilities may include not only assets and liabilities relating exclusively to that segment, but also an allocated portion of assets and liabilities that are shared by it with other segments. SSAP 25 suggests that shared assets and liabilities should be allocated among segments on a reasonable basis. As the words 'reasonable basis' are not further explained, the guidance on the allocation of common costs discussed in paragraph 44 would seem equally relevant to the allocation of shared assets and liabilities. SSAP 25:25 Author

47 Where associated undertakings account for 20 per cent of the total result or 20 per cent of the total assets of the group, the following information should be disclosed segmentally for the undertakings: SSAP 25:36

(a) the group's share of results of associated undertakings before taxation, minority interests and extraordinary items; and

(b) the group's share of net assets of associated undertakings (including goodwill to the extent not written off) stated, where possible, after attributing fair values to the net assets at the date of acquisition of the interest in each associated undertaking.

The segmental disclosure should be of the aggregate amounts for all associated undertakings and should be shown separately in the segment report. However, the information need not be disclosed if it is unobtainable or its disclosure would be prejudicial to the business of the associate. Where disclosure is not made for either of these reasons, the reason for non-disclosure should be stated in the notes, together with a brief description of the omitted business or businesses.

48 For listed companies The International Stock Exchange requires information broadly similar to the above, and in addition a geographical analysis of net turnover and trading profit derived from operations outside the UK and the Republic of Ireland should be given. The disclosures required are: ASL 21(c)

(a) an analysis of turnover by continent and, if any continent accounts for more than 50 per cent of turnover derived from such overseas operations, a more detailed breakdown (e.g. by country). For this purpose overseas operations include direct exports and activities carried out otherwise than in the country where the main place of business of the company (or group) is situated; and

(b) an appropriate statement, where necessary for a proper appraisal of the business, of significant contributions to trading results derived from activities carried out in any territory if the contribution from a specific area is abnormal, i.e. out of line with the normal ratio of profit to turnover.

49 Where an acquisition, or a sale or a termination, has a material impact on a major business segment this should be disclosed and explained. FRS 3:15

50 Where both parent and consolidated accounts are presented, segmental information should be presented on the basis of the consolidated figures only. SSAP 25:35

51 The total of the amounts in the segmental analysis should agree to the related total in the accounts. If it does not, a reconciliation between the two figures should be given, together with an explanation of the reconciling items. SSAP 25:37

52	Comparative figures are required. Where a change is made to the definitions of segments or to the accounting policies for reporting segmental information, the nature of the change should be disclosed, together with the reasons for, and effect of, the change. Comparative figures should be adjusted to reflect the change.	SSAP 25:38,39
53	Segmental information required by the Act or by the standard need not be disclosed if, in the opinion of the directors, disclosure would be seriously prejudicial to the interests of the company. However, the fact that the information has not been disclosed must be stated.	1985 4 sch 55(5) SSAP 25:43
54	A subsidiary that is not a public limited company or a banking or insurance company need not comply with the provisions of SSAP 25 if its parent provides segmental information in accordance with the standard.	SSAP 25:41
	Income from finance and operating leases	
55	There should be disclosed:	
	(a) the aggregate rentals receivable in the accounting period, analysed between amounts receivable under finance leases and under operating leases;	SSAP 21:60(b)
	(b) the rentals included above in respect of land and buildings (after deduction of ground rents, rates and other outgoings), if such rents form a substantial part of the company's revenue; and	1985 4 sch 53(5)
	(c) the accounting policy adopted for recognising finance lease income.	SSAP 21:60(a)
	In respect of (c), where tax free grants available to the lessor have been grossed up and included in arriving at the profit before tax, the lessor should disclose the amount by which the profit before tax and the tax charge have been increased.	SSAP 21:41
56	Income from hire purchase contracts should be included as part of the disclosure required above in respect of finance leases or operating leases depending on its characteristics.	SSAP 21:60
	Income from investments	
57	Income from listed investments, including any tax credit in respect of incoming dividends from UK resident companies, must be disclosed.	1985 4 sch 53(4) SSAP 8:25
58	Income derived from fixed asset investments must be split between that derived from group undertakings and that derived from other sources.	1985 4 sch format, note 15
59	In an investing company's individual profit and loss account income from shares in group undertakings and from participating interests (including associated undertakings) should include only dividends received and receivable from those undertakings.	SSAP 1:18 1985 4 sch format (1989 1 sch 3(1))

Associated undertakings

60 The Act defines associated undertakings only in relation to the consolidated accounts of a group. The definition of associated undertaking and the treatment in consolidated accounts is explained in Chapter 8. An investing company which does not prepare consolidated accounts should show the information required by SSAP 1 in respect of associated undertakings by preparing a separate profit and loss account or by adding the information in supplementary form to its own profit and loss account unless the investing company is exempt from preparing consolidated accounts, or would be exempt, if it had subsidiaries. The information should be reported in such a way that its share of profits of associated undertakings is not treated as realised for the purposes of the Act (see also Chapter 5 regarding the balance sheet treatment of associated undertakings). SSAP 1:24 (as amended by Interim Statement-Consolidated Accounts)

Interest receivable

61 Other interest receivable and similar income must be distinguished between that due from group undertakings and that derived from other sources. 1985 4 sch format, note 15

62 Where material revenue based government grants have been credited to the profit and loss account, this fact, and the amount involved, should be disclosed. Author

Auditors' remuneration

63 There must be stated in the notes, the amount of the remuneration of the company's auditors in their capacity as auditors, including expenses and the estimated money value of any benefits in kind. 1985 s 390A (1989 s 121)

64 The Act strictly requires disclosure of the remuneration of the company's auditors for the audit of the company. However, it remains common practice to disclose the aggregate remuneration of the auditors of all group companies and not merely that of the parent. At the time of writing, the DTI has issued for comments a draft statutory instrument which is designed to clarify the requirements of the law to disclose group remuneration. Until such time as the new statutory instrument is implemented, disclosure should be made both of the auditors' remuneration for the company to comply with the strict requirements of the Act, as well as the auditors' remuneration for the group, if applicable, in order to give a more meaningful disclosure and to anticipate the clarification of the law. Author

65 For accounting periods beginning on or after 1 October 1991, there must also be disclosed in the notes the amount of remuneration (including expenses) payable to the company's auditors or their associates for non-audit services provided to the company and any subsidiary undertakings audited by the same auditor (or by the auditor's associates) as the company. Non-audit fees include, for example, fees for accountancy or taxation services, investigations or other corporate finance work or management consultancy. SI 1991 No 2128

The disclosure requirement does not apply to small and medium-sized companies and groups nor is any disclosure required of remuneration for services rendered to subsidiaries not audited by the parent company's auditors or to subsidiaries incorporated outside the UK.

Emoluments, pensions and compensation paid to directors and past directors

66 The amounts described in the three categories set out below must be disclosed in a note to the accounts, irrespective of materiality, distinguishing in each case between amounts paid to or receivable by any person in respect of (i) his services as director of the company or its subsidiaries (e.g. fees, percentages and remuneration for special services), and (ii) otherwise in connection with the management of the affairs of the company or its subsidiaries. Directors are to apportion payments, where necessary, to analyse them into the appropriate categories. The amounts to be disclosed are as follows: 1985 5 sch 12 (1989 4 sch)

(a) aggregate of directors' emoluments, including fees, percentages, expense allowances (so far as chargeable to UK income tax), pension scheme contributions paid and the estimated money value of any other benefits received otherwise than in cash. Emoluments in respect of accepting office as director (e.g. payments in advance of becoming a director: 'golden hellos') must be treated as being emoluments for services as director; 1985 6 sch 1 (1989 4 sch)

(b) aggregate of pensions receivable by directors, past directors or their nominees or dependants, including the estimated money value and nature of any non-cash benefits, but excluding pensions receivable under a pension scheme where the contributions are substantially adequate for the maintenance of the scheme; 1985 6 sch 7 (1989 4 sch)

(c) aggregate of compensation in respect of loss of office, including retirement, receivable by directors or past directors including the estimated money value and nature of any non-cash benefits; (The payment to a director of compensation, except as indicated below, is illegal unless particulars and the amount of the proposed payment have been disclosed to and approved by the company in general meeting. For the purpose of prior approval in general meeting, compensation for loss of office does not include any bona fide payment representing damages for breach of contract or consideration for the premature termination of a service agreement, or a pension in respect of past services.); and 1985 6 sch 8 (1989 4 sch) 1985 s 312,316 1985 s 316(3)

(d) aggregate of consideration payable to third parties for making available the services of any person as a director, including the estimated money value and nature of non-cash benefits. Third parties do not include the director himself, a person connected with him, or a company controlled 1985 6 sch 9 (1989 4 sch) by him or the company or its subsidiary undertakings. Separate disclosure of amounts in respect of services as director and in respect of other services is not required.

67 The disclosures required by the preceding paragraph must include sums paid by or receivable from:

1985 6 sch 10(2)
(1989 4 sch)

(a) the company;

(b) the company's subsidiary undertakings; and

(c) any other person,

but not sums for which the recipient has to account to the company or its subsidiaries, unless that liability is released or not enforced within two years. In regard to compensation for loss of office, there must be shown separately the amounts received from each of the above sources.

6 sch 11(2)
(1989 4 sch)
1985 6 sch 10(3)
(1989 4 sch)

68 The disclosures required by the preceding two paragraphs must include any amounts paid to or receivable by a person connected with the director or a company controlled by him, but not so as to require an amount to be counted twice.

1985 6 sch 10(4)
(1989 4 sch)

69 The amounts to be disclosed in a financial year are the amounts receivable in respect of that year or, in the case of amounts not receivable in respect of a year, amounts paid in the year. Where an expense allowance has been charged to UK income tax at a later date, the relevant sums must be included in the next succeeding accounts, and shown separately.

1985 6 sch 11
(1989 4 sch)

70 There is a special definition of a subsidiary for the purpose of this part of the Act. When any director of the company is or was by virtue of the company's direct or indirect nomination at the same time a director of any other undertaking, that undertaking must for this purpose be treated as a subsidiary undertaking. For example, an associated undertaking of a parent undertaking is deemed to be a subsidiary undertaking for the purpose of this part of the Act where a director of the parent undertaking has been nominated to the board of the associated undertaking. Consequently, any remuneration received by the director from the associated undertaking will fall to be disclosed in the accounts of the parent.

1985 6 sch 13(2)
(1989 4 sch)
Author

71 In respect of the emoluments of the directors (excluding for this purpose contributions paid in respect of a person under a pension scheme) there must be stated:

1985 6 sch 2-5
(1989 4 sch)

(a) the number of directors (including the chairman and the highest paid director) whose emoluments fall into each bracket of a scale in multiples of £5,000. Individual brackets need only be shown where the emoluments of at least one of the directors fall within the bracket in either the current or previous year. Directors who have no emoluments should be included in the bracket from £nil to £5,000;

(b) the emoluments while chairman of each person so acting during the year; and

(c) the emoluments of the highest paid director if not the chairman. It is not necessary to give the name of such director. Author

Items (a), (b) and (c) are not applicable to a director whose duties were carried out wholly or mainly outside the UK. Nor are these disclosures required if the company is neither a parent company nor a subsidiary and the aggregate directors' emoluments (excluding for this purpose pensions and any compensation for loss of office) do not exceed £60,000.

72 The Cadbury Committee's Report on 'The financial aspects of corporate governance' incorporating 'The code of best practice' recommends that listed companies reporting in respect of years ending after 30 June 1993 should give a full and clear disclosure of director's total emoluments and those of the chairman and highest-paid UK director, including pension contributions and stock options. Separate figures should be given for salary and performance-related elements and the basis on which performance is measured should be explained. Although the Code is generally aimed at listed companies, other companies are encouraged to comply with its requirements. Cadbury Report

73 The number of directors who have waived rights to receive emoluments, including pension contributions, during the year and the aggregate amount thereof must be shown. This is not applicable to a company which is neither a holding company nor a subsidiary company and the aggregate directors' emoluments of which (excluding for this purpose pensions and compensation for loss of office) do not exceed £60,000. Listed companies are to give details of waivers of future emoluments by directors, whether receivable from the company or its subsidiaries. 1985 6 sch 6(1) (1989 4 sch) ASL 21(n)

74 Annual accounts of a parent company need only disclose the details relating to the parent company directors. Note however that this includes amounts paid to them by subsidiaries. 1985 6 sch 1(2) (1989 4 sch)

75 If the company fails to make adequate disclosure of directors' emoluments, the auditors must include the relevant information in their report. 1985 s 237(4) (1989 s 9)

Staff

76 There must be stated:

(a) the average number of persons employed in the financial year (whether in the UK or abroad); and 1985 4 sch 56(1)(a)

(b) the average number of such employees within each category of persons employed. Categories must be determined by the directors having regard to the manner in which the company's activities are organised. It is not clear what sorts of categories are envisaged. The options appear to be: 1985 4 sch 56(1)(b),(5) Author

(i) a geographical analysis;

(ii) a functional analysis (production, marketing, administration etc); or

(iii) an analysis by product group.

The 'average number' must be calculated by dividing the total of the numbers of staff employed under contracts of service in each week of the financial year by the number of weeks in the financial year. It seems clear that this information must be given in respect of all employees, both in the UK and abroad. The disclosure in respect of emoluments and the average number of employees should make it clear whether or not executive directors have been included. 1985 4 sch 56(2),(3) Author

77 In respect of the same persons taken into account in the preceding paragraph, there must be stated separately the aggregate amounts of: 1985 4 sch 56(4)

(a) wages and salaries paid or payable for the year in respect of those persons;

(b) social security costs incurred by the company on their behalf; and

(c) other pension costs so incurred,

insofar as any of these amounts are included in the profit and loss account.

Pension costs

78 The pension cost charge for the period should be disclosed together with, in the case of a defined benefit scheme, explanations of significant changes in the charge compared to that in the previous accounting period. SSAP 24:87(c),88(e)

79 For defined contribution schemes the charge against profits should be the amount of contributions payable to the pension scheme in respect of the accounting period. SSAP 24:78

80 For defined benefit schemes the pension cost should be calculated using actuarial valuation methods designed to provide the actuary's best estimate of the cost of providing the pension benefits promised. The method should be such that regular pension cost is a substantially level percentage of current and expected future pensionable payroll in the light of the current actuarial assumptions. SSAP 24:79

81 Variations from the regular cost should be allocated over the expected remaining service lives of current employees in the scheme, except as stated in paragraphs 82 and 83 below. SSAP 24:80

82 Where the significant reduction in the number of employees is related to the sale or termination of an operation, the associated pension cost or credit should be recognised immediately to the extent necessary to comply with the requirements of FRS 3 (see paragraph 14 above). In all other cases where there is a reduction in contributions arising from a significant reduction in employees the reduction of contributions should be recognised as it occurs. SSAP 24:81 (amended by FRS 3)

83 Where a company takes a cash refund as part of a scheme to reduce a surplus in accordance with the provisions of the Finance Act 1986, or equivalent legislation, the refund may be credited to the profit and loss account in the year of receipt, rather than spreading forward the effects of the variation which has given rise to the surplus. SSAP 24:83

84 In certain very limited circumstances prudence may require that a material deficit which has necessitated the payment of significant additional contributions be recognised over a period shorter than the expected remaining service lives of current employees in the scheme. SSAP 24:82

85 Where *ex gratia* pensions or *ex gratia* pension increases not allowed for in the actuarial assumptions are granted, the capital cost, to the extent not covered by a surplus, should be recognised in the accounting period in which they are granted. SSAP 24:84,85

86 Where the company or group has pension obligations in respect of overseas operations, the pension charge should reflect that obligation in accordance with SSAP 24. A consolidation adjustment may be necessary to achieve conformity with SSAP 24 unless the nature of the commitment is very different from that which is customary in the UK. If, because of the difficulties and cost of obtaining the actuarial information, this is impractical, the amount charged to the profit and loss account and the basis of charge should, as a minimum, be disclosed. SSAP 24:91

Post-retirement benefits other than pensions

87 In addition to pensions, some employers also provide post-retirement health care or other benefits. Although these arrangements are relatively uncommon in the UK, they are quite common in some countries, notably the US. UK holding companies with overseas subsidiaries have to consider the question of accounting for them even if they have no material obligations in the UK. Author

88 Abstract 6 states that, as a matter of principle, such benefits are liabilities and that the principles of SSAP 24 should be applied to their measurement and disclosure in accounts relating to accounting periods ending on or after UITF Abstract 6

23 December 1994. Where a UK parent undertaking has US subsidiaries which are governed by the requirements of US Statement of Financial Accounting Standard 106 'Accounting for post-retirement benefits other than pensions', measurement in accordance with this statement will be deemed to satisfy SSAP 24 principles.

89 Where employers have not yet applied SSAP 24 to post-retirement benefits other than pensions, the abstract requires certain disclosures to be made during the transitional period, before full recognition becomes mandatory, beginning with accounts relating to accounting periods ending on or after 23 December 1992 (see Chapter 5). UITF Abstract 6

Depreciation

90 Any charges for depreciation and diminution in value of fixed assets must be stated by note, if not otherwise required to be shown by the profit and loss account format adopted. In addition there must be stated separately the aggregate amount of: 1985 4 sch format, note 17

(a) any provision against a fixed asset investment for diminution in value; 1985 4 sch 19(1)

(b) any provision against a fixed asset for permanent diminution in value; and 1985 4 sch 19(2)

(c) any write back of a provision made under (a) or (b) above which is no longer necessary. 1985 4 sch 19(3)

Research and development

91 Other than for companies described below, the total amount of research and development expenditure charged in the profit and loss account should be disclosed, analysed between the current year's expenditure and amounts amortised from deferred expenditure. SSAP 13:31

92 A company is exempt from the above disclosure if it satisfies both the following conditions: SSAP 13:22

(a) it must not be a public limited company nor a banking or insurance company, nor be a holding company which has such a company as a subsidiary; and

(b) it satisfies the Act's criteria, multiplied in each case by 10, for defining a medium-sized company. (See Chapter 9).

Foreign currency translation

93 The net amount of exchange gains or losses on foreign currency borrowings less deposits should be disclosed, identifying separately: SSAP 20:60

(a) the amount offset in reserves as permitted by SSAP 20; and

(b) the net amount charged/credited to profit and loss account.

Goodwill

94 The amount of goodwill amortised through the profit and loss account during the year should be disclosed (where the amortisation policy is followed). SSAP 22:45(a)

Interest payable and similar charges

95 Interest payable (gross) must be disclosed showing separately the totals of interest payable on loans from group undertakings, and all other interest payable or any similar charges. In the latter case, the totals in each of the following categories must be shown separately: 1985 4 sch 53(2) 1985 4 sch format, note 16

(a) all bank loans and overdrafts, together with other loans (other than from group undertakings) either:

   (i) not repayable by instalments and due for repayment within five years of the year end; or

   (ii) repayable by instalments the last of which falls due within five years of the year end;

(b) loans of any other kind (other than from group undertakings); and

(c) aggregate finance charges allocated for the period in respect of finance leases, including hire purchase contracts of a financing nature. SSAP 21:53

Examples of 'other similar charges' might include arrangement fees on loans, foreign currency losses relating to financing or 'financing costs' of deep discount or zero coupon bonds.

96 Reference to such complex capital instruments is contained in Chapter 5. In accordance with FRED 3, the finance costs of debt should be allocated to periods over the term of the debt at a constant rate on the carrying amount and charged to the profit and loss account. The carrying amount of debt should be increased by the finance cost in respect of the reporting period and reduced by payments made in respect of the debt in that period. FRED 3:25,26

97 The premium (supplementary interest) payable when a convertible bond is redeemed should be accrued over the period to redemption and charged to the profit and loss account along with the coupon rate even where it is likely that the bond will be converted into shares. A change of accounting policy to comply with this requirement should be treated as a prior year adjustment in accordance with FRS 3. Under FRED 3, the premium would fall to be included in the calculation of the finance cost for the debt as stated in the preceding paragraph. UITF Abstract 1

Operating lease rentals

98 The total of operating lease rentals (including charges under a hire purchase agreement similar in nature to an operating lease) charged as an expense in the profit and loss account should be disclosed, analysed between amounts payable in respect of hire of plant and machinery and in respect of other operating leases (e.g. for land and buildings). The accounting policy for operating leases should be disclosed. 1985 4 sch 53(6) SSAP 21:55 SSAP 21:57

99 The words 'plant and machinery' should be construed to cover whatever items in the nature of fixed assets (other than land and buildings) are hired for use in the business (e.g. vehicles, ships or other equipment). Author

Taxation

100 Tax effects should be shown in the accounts separately from the items or transactions to which they relate. SSAP 15:16

101 The charge for taxation must be shown, distinguishing between: 1985 4 sch 54 SSAP 8:22

(a) UK corporation tax, showing the extent of any relief from double taxation;

(b) any material transfers between the deferred taxation account and the profit and loss account. The statutory provisions on deferred tax are extended by SSAP 15 (revised), which requires that deferred taxation dealt with in the profit and loss account should be shown separately as part of the total tax charge or credit in the profit and loss account, or by way of note to the accounts; SSAP 15:33

(c) UK income tax (e.g. tax attributable to franked investment income);

(d) overseas taxation of profits, income and capital gains (so far as the tax is charged to revenue), relieved and unrelieved, specifying that part of the unrelieved overseas taxation which arises from the payment or proposed payment of dividends; and

(e) irrecoverable ACT.

The amounts shown above must be stated separately in respect of 'tax on profit or loss on ordinary activities' and 'tax on extraordinary profit or loss', either on the face of the profit and loss account or in a note to the accounts. 1985 4 sch 54(3) SSAP 15:33,34

102 The amount of tax attributable to exceptional items described in paragraph 14 above should also be disclosed in a note in aggregate. The tax attributable to such items should be calculated by computing the tax on the profit or loss on ordinary activities as if the items did not exist and comparing this notional tax with the tax on the profit or loss for the year FRS 3:20,24

after extraordinary items. Any additional tax charge or credit (including deferred tax) that arises should be attributable to the items.

103 The tax attributable to any extraordinary items should also be computed in a manner similar to that outlined above, that is, with and without the extraordinary items. However, if there are both exceptional items of the kind described in paragraph 14 above and extraordinary items in the same period, the tax attributable to the items combined should be calculated and then apportioned between the two groups in relation to their respective amounts. If a more appropriate basis is adopted, the method of apportionment should be disclosed. In practice, it is unlikely that under the FRS there will ever be extraordinary items and so this situation should not arise. FRS 3:24 Author

104 The basis on which UK corporation tax is computed must be stated; SSAP 8 requires the tax to be based on the profit of the year. 1985 4 sch 54(1) SSAP 8:22(a)

105 If the rate of corporation tax is not known for the whole or part of the year, the latest known rate should be used and disclosed. SSAP 8:23

106 Any material adjustment in respect of amounts charged in previous years should be shown separately but normally included in arriving at the tax charge or credit for the year. Author

107 If material trading losses are set against chargeable capital gains for corporation tax purposes, appropriate adjustments should be made in the accounts to make clear the true incidence of tax suffered and relieved. Author

108 Particulars are required of any special circumstances that affect the overall tax charge or credit for the period (including taxation on exceptional items described in paragraph 14 above) or that may affect those of future periods. If there is more than one circumstance that affects the overall tax charge, the effect of each separate factor should be quantified in the notes. These might include such items as: 1985 4 sch 54(2) FRS 3:23 Author

(a) disallowable expenses;

(b) tax free income;

(c) losses, either revenue or capital and including previously unutilised allowances or reliefs, brought forward and utilised in the year;

(d) losses, as described in (c) above, incurred during the year but not utilised and therefore available for use in future years. The tax effect of such losses may be:

  (i) carried forward in the accounts by deduction from a deferred tax liability or as an asset; or

  (ii) disclosed by way of note. Such note should make it clear that any tax relief is dependent on there being future profits (revenue or capital, as the case may be) of sufficient amount;

(e) losses set off against the profits of the preceding accounting period;

(f) the surrender or claim of losses by way of group relief, or the surrender or claim of ACT (to be disclosed in the accounts of the companies concerned) either:

  (i) paid for (or to be paid for) by the claiming company; or

  (ii) surrendered free of charge;

(g) the potential recovery in future years of presently irrecoverable ACT, or a potential tax credit on surplus franked investment income. The disclosure of the potential benefit should be such that it is clear that the benefit depends:

  (i) in the case of irrecoverable ACT, on there being future taxable profits of sufficient amount; and

  (ii) in the case of surplus franked investment income, on the company making future distributions;

(h) the realisation in the year of the benefits described in (g) brought forward from previous years;

(i) the deferral of tax on capital gains under 'rollover' provisions; and

(j) the effect on potential tax liabilities arising from the apportionment of income of a close company.

Disclosure of such matters should be restricted to those where the tax effect is significant. Author

109 The amount of any unprovided deferred tax in respect of the period should be disclosed in a note, analysed into its major components. SSAP 15:35

110 Adjustments to deferred tax arising from changes in tax rates and tax allowances should normally be disclosed separately as part of the tax charge for the period. SSAP 15:36 The effect of a fundamental change in the basis of taxation should also be included in the tax charge or credit for the period and separately disclosed on the face of the profit and loss account. FRS 3:23

Dividends

111 The aggregate amount of dividends paid and proposed must be shown in the profit and loss account. 1985 4 sch 3(7),51(3) SSAP 8:24

112	Where there is more than one class of shares ranking for dividends, it is preferable to show dividends in relation to each class of share, distinguishing between dividends already paid and dividends recommended. The rates (per cent or pence per share) should preferably be stated and it may be helpful to shareholders to state the date of payment of the dividends.	Author
	Redemption of share capital or loans	
113	Amounts set aside for redemption of share capital and loans must be shown separately.	1985 4 sch 53(3)
	Earnings per share (listed companies only)	
	Basic earnings per share	
114	The definition of earnings per share in SSAP 3 has been amended by FRS 3 to be based on profit after extraordinary items, whereas previously under SSAP 3 it was based on profit before extraordinary items.	FRS 3:25
115	Earnings per share on the 'net' basis, together with corresponding figures for the previous year, should be shown on the face of the profit and loss account.	SSAP 3:14
116	Where there is a material difference between earnings per share calculated on the net basis and on the 'nil distribution' basis, the latter should also be shown. In this case, 'material' is not defined by the standard, but a difference in excess of five per cent might be regarded as such.	SSAP 3:9 Author
117	The basis of calculation should be shown either in the profit and loss account or in a note. Disclosure should include: (a) the amount of earnings; and (b) the number of equity shares used in the calculation.	SSAP 3:15
	Additional earnings per share	
118	It is likely that earnings per share calculated in the way required by FRS 3 will be volatile because it will be affected by items such as profits or losses on disposals of business segments (previously extraordinary and therefore excluded under the original SSAP 3 definition - now exceptional and included under the revised SSAP 3 definition). For this reason, FRS 3 permits disclosure of an additional alternative earnings per share calculated at any other level of profit.	Author
119	Where such an additional earnings per share is presented, the following requirements should be observed: (a) the earnings per share required by FRS 3 should be disclosed at least as prominently as the additional earnings per share;	FRS 3:25

(b) a reconciliation should be given between the earnings per share required by FRS 3 and the additional earnings per share listing the items for which an adjustment is made and disclosing their individual effect; and

(c) the reason for calculating the additional earnings per share should be explained.

In addition, the additional earnings per share should be calculated on a consistent basis each year. It is not possible to do it at a certain level one year, because profits at that level are good, and then not to disclose it on the same basis the next year. FRS 3:25 Author

Fully diluted earnings per share

120 Fully diluted earnings per share should be shown, in addition to basic earnings per share, if there are in issue: SSAP 3:16

(a) a separate class of equity shares which does not rank for dividend in the year under review but will do so in the future; or

(b) debentures, loan stock or preference shares convertible into equity shares of the company; or

(c) options or warrants to subscribe for equity shares of the company.

However, the fully diluted earnings per share need not be given unless dilution is material. Dilution amounting to five per cent or more is regarded as material for this purpose.

121 Where fully diluted earnings per share is shown: SSAP 3:16

(a) the basis of calculation of fully diluted earnings per share should be disclosed;

(b) the corresponding amount for the previous year should not be shown unless the assumptions on which it was based still apply; and

(c) equal prominence should be given to basic and fully diluted earnings per share.

7 Cash Flow Statements

General

1 In September 1991, the ASB published its first FRS on 'Cash flow statements'. FRS 1 supersedes SSAP 10 'Statement of source and application of funds' and requires reporting entities to include a cash flow statement as a primary financial statement for accounting periods ending on or after 23 March 1992. The FRS exempts most reporting entities that satisfy the size criteria specified in Chapter 9 for small-sized companies and wholly-owned subsidiaries of EC parent companies (subject to certain conditions) from the requirement to prepare a cash flow statement. FRS 1:7 FRS 1:8

Form and content of cash flow statements

2 FRS 1 sets out a prescribed format for presenting the movement in the entity's cash and cash equivalents - defined as short-term, highly liquid investments which are readily converted into known amounts of cash without notice and which were within three months of maturity when acquired. FRS 1:3

3 The elements of cash flow should be classified under the following standard headings according to the activity that gave rise to them: FRS 3:12

(a) operating activities;

(b) returns on investment and servicing of finance (including interest and dividends paid and received);

(c) taxation (arising on revenue and capital profits);

(d) investing activities; and

(e) financing.

A total must be shown for each standard heading and for the net cash flow before financing. Possible formats for cash flow statements for various types of entities are provided in the illustrative examples annexed to the FRS. FRS 1:12 Appendix

4 The format also sets out the various sub-headings of cash inflows and outflows within each of the standard headings other than operating activities.

Reporting entities are required to follow this classification and only in exceptional circumstances are allowed to use an alternative presentation. The cash inflows and outflows that should be included under each of the standard headings are considered in paragraphs 5 to 10 below. FRS 1:13

Cash flows - operating activities

5 Operating cash flows may be reported on a net or gross basis. The net cash flow from operating activities should represent the net movement in cash and cash equivalents resulting from operations shown in the profit and loss account in arriving at operating profit (for non-financial companies normally profit before interest). However, whichever method is used, a reconciliation between the operating profit reported in the profit and loss account and the net cash flow from operating activities should be given in a note to the cash flow statement. Analysis of net cash flow from operating activities on a gross basis (the so called 'direct method') is encouraged but not required. FRS 1:15-17

Cash flows - returns on investments and servicing of finance

6 The following categories of cash inflow and outflow should be shown under the standard heading 'returns on investments and servicing of finance': FRS 1:18-20

(a) interest received, including any related tax recovered;

(b) dividends received net of tax credits;

(c) interest paid (whether or not the charge is capitalised), including any tax deducted and paid to the relevant tax authority;

(d) dividends paid, excluding advance corporation tax; and

(e) the interest element of finance lease rentals.

Cash flows - taxation

7 The cash flows included under the heading 'taxation' should only relate to cash flows in respect of taxation arising from revenue and capital profits. FRS 1:21-23

These include:

(a) cash receipts from tax rebates, claims or overpayment; and

(b) cash payments for corporation tax, including payments of ACT and purchases of certificates of tax deposit.

Cash flows in respect of other taxation, including payments and receipts in respect of VAT, other sales taxes, property taxes and other taxes not assessed on the profits of the reporting entity should be dealt with as set out in paragraph 12 below.

Cash flows - investing activities

8 The following categories of cash inflows and outflows should be shown separately under the heading 'investing activities': FRS 1:24-26

(a) receipts from sales or disposals of fixed assets;

(b) receipts from sale of investments in subsidiary undertakings net of any balances of cash and cash equivalents transferred as part of the sale;

(c) receipts from sales of investments in other entities;

(d) receipts from repayment or sales of loans made to other entities by the reporting entity or of other entities' debt (other than cash equivalents) which were purchased by the reporting entity;

(e) payments to acquire fixed assets;

(f) payments to acquire investments in subsidiary undertakings net of balances of cash and cash equivalents acquired;

(g) payments to acquire investments in other entities; and

(h) loans made by the reporting entity and payments to acquire debt of other entities (other than cash equivalents).

9 Purchases and sales of securities that are treated as cash equivalents should be disclosed net. For example, if a short-term deposit is rolled over at the end of its term or is reinvested in another cash equivalent, this should not be recorded as cash outflows and inflows, but should be shown as part of the movements in cash and cash equivalents. However, purchases and sales of securities that fall outside the definition of cash equivalents should be shown in the investing section on a gross basis. FRS 1:11 Author

Cash flows - financing

10 The following categories of cash inflows and outflows should be shown separately under the heading 'financing': FRS 1:27-29

(a) receipts from issuing shares or other equity instruments;

(b) receipts from issuing debentures, loans, notes, and bonds and from other long and short-term borrowings (other than those included within cash equivalents);

(c) repayments of amounts borrowed (other than those included within cash equivalents);

(d) the capital element of finance lease rental payments;

(e) payments to re-acquire or redeem the entity's shares; and

(f) payments of expenses or commissions of any issue of shares, debentures, loans, notes, bonds or other financing.

Cash flows - exceptional and extraordinary items

11 Where cash flows relate to items that are classed as exceptional or extraordinary, the cash flows should be included under the appropriate cash flow heading, according to the nature of the items and disclosed separately. In the extremely rare circumstances where it is inappropriate to include extraordinary cash flows under one or more of the standard headings, such cash flows should be shown within a separate section in the cash flow statement. FRS 1: 31-33

Cash flows - VAT and other taxes

12 In respect of VAT and other sales taxes, the cash flows should be dealt with in the following ways: FRS 1:34,35

(a) all cash flows should be reported net of VAT and other sales taxes;

(b) the net movement on the amount payable or receivable in respect of VAT and other sales taxes should be included in cash flows from operating activities unless a different treatment is more appropriate in the particular circumstances concerned;

(c) cash flows should be reported gross of any irrecoverable VAT and other sales taxes. Where it is impracticable to show cash flows gross of the irrecoverable tax, the irrecoverable tax should be shown under the most appropriate standard heading; and

(d) other taxation cash flows, excluding those relating to income taxes, corporation taxes, VAT or other sales taxes, should be shown under the same standard heading as the cash flows that give rise to them.

Cash flows - foreign currencies

13 Companies with foreign currency transactions or foreign operations should present the reporting currency equivalent of foreign currency cash flows, using the same exchange rate as used in the profit and loss account. FRS 1:36

14 Cash flows that result from transactions undertaken to hedge another transaction should be reported under the same standard heading as the transaction which is the subject of the hedge. This treatment applies to futures contracts, forward contracts, options and swaps that are taken out as hedges of identifiable transactions or events. FRS 1:37 Author

Consolidated cash flow statements

15 When presenting a consolidated cash flow statement, the following requirements should be followed:

(a) the statement should deal with flows of cash and cash equivalents that are external to the group. Therefore, all intra-group cash flows should be eliminated; FRS 1:38

(b) dividends paid to minority shareholders should be included under the heading 'returns on investments and servicing of finance' and separately disclosed; FRS 1:38

(c) where a group has investments in entities that are included in the consolidation under the equity method, the cash flows between the group and the entities concerned should be dealt with in the following ways:

  (i) only the actual cash flows between the group and the entities concerned (i.e. not the cash flows of the equity accounted entity itself) should be reported; FRS 1:39

  (ii) any dividends received should be separately disclosed under 'returns on investments and servicing of finance'; FRS 1:19(b)

  (iii) the cash flows relating to acquisitions and divestments should be separately disclosed under 'investing activities'; and FRS 1:25(c),26(c)

  (iv) the amounts of any finance cash flows received from or paid to the entities concerned should be disclosed under 'financing'; FRS 1:30

(d) where a group acquires or disposes of a subsidiary undertaking during the year, the cash flows relating to the acquisition and disposal should be dealt with in the following ways:

  (i) the amount of the consideration paid or received should be reported *net* of any cash and cash equivalents transferred as a result of the acquisition or disposal; FRS 1:40

  (ii) the cash flows of the subsidiary joining or leaving the group during the financial year should be included for the same period as that for which the group's profit and loss account includes the results of the subsidiary; FRS 1:41

  (iv) a summary of the effects of acquisitions and disposals indicating how much of the consideration comprised cash and cash equivalents and the amounts of cash and cash equivalents transferred as a result of the acquisitions or disposals should be disclosed in a note to the cash flow statement. FRS 1:40 In practice, the summary of the effects of acquisitions and disposals required by the standard could be combined with that required by the Act (see Chapter 8) and SSAP 23 (see Chapter 6); and Author

(v) where material, the extent to which the amounts reported under each of the standard headings have been affected by the cash flows of the subsidiary acquired or disposed of should be disclosed in a note to the cash flow statement. This information need only be given for the period in which the acquisition or disposal occurs. FRS 1:42

Other note disclosures

16 The standard requires other disclosures that are necessary to supplement the information presented in the cash flow statement. These disclosures, which should be provided in a note to the cash flow statement, are as follows: FRS 1:44

(a) a reconciliation between the opening and closing balances of cash and cash equivalents shown in the balance sheets;

(b) a reconciliation between the items shown in the financing section of the cash flow statement and the related items in the opening and closing balance sheets;

(c) the reconciliations in sub-paragraphs (a) and (b) above should disclose separately the following items:

(i) exchange differences arising from the retranslation of any opening balances of cash and cash equivalents and financing items;

(ii) exchange differences arising from the translation of the cash flows of foreign entities at exchange rates other than the year end rate; and

(iii) other movements;

(d) where several balance sheet amounts or parts thereof have to be combined to permit a reconciliation under sub-paragraphs (a) and (b) above, sufficient detail should be given to enable the movements to be understood. For example, short-term highly liquid investments and borrowings that are treated as cash equivalents but are included elsewhere within current assets and liabilities, must be separately identified; and Author

(e) material non-cash transactions should be disclosed in the notes to the cash flow statement. These do not involve any cash flows, but have the same effect as if several notional cash transactions were made together (e.g. conversion of debt to equity, assets acquired under finance leases). FRS 1:43 Author

Comparatives

17 Comparative figures should be given for all items in the cash flow statements and the related notes. FRS 1:45

8 Consolidated Accounts

The legal requirement for group accounts

1 Where at the end of any financial year a company is a parent company, group accounts must be prepared in the form of consolidated accounts dealing with the parent company and its subsidiary undertakings (see paragraph 27). 1985 s 227(1),(2) (1989 s 5(1)) FRS 2:20

2 There is an overriding requirement that consolidated accounts must give a true and fair view of the state of affairs and profit or loss of the undertakings included in the consolidation as a whole, so far as concerns members of the company. The meaning of 'true and fair' and its relationship to the detailed requirements of the Act is discussed briefly in Chapter 1. 1985 s 227(3)-(6) (1989 s 5(1))

3 The ASB issued FRS 2 'Accounting for subsidiary undertakings' in July 1992. FRS 2 supersedes SSAP 14 'Group accounts'. The need to revise SSAP 14 for changes in the law provided the ASB with an opportunity to conduct a thorough review of the standard. This was undertaken initially by the ASC whose proposals were issued as ED 50 'Consolidated Accounts' in June 1990. The ASB issued the 'Interim statement: Consolidated Accounts' in December 1990, to give timely guidance on how certain provisions of the Act were to be interpreted in the preparation of consolidated accounts. The interim statement also made changes to SSAP 14 that were required as a consequence of the statutory changes. The issue of FRS 2 which is based on the proposals contained in ED 50 and the ASB's interim statement relating to subsidiary undertakings completes this review process. FRS 2 also supersedes the interim statement except for those parts that relate to associated undertakings and joint ventures.

4 FRS 2 applies to all parent undertakings that prepare consolidated accounts intended to give a true and fair view of the financial position and profit or loss (or income and expenditure) of their group relating to periods ending on or after 23 December 1992. FRS 2:18

5 Parent undertakings that do not report under the Act should also comply with the requirement of FRS 2, and of the Act where referred to in the FRS, except to the extent that these requirements are not permitted by any statutory framework under which such undertakings report. FRS 2:19

6 The objective of FRS 2 is to require parent undertakings to provide financial information about the economic activities of a group. It sets out the conditions under which a parent undertaking is required to prepare consolidated accounts and the manner in which consolidated accounts are to be prepared. FRS 2:1

Definition of parent and subsidiary undertakings

7 An undertaking is the parent undertaking (P) of a subsidiary undertaking (S) if:

(a) P holds a majority of the rights to vote at general meetings of S on all or substantially all matters or has the right to direct its overall policy or alter its constitution; or 1985 s 258(2)(a) (1989 s 21(1)) 1985 10A sch 2 (1989 9 sch 2)

(b) P is a member of S and has the right to appoint or remove directors holding a majority of the voting rights at meetings of the board; or 1985 s 258(2)(b) (1989 s 21(1)) 1985 10A sch 3 (1989 9 sch 3)

(c) P has the right to exercise a dominant influence over S:

(i) by virtue of provisions contained in S's memorandum or articles; or 1985 s 258(2)(c) (1989 s 21(1))

(ii) by virtue of a written control contract; or

(d) P is a member of S and controls alone, pursuant to an agreement with other members, a majority of the voting rights in S; or 1985 s 258(2)(d) (1989 s 21(1))

(e) P has a participating interest in S and:

(i) P actually exercises a dominant influence over S; or 1985 s 258(4)(a) (1989 s 21(1))

(ii) P and S are managed on a unified basis; or 1985 s 258(4)(b) (1989 s 21(1))

(f) P is the parent of any undertaking which is S's parent. 1985 s 258(5) (1989 s 21)

FRS 2 adopts the above definitions but provides further elaboration of specific terms as discussed in paragraphs 11 to 16 below.

8 Rights held by a person as nominee for P (i.e. exercisable only on P's instructions or with P's consent) or held by any subsidiary of P shall be treated as held by P. P shall be treated as a member of S if any shares in S are held by a person acting on behalf of P or by any of its subsidiaries. 1985 10A sch 7,9 (1989 9 sch) 1985 s 258(3) (1989 s 21(1))

9 'Undertaking' means: 1985 s 259(1) (1989 s 22)

(a) a body corporate (wherever incorporated) or partnership; or

(b) an unincorporated association carrying on a trade or business, with or without a view to profit.

10 'Participating interest' means an interest held by an undertaking in the shares of another undertaking which it holds on a long-term basis for the purpose of securing a contribution to its activities by the exercise of control or influence arising from or related to that interest. A holding of 20 per cent or more shall be presumed to be a participating interest unless the contrary is shown. An interest in shares includes convertible securities and options to acquire shares, whether or not those shares are already issued. An interest held on behalf of an undertaking is treated as held by that undertaking. 1985 s 260 (1989 s 22)

11 The terms 'control', 'dominant influence', 'actual exercise of dominant influence' and 'managed on a unified basis' are not defined in the Act because the legislators wished 'the ordinary spirit of the language of the legislation' to be followed. The intention is to bring within the consolidation all undertakings which are controlled by the parent undertaking. However, definitions of these terms and how they should be interpreted in the preparation of consolidated accounts are contained in FRS 2 and are considered below.

Control

12 Control is defined as "the ability of an undertaking to direct the financial and operating policies of another undertaking with a view to gaining economic benefits from its activities". FRS 2:6

Dominant influence

13 Dominant influence is defined as "influence that can be exercised to achieve the operating and financial policies desired by the holder of the influence, notwithstanding the rights or influence of any other party". This definition does not specifically refer to control, although FRS 2 notes that "the effect of dominant influence is the same as control". In the context of sub-paragraph 7(c) above and section 258(2)(c) 'the right to exercise a dominant influence' means that P at least has a right to give directions on the operating and financial policies of S which its directors are obliged to follow whether or not they are for the benefit of S. FRS 2:7(a) 1985 10A sch 4(1) (1989 9 sch)

Actual exercise of dominant influence

14 The definition of dominant influence in the preceding paragraph does not apply for the purpose of sub-paragraph 7(e)(i) above and section 258(4)(a) 'actually exercises a dominant influence'. The FRS defines 'actual exercise of dominant influence', as "the exercise of an influence that achieves the result that the operating and financial policies of the undertaking influenced 1985 10A sch 4(3) (1989 9 sch) FRS 2:7(b)

are set out in accordance with the wishes of the holder of the influence and for its benefit (whether or not those wishes are explicit). The actual exercise of dominant influence is identified by its effect in practice rather than the means by which it is exercised". The explanatory section of FRS 2 provides further guidance on this definition. Consequently, in determining whether P actually exercises a dominant influence many factors will have to be considered, including the holding of a power of veto or any other reserve powers, special or contingent voting rights, economic dependency and any other formal or informal agreements. It is understood that the legislation is not intended to include influence which may be exerted merely by being a major customer or supplier of the undertaking. FRS 2:71-73 Author

15 The word 'dominant' implies a single investing undertaking which has more influence than any other and whose influence prevails in the face of opposition from other parties; there could not be two dominant undertakings. Accordingly, where the tests of the Act identify more than one undertaking as a parent of one subsidiary undertaking, not more than one of those parents can have control as defined in paragraph 12 above. Where this is the case, it is probably likely that they share control and, therefore, their interests in the subsidiary undertaking are in effect interests in a joint venture and should be treated accordingly (see paragraph 134). Alternatively, one of the parent undertakings may have a non-controlling but significant influence, in which case it would be more appropriate to treat that subsidiary undertaking in the same way as an associated undertaking rather than to consolidate it in full. Author

Managed on a unified basis

16 Two or more undertakings are managed on a unified basis if the whole of the operations of the undertakings are integrated and they are managed as a single unit. Unified management does not arise solely because one undertaking manages another. FRS 2:12

17 An undertaking is a 'fellow subsidiary' of another undertaking if both are subsidiaries of the same parent undertaking, but neither is the other's subsidiary. 1985 s 259(4) (1989 s 22)

18 A 'group undertaking' is defined as a parent, a subsidiary or a fellow subsidiary undertaking. 1985 s 259(5) (1989 s 22)

19 As stated in Chapter 4, quasi subsidiaries are not specifically dealt with in FRS 2, but FRED 4 will require a quasi subsidiary to be treated in the consolidated accounts of the group that controls it in the same way as if it were a legally defined subsidiary. Control is defined in the same way as discussed in paragraph 12 above. However, quasi subsidiaries should be excluded from consolidation only where they are held exclusively with a view to subsequent resale and they have not been previously included in the consolidated accounts (see paragraph 31(d)). The disclosures relating to quasi subsidiaries are considered in paragraph 41 below. FRED 4:30 FRED 4:31

Exemptions

20 Consolidated accounts need not be prepared by a company which is itself a subsidiary undertaking whose immediate parent undertaking is established under the law of an EC country, and either: 1985 s 228(1) (1989 s 5)

(a) it is a wholly-owned subsidiary of that parent; or FRS 2:21(b)

(b) that parent owns more than 50 per cent of the shares and a request for group accounts has not been received from shareholders holding more than half of the remaining shares, or five per cent of the total shares of the company. The request must be served within six months of the end of the previous financial year (that is, during the first six months of the financial year for which consolidated accounts are being considered). FRS 2:21(c) 1985 s 228(1)(b) (1989 s 5)

21 This exemption does not apply to a company any of whose securities (including shares, debentures, convertible rights) are listed on a stock exchange in the EC countries. 1985 s 228(3) (1989 s 5)

22 This exemption is only available to companies included in consolidated accounts for a larger group, drawn up and audited under the law of an EC country in accordance with the Seventh Directive, by a parent undertaking established in an EC country. 1985 s 228(2) (1989 s 5)

23 Where advantage is taken of this exemption, the company must: 1985 s 228(2) (1989 s 5)

(a) state in its individual accounts that it is exempt from the obligation to prepare and deliver group accounts, and give the name of the parent undertaking in whose group accounts it is included, giving the country of incorporation (if other than Great Britain), the country of registration (England and Wales or Scotland) if incorporated in Great Britain or, if it is unincorporated, the address of its principal place of business; and

(b) deliver to the registrar copies of those group accounts, directors' report and auditors' report, including a certified translation into English where any part of those documents is not already in English.

24 Small and medium-sized groups may claim exemption from the requirement to prepare group accounts if certain conditions are met. This exemption is explained in Chapter 9. 1985 s 248 (1989 s 13) FRS 2:21(a)

25 Consolidated accounts need not be prepared where all of the parent's subsidiary undertakings are permitted or required to be excluded from consolidation. The conditions for excluding a subsidiary undertaking from consolidation are dealt with in paragraphs 31 to 37 below. 1985 s 229(5) (1989 s 5) FRS 2:21(d)

26 The Act sets out disclosure requirements for parent companies not required to prepare group accounts. These requirements are considered in Chapter 5.

The form of group accounts

27	Group accounts are required to be presented in the form of a single set of consolidated accounts complying with the provisions of schedule 4A to the Act and accounting standards in all material respects, and comprising:	1985 s 227(2),(4) (1989 s 5) 1985 4A sch 5 (1989 2 sch)
	(a) a consolidated balance sheet;	
	(b) a consolidated profit and loss account;	
	(c) a consolidated statement of total recognised gains and losses;	FRS 3
	(d) a consolidated cash flow statement; and	FRS 1
	(e) additional information to be provided by way of notes.	
28	A description should be given of the bases on which subsidiary undertakings have been dealt with in the consolidated accounts. A note included to meet this requirement would normally state whether all subsidiary undertakings have been consolidated or, if they have not, would explain the position regarding subsidiaries not consolidated. Such a note may be included under the heading 'accounting policies', and be confined to a general statement as indicated above, or the matter may be dealt with in a note giving the required information about the subsidiary undertakings.	Author
29	Consolidated accounts should deal with the parent company and all its subsidiary undertakings except as set out below.	1985 s 229(1) (1989 s 5) FRS 2:23

Parent's profit and loss account

30	A parent company need not publish its individual profit and loss account where:	1985 s 230 (1989 s 5(4))
	(a) it prepares group accounts in accordance with the Act;	
	(b) the company's profit or loss for the financial year determined in accordance with the Act is disclosed in the notes to the company's individual balance sheet; and	
	(c) a note in the company's annual accounts states that the exemption applies.	
	The company's individual profit and loss account (but not the notes supplementing the profit and loss account) must still be prepared, approved by the Board of Directors and signed by a director. The company's statement of total recognised gains and losses may also be excluded from the consolidated accounts in these circumstances.	Author

Subsidiary undertakings excluded from consolidation

31 The circumstances in which the Act permits or requires a subsidiary undertaking to be excluded from consolidation are the following:

Permissive exclusion

(a) if its inclusion is not material for the purpose of giving a true and fair view; but two or more undertakings may be excluded only if they are not material taken together; or 1985 s 229(2) (1989 s 5)

(b) where the information necessary for the preparation of group accounts cannot be obtained without disproportionate expense or undue delay; or 1985 s 229(3)(b) (1989 s 5)

(c) where severe long-term restrictions substantially hinder the exercise of the rights of the parent company over the assets or management of that undertaking; or 1985 s 229(3)(a) (1989 s 5)

(d) where the interest of the parent company is held exclusively with a view to subsequent resale and the undertaking has not previously been included in consolidated accounts prepared by the parent company. 1985 s 229(3)(c) (1989 s 5)

Required exclusion

(e) where the activities of the subsidiary are so different from those of other undertakings to be included in the consolidation that its inclusion would be incompatible with the obligation to give a true and fair view. This exception does not apply merely because some of the undertakings are industrial, some commercial and some provide services, or because they carry on industrial or commercial activities involving different products or provide different services. 1985 s 229(4) (1989 s 5)

32 Within the statutory framework, FRS 2 elaborates on the conditions for exclusion set out in the Act. In this context, it goes further than the Act with regard to excluding subsidiaries from consolidation and requires that the statutory grounds for exclusion should only be used exceptionally. In these limited circumstances that undertaking should be required, not merely allowed, to be excluded from consolidation. FRS 2:77

Materiality

33 The FRS deals only with material items. Thus this ground for exclusion requires no further elaboration. The Act only allows exclusion for two or more subsidiary undertakings if they are not material taken together. FRS 2:78(a)

Disproportionate expense and undue delay

34 The FRS tightens the Act's permissive exclusion from consolidation by stating that in principle neither expense nor delay can justify excluding from consolidation subsidiary undertakings that are individually or collectively material in the context of the group. Consequently, exclusion on this ground can only apply to immaterial subsidiaries. FRS 2:24,78(b)

Severe long-term restrictions

35 Where severe long-term restrictions substantially hinder the exercise of the rights of the parent undertaking over the management of its subsidiary undertaking, the FRS requires that such a subsidiary should not be consolidated. In order to take advantage of this exclusion, the following points should be noted: FRS 2:25(a),78(c)

(a) the rights restricted must be those by virtue of which it is a subsidiary undertaking of the parent undertaking and without which it would not be a subsidiary undertaking;

(b) the effect of the restrictions must be that the parent undertaking does not control the subsidiary undertaking; and

(c) the restrictions must have an effect in practice. Threats or powers held by other parties to impose restrictions do not justify exclusion unless they have a restricting effect in practice in the long-term over the parent's rights.

Generally restrictions are dealt with better by disclosure rather than by non-consolidation. Examples of circumstances that may be indicative of severe long-term restrictions are where a subsidiary undertaking is subject to the control of an administrative receiver or liquidator or where severe difficulties exist in making remittances to the parent undertaking.

Interest held exclusively with a view to subsequent resale

36 This exclusion applies only to those undertakings that have never formed a continuing part of group activities and have not previously been included in the consolidated accounts prepared by the parent undertaking. The FRS has restricted further this exclusion by adding that it can only be used where one of the following conditions is satisfied: FRS 2:11,25(b),78(d)

(a) a purchaser has been identified or is being sought, and the interest is reasonably expected to be disposed of within approximately one year of its date of acquisition. An interest for which a sale is not completed within a year of its acquisition may still be excluded from consolidation if, at the date the accounts are signed, the terms of the sale have been agreed and the process of disposing of that interest is substantially complete; or

(b) the interest was acquired as a result of the enforcement of a security, unless the interest has become part of the continuing activities of the group or the holder acts as if it intends the interest to become so. The provisions of paragraph 8(b) of schedule 10A may be relevant in determining whether such an interest has been acquired.

Different activities

37 FRS 2 goes further than the Act with regard to excluding subsidiaries where their activities are different from those of the rest of the group. It takes the FRS 2:25(c),78(e)

view that the circumstances under which a subsidiary undertaking's activities are so different that its inclusion in the consolidation would be incompatible with the obligation to give a true and fair view, are so exceptional that it would be misleading to link in general to any particular contrast of activities. For example, the contrast between Schedule 9 or 9A companies (banking or insurance companies and groups) and other companies or between profit and not-for profit undertakings is not sufficient of itself to justify non-consolidation. This has closed a 'loophole' which had been used by a relatively small number of such groups. FRS 2 points out that completeness of information is critical and that different activities are best dealt with by segmental disclosure. Author

Disclosures regarding subsidiary undertakings

All subsidiaries

38 In addition to the disclosure requirements that apply to all subsidiary undertakings whether or not consolidated accounts are prepared and explained in Chapter 5, the following information must be given in respect of each subsidiary:

(a) whether the subsidiary undertaking is included in the consolidation and, if it is not, the reasons for its exclusion; and 1985 5 sch 15(4) (1989 3 sch)

(b) which of the conditions specified in paragraph 7 above cause the undertaking to be treated as a subsidiary of its immediate parent undertaking. This disclosure is not required if the relevant condition is that specified in sub-paragraph 7(a) above (the immediate parent holds a majority of the voting rights) and the proportion of voting rights held by the immediate parent is the same as the proportion of shares held. 1985 5 sch 15(5) (1989 3 sch)

39 FRS 2 also requires the following information to be disclosed for each subsidiary undertaking whose results or financial position principally affects the figures in the consolidated accounts: FRS 2:33

(a) the proportion of the voting rights held by the parent and its subsidiary undertakings; and

(b) an indication of the nature of its business.

40 Furthermore, where a subsidiary undertaking has been included in the consolidation by virtue of the parent undertaking satisfying the condition specified in sub-paragraph 7(e)(i) above (participating interest and actually exercises a dominant influence), the consolidated accounts must disclose the basis of the parent undertaking's dominant influence. FRS 2:34

Quasi subsidiaries

41 Where one or more quasi subsidiaries are included in the consolidation, it is proposed that this fact should be stated. In addition, FRED 4 proposes that summary financial statements for quasi subsidiaries showing separately each FRED 4:33

major balance sheet, profit and loss account and cash flow statement headings must be provided in the notes to the consolidated accounts. This information may be combined if there is more than one quasi subsidiary of a similar nature. Comparative figures are required. In certain circumstances, the assets and liabilities of a quasi subsidiary should be included in consolidated accounts using the linked presentation described in Chapter 4. FRED 4:32

Subsidiary undertakings excluded from consolidation

42 The following information should be disclosed in respect of each subsidiary excluded from consolidated accounts, whatever the reason for its exclusion:

(a) the name of the subsidiary; 1985 5 sch 15(2) (1989 3 sch) FRS 2:26

(b) the reason for excluding the subsidiary from the consolidation; 1985 5 sch 15(4) (1989 3 sch) FRS 2:26

(c) the aggregate capital and reserves at the subsidiary's most recent financial year end; 1985 5 sch 17(a) (1989 3 sch)

(d) the profit or loss for that year; 1985 5 Sch 17(b) (1989 3 sch)

(e) particulars of the balances between the excluded subsidiary undertakings and the rest of the group; FRS 2:31(a)

(f) the nature and extent of transactions of the excluded subsidiary undertakings with the rest of the group; FRS 2:31(b)

(g) an indication of the extent of any group liability for the excluded subsidiary undertakings, for example as a result of guarantees; and FRS 2:79(d)

(h) any qualification contained in the auditors' report on the subsidiaries' accounts for the relevant financial year. This includes any additional information included in a note to those accounts that draws attention to a matter which would otherwise have been included in the qualification itself. This applies to the extent that the qualification is not covered by the group's consolidated accounts, and to the extent that it is material from the point of view of the parent undertaking's shareholders. If the required information is not obtainable, a statement must be given in the notes to the consolidated accounts. 1985 5 Sch 18 (1989 3 sch)

43 The information in (c) and (d) of the preceding paragraph is not required if: 1985 5 sch 17 (1989 3 sch)

(a) the subsidiary is included in the accounts by way of the equity method of valuation;

(b) the company holds less than one half of the nominal value of the allotted share capital of the subsidiary, and the subsidiary is not required by the Act to file its balance sheet for its most recent financial year with the registrar (e.g. because it is unincorporated or is incorporated outside Great Britain) and does not otherwise publish that balance sheet in Great Britain or elsewhere; or

(c) the information is not material.

44 Where a subsidiary undertaking is excluded from the consolidation because of severe long-term restrictions, it should be treated as a fixed asset investment. If the restrictions were in force at the acquisition date, the subsidiary should be carried initially at cost. If the restrictions came into force at a later date, the amount of the group's investment in the subsidiary should be stated in the consolidated balance sheet at the amount at which it would have been included under the equity method of accounting at that date. While the restrictions are in force, no further accruals should be made for its profits or losses, unless the parent still exercises a significant influence over it. In that case, it should be treated as an associated undertaking under the equity method. FRS 2:27

45 A review of the value of subsidiary undertakings subject to severe long-term restrictions should be carried out to assess whether they have suffered a permanent diminution in value. Where any permanent diminution in value has occurred, this should be reflected by providing against the carrying amount of the relevant subsidiary and charging the provision to the consolidated profit and loss account. In assessing diminution in value, each subsidiary should be considered individually. The intra-group balances with subsidiary undertakings excluded on the grounds of severe long-term restrictions should also be reviewed and written down, if necessary. FRS 2:27

46 When the severe restrictions cease and the parent undertaking's rights are restored, the amount of the unrecognised profit or loss that accrued during the period of restriction should be dealt with in the consolidated profit and loss account of the period in which control is resumed and disclosed separately. Similarly, any provision previously charged for permanent diminution in value that needs to be written back must be separately disclosed. FRS 2:28

47 Where a subsidiary is excluded from consolidation because it is held exclusively with a view to subsequent resale (in accordance with paragraph 31(d) above), the investment in the subsidiary should be stated in the consolidated balance sheet as a current asset at the lower of cost and net realisable value. FRS 2:29

48 Where a subsidiary is excluded from consolidation because its activities are so different that its inclusion would be incompatible with the obligation to give a true and fair view, the interest of the group in the subsidiary and the 1985 4A sch 18 (1989 2 sch) FRS 2:30

amount of profit or loss attributable to that interest must be shown in the consolidated accounts by the equity method of accounting (including dealing with any goodwill arising in accordance with the Act and SSAP 22 (see Chapter 5)). The equity method of accounting is described in paragraph 124.

49 Where a subsidiary is excluded because of different activities, separate accounts for that subsidiary should be appended to the consolidated accounts. Summarised information may be provided for subsidiaries that individually, or in combination with those with similar operations, do not account for more than 20 per cent of any one or more of operating profits, turnover or net assets of the group. The group amounts should be measured by including any excluded subsidiary undertakings. FRS 2:31(d)

50 Where a subsidiary undertaking is excluded from consolidation because of different activities, and it is either an unincorporated undertaking or is incorporated outside Great Britain (with no established place of business in Great Britain), there is an additional requirement that a copy of the undertaking's latest accounts be appended to the parent company's accounts. The accounts must be for a period ending not more than 12 months before the parent company's year end and must include: 1985 s 243 (1989 s 11)

(a) if it is a parent undertaking, its group accounts;

(b) if the accounts are required by law to be audited, a copy of the auditors' report; and

(c) if the accounts are not in English, a translation.

This paragraph does not apply if accounts for the subsidiary undertaking would not otherwise be prepared or would not otherwise be required to be published, or if the subsidiary's accounts are included in the consolidated group accounts of an excluded sub-group whose group accounts are appended.

51 Where an excluded subsidiary undertaking is carried in the consolidated balance sheet other than by the equity method, there should be stated any amounts included in the consolidated profit and loss account in respect of: FRS 2:31(c)

(a) dividends received and receivable from that undertaking; and

(b) any write downs in the period in respect of the investment in that undertaking or amounts due from that undertaking.

52 The general disclosure requirements listed above are required for individual subsidiaries excluded. However, if the information about excluded subsidiary undertakings is more appropriately presented for a sub-unit of the group made up from more than one excluded subsidiary undertaking, the disclosures may be made on an aggregate basis. These sub-units for which FRS 2:32

these disclosures should be given are to be made up from subsidiary undertakings excluded under the same sub-section of section 229(3). Individual disclosures should be given for any excluded subsidiary undertaking that alone accounts for more than 20 per cent of any one or more of the following:

(a) group operating profits;

(b) group turnover; and

(c) group net assets.

The group amounts should be measured by including any excluded subsidiary undertakings.

Accounting principles

53 Consolidated accounts must incorporate in full the information contained in the individual accounts of the parent company and its subsidiaries as if they were the accounts of a single entity, after making such adjustments set out below. 1985 4A sch 2(1) (1989 2 sch)

54 Consolidated accounts must comply so far as practicable with the provisions of schedule 4 to the Act as if the parent and subsidiary undertakings were a single company. This requirement does not extend to the other requirements of the Act, such as schedule 6 (disclosure of directors' emoluments and loans and other transactions in favour of directors). 1985 4A sch 1(1) (1989 2 sch)

55 *Coterminous financial years*
The directors of a parent company must ensure, except where there are good reasons to the contrary, that the financial years of the parent and subsidiary undertakings coincide. Where a subsidiary or parent undertaking changes its accounting reference date to coincide with that of its parent or subsidiary, this is an exception to the general rules that accounting reference periods may not be changed retrospectively and may not be extended until five years have elapsed since any previous extension. 1985 s 223(5) (1989 s 3) FRS 2:42 1985 s 225(2),(4) (1989 s 3)

56 If the financial year of a subsidiary does not coincide with that of the parent, the directors may use for consolidation either: 1985 4A sch 2(2) (1989 2 sch)

(a) the subsidiary's accounts for its last financial year, provided it ended within the three months preceding the parent company's year end; or

(b) interim accounts prepared as at the end of the parent company's financial year.

57 Although the Act provides a choice of accounts to be used in the consolidation where the year ends are not coterminous, FRS 2 actually requires the preparation of interim accounts for use in the consolidation process wherever practicable. Only if it is not practicable to prepare such FRS 2:43

interim accounts should the subsidiary's accounts for its last financial year be used, provided that year ended not more than three months before the relevant year end of the parent undertaking of the group. In this case any changes that have taken place in the intervening period that materially affect the view given by the consolidated accounts should be taken into account by adjustments in the preparation of the consolidated accounts. In effect, this means that the consolidated accounts must present within the limits of materiality the same position as if coterminous year ends had been adopted. Author

58 Where the accounting period of any subsidiary (whether or not dealt with in the consolidated accounts) does not end with that of the parent company, the accounts must explain for each such subsidiary the reasons why the directors consider that its financial year should not end with that of the parent company, and give either the date of the end of each such subsidiary's year ending last before that of the parent company, or the earliest and latest of those year end dates. Additionally, the names of the principal subsidiaries concerned should be stated. Where the accounting period of a principal subsidiary is of a different length from that of the parent company, the accounting period of the subsidiary should be stated. 1985 5 sch 19 (1989 3 sch) FRS 2:44

Uniform accounting policies

59 Assets and liabilities to be included in the group accounts should be adjusted, wherever necessary, so as to accord with group accounting policies. 1985 4A sch 3(1) (1989 2 sch) FRS 2:40

60 If there are special reasons for departing from the requirement for uniform accounting policies, for example where in exceptional cases it is impracticable to make adjustment, there shall be disclosed: 1985 4A sch 3(2) (1989 2 sch) FRS 2:41

(a) particulars of the different accounting policies used;

(b) the reasons for the different treatment; and

(c) the effect of the departure, indicating the amount of the assets and liabilities involved and, where practicable, the effect on the results and net assets.

The way in which the above disclosures should be made is explained in Chapter 4. UITF Abstract 7

61 If there are differences between the accounting policies used in the parent company's individual accounts and those used in the group accounts, those differences shall be disclosed together with the reasons. 1985 4A sch 4 (1989 2 sch)

62 Where a new subsidiary is acquired by a group that applies a different accounting policy to the subsidiary acquired, the new subsidiary has sufficient reason to change its accounting policy and make a prior-year adjustment in accordance with FRS 3. Alternatively the new subsidiary may continue with its original accounting policy in its entity accounts and an Author

adjustment made on consolidation to reflect the subsidiary's results in accordance with the group's accounting policy.

Elimination of intra-group transactions

63 The following amounts shall be eliminated in preparing group accounts in respect of undertakings included in the consolidation: 1985 4A sch 6 (1989 2 sch) FRS 2:39,83

(a) amounts owed by and to group undertakings or other debts and claims between such undertakings;

(b) income and expenditure relating to transactions between group undertakings; and

(c) profits and losses resulting from transactions between group undertakings which are included in the book value of assets.

64 In the context of sub-paragraph 63(c) above, the Act permits this elimination to be effected in proportion to the group's interest in the shares of the undertakings, but FRS 2 requires elimination in full. The elimination of profit or loss relating to intra-group transactions should be set against the interests held by the parents and its other subsidiary undertakings and against the minority interest in proportion to their respective holdings in the undertaking whose individual accounts recorded the eliminated profits or losses. This means that the minority shareholders will bear a proportion of the unrealised profit or loss arising on intra-group transactions. FRS 2:39,83

65 Transactions with subsidiary undertakings excluded from consolidation because of dissimilar activities, which would be eliminated if they related wholly to subsidiary undertakings included in the consolidation, should also be eliminated. Profits or losses arising on transactions with undertakings excluded from consolidation because they are held exclusively with a view to subsequent resale or because of severe long-term restrictions need not be eliminated, except to the extent appropriate where significant influence is retained and the subsidiary undertaking is treated as an associated undertaking. However, it is important to consider whether it is prudent to record any profit arising from transactions with subsidiaries excluded on these grounds. FRS 2:39,83 FRS 2:83

Minority interests

66 Minority interest in the balance sheet is defined as the amount of capital and reserves attributable to shares in subsidiary undertakings included in the consolidation and held by or on behalf of persons other than the parent company and its subsidiaries. The FRS states that the effect of the existence of minority interests on the returns to investors in the parent is best reflected by presenting the net identifiable assets attributable to minority interests on the same basis as those attributable to group interests. 1985 4A sch 17(2) (1989 2 sch) FRS 2:35 FRS 2:80

67 However, the consistency of valuing minority interest on the same basis as those attributable to the parent and its other subsidiary undertaking does not extend to goodwill arising on acquisition. When a parent purchases a controlling, but not 100 per cent, stake in a subsidiary undertaking goodwill may arise. That goodwill relates only to the parent's share of the subsidiary undertaking and not to the minority. Consequently, no goodwill should be attributable to the minority interest. FRS 2:38

68 Minority interests in the capital and reserves of undertakings included in the consolidation are required to be shown separately in the consolidated balance sheet either after capital and reserves (formats 1 and 2) or after accruals and deferred income (format 1 only). The former position is usually adopted to show that minority interest is not a liability or provision. 1985 4A sch 17(2) (1989 2 sch) FRS 2:35 Author

69 The amount of any profit or loss on ordinary activities attributable to minority interests shall be shown separately in the consolidated profit and loss account after group profit or loss on ordinary activities after tax and before extraordinary items. 1989 4A sch 17(3) (1989 2 sch) FRS 2:36

70 The minority interest relating to the three types of exceptional items that are required to be disclosed after operating profit (see paragraph 14 of Chapter 6) must also be calculated and disclosed in aggregate in a note to the profit and loss account, unless the effect of the minority interest on each of the items differs, when further information should be given, where practicable. FRS 3:20

71 The amount of any profit or loss on extraordinary activities attributable to minority interests should be shown separately in the consolidated profit and loss account as a deduction from extraordinary profit or loss after tax. 1985 4A sch 17(4) (1989 2 sch) FRS 2:36

72 Where a subsidiary undertaking incurs a loss during the current year, a proportion of the loss should be attributable to the minority interest regardless of whether or not this leads to a debit balance for the minority interest. This is a change from the previous SSAP 14 position that required recognition of debit minority interest balance only if the minority was obliged (and able) to make good its share of any losses. However, the FRS makes it clear that the group should provide for any commercial or legal obligation, whether formal or implied, to provide finance that may not be recoverable in respect of the accumulated losses attributable to the minority interests. Provisions of this sort would include the minority's share of any liability guaranteed by the group, or any liability that the group itself would be likely to settle for commercial or other reasons, if the subsidiary undertaking could not do so itself. Any provision made with respect to minority debit balances should be set directly against the minority interest amount in the profit and loss account and balance sheet. FRS 2:37,81 Author

73 Despite the title 'Minority interest', there is in principle no upper limit to the proportion of shares in a subsidiary undertaking which may be held as minority interest while the parent undertaking still qualifies as such under

section 258 of the Act (described in paragraph 7 above). It is possible for a minority interest to represent more than 50 per cent of the capital and reserves and profit or loss of a subsidiary undertaking, for example where the parent company owns shares carrying more than 50 per cent of the voting rights, but less than 50 per cent of the rights to participate in distributions or where, say, a 51 per cent held subsidiary in turn holds 51 per cent of a sub-subsidiary. If such a subsidiary is significant, it may be necessary to provide additional disclosure of the circumstances to prevent misunderstanding. Author

Additional disclosures

74 The following disclosures have to be made concerning the group's profit for the year:

(a) the parent company's profit for the financial year (i.e. before dividends); and 1985 s 230(1)(b)

(b) share of net assets retained by associated undertakings. SSAP 1:22,31

If there are significant restrictions on the ability of the parent company to distribute the retained profits of the group (other than those shown as non-distributable), because of statutory, contractual or exchange control restrictions on distributions by subsidiary undertakings, the nature and extent of the restrictions should be disclosed. FRS 2:53

75 The extent to which deferred tax has been accounted for in respect of future remittances of the accumulated reserves of overseas subsidiary undertakings should be disclosed. Where deferred tax has not been provided in respect of all the accumulated reserves of overseas subsidiary undertakings the reasons for not fully providing should be given. FRS 2:54

Changes in composition

76 This section deals with changes in group membership following acquisitions and disposals of subsidiary undertakings. 'Accounting for acquisitions and mergers' is dealt with by SSAP 23. The term 'acquisition' is used to describe any event the result of which is that an undertaking becomes a subsidiary of the parent company. This section deals only with the treatment of acquisitions and disposals in the consolidated accounts and not their effect on the parent company's individual accounts (see Chapter 5). 1985 4A sch 7 (1989 2 sch) SSAP 23:6

77 An acquisition must be accounted for using acquisition accounting unless all the conditions for treating it as a merger are met, in which case it may be accounted for using merger accounting. Merger accounting is, therefore, optional even where all the merger accounting conditions are met. 1985 4A Sch 8 (1989 2 sch) SSAP 23:11,15

78 The flexibility in treatment offered by SSAP 23 has led to criticism about the ease with which companies can, on occasion, adopt the method which Author

appeals most to them and there have been calls to tighten the rules. In view of this criticism, the ASC issued ED 48 'Accounting for acquisitions and mergers' in February 1990. ED 48 proposes to tighten considerably the existing criteria for merger accounting by requiring that merger accounting should be used in future only for business combinations in which no acquirer or acquiree can be identified. It proposes mandatory use of the merger method where the criteria for merger accounting are met. At the time of writing, ED 48 has not been converted into an accounting standard but the ASB is currently working on this project. This edition of the book only deals with the requirements and implications of the current version of SSAP 23.

79 Where a group of undertakings is acquired, the Act's rules on acquisition and merger accounting set out in paragraphs 81 to 91 should be interpreted as follows: 1985 4A sch 12 (1989 2 sch)

(a) reference to shares in the undertaking acquired are to shares in the parent undertaking; and

(b) references to the assets, liabilities, income and expenditure of the undertaking acquired and any other references, are to those of the acquired group, after making consolidation adjustments.

Date of changes in group membership

80 The Act defines an acquisition as taking place 'where an undertaking becomes a subsidiary undertaking'. That event will therefore determine the date from which the results should be brought into the consolidated accounts. SSAP 14 specified that the effective date of acquisition or disposal of a subsidiary was the earlier of the date on which consideration passed or the date on which an offer became unconditional. This is replaced in FRS 2 by a single triggering date which is the date control of the undertaking passes. Consequently, an undertaking becomes a subsidiary undertaking on the date control passes to the new parent and it ceases to be a subsidiary undertaking on the date the former parent relinquishes control. This date is a matter of fact and cannot be backdated or otherwise altered. The definition applies even if the acquirer has a right to share in profits from a date earlier than the date control passes. The explanatory section of the FRS provides further guidance on determining the effective date of a change in composition of a group. 1985 4A sch 9(3) (1989 2 sch) FRS 2:45 FRS 2:85

Acquisition accounting

81 Where acquisition accounting applies, the fair value of the purchase consideration should be allocated between the underlying net tangible and intangible assets other than goodwill, on the basis of their fair values to the acquiring company as at the date of acquisition. Any difference between the fair value of the consideration and the aggregate of the fair values of the underlying net assets will represent goodwill. Any goodwill arising should be accounted for in accordance with the Act and SSAP 22 (see Chapter 5). SSAP 23:16

2 Although it has been taken for granted for many years that fair values are a key part of acquisition accounting, the principles of fair valuing were not sufficiently well defined to ensure that the treatment of assets and liabilities in acquisition accounting was consistent and correct. Consequently, in July 1990, the ASC issued ED 53 'Fair value in the context of acquisition accounting' that deals in detail with both the fair value of purchase consideration (including deferred and contingent consideration) and the fair value of assets and liabilities (including provisions and contingencies). At the time of writing, ED 53 has not been converted into an accounting standard. As the ASB is currently working on this project and will issue new rules on fair value accounting in due course, the provisions of ED 53 have not been considered further. — Author

3 The identifiable assets and liabilities of the acquired subsidiary should be included in the consolidated balance sheet at their fair values. Identifiable assets or liabilities are those assets or liabilities of the subsidiary which are capable of being disposed of or discharged separately, without disposing of the business of the subsidiary. They include identifiable intangibles, but not goodwill and other similar intangible assets which can only be acquired or sold as part of the business. — 1985 4A sch 9(2) (1989 2 sch) SSAP 22:27

4 Goodwill or negative consolidation difference ('negative goodwill') is the difference between: — 1985 4A sch 9(4),(5) (1989 2 sch)

(a) the acquisition cost of the group's interest in the subsidiary, being the amount of any cash consideration and the fair value of any other consideration together with any fees or other expenses of the acquisition as the company may determine; and — SSAP 23:16

(b) the group's interest in the capital and reserves of the subsidiary at the date of acquisition, after adjusting the identifiable assets and liabilities to fair values. This will be equal to the aggregate of the fair values of the identifiable assets and liabilities of the subsidiary.

5 As stated in paragraph 80 above, the income and expenditure of the acquired subsidiary should be brought into the consolidated accounts from the date of acquisition only. It is therefore necessary to apportion the results between pre-acquisition and post-acquisition on an accurate basis. In practice, this is often achieved by using the subsidiary's management accounts. — SSAP 23:17 Author

Merger accounting

6 Both the Act and SSAP 23 set out conditions which must be met before merger accounting may be used. The Act requires that adoption of merger accounting must accord with 'generally accepted accounting principles or practice'. This is understood to be a reference to the conditions expressed in SSAP 23 (or a successor to that standard). An acquisition *may* therefore be accounted for using merger accounting only if all of the following conditions are met: — 1985 4A sch 10(1)(d) (1989 2 sch) Author

(a) the acquisition must result from an offer to holders of all equity shares and holders of all voting rights which are not already held by the group; SSAP 23:11(a)

(b) at least 90 per cent of the nominal value of relevant shares in the subsidiary must be held by or on behalf of group undertakings. Relevant shares are those carrying unrestricted rights to participate both in distributions and in the assets of the subsidiary upon liquidation; 1985 4A sch 10(1)(a), 10(2)

(c) at least 90 per cent of all equity shares (taking each class of equity separately) and shares carrying at least 90 per cent of the votes (excluding shares which carry votes only in special circumstances), must be held by group undertakings; SSAP 23:11(b)

(d) immediately prior to the offer, the group must not hold: SSAP 23:11(c)

  (i) 20 per cent or more of all equity shares of the subsidiary (taking each class of equity separately); or

  (ii) shares carrying 20 per cent or more of the votes of the subsidiary;

(e) the 90 per cent holding referred to in sub-paragraph (b) above must have been attained pursuant to an arrangement providing for the issue of equity shares by the parent company or one or more of its subsidiaries; and 1985 4A sch 10(1)(b), (c)

(f) the fair value of any consideration other than the issue of equity shares must not exceed 10 per cent of the *nominal* value of the equity shares issued. (This condition will generally be more restrictive than the corresponding condition in SSAP 23 discussed in sub-paragraph (g) below.); and Author

(g) not less than 90 per cent of the fair value of the consideration given for any voting non-equity share capital must be in the form of equity and/or voting non-equity share capital. SSAP 23:11(d)

87 Any convertible stock outstanding at the time of the offer is not to be regarded as equity except to the extent that it is converted into equity as a result of and at the time of the acquisition. SSAP 23:12

88 If merger accounting is adopted, the carrying values of the subsidiary's assets and liabilities will not be adjusted to fair value. The subsidiary's assets and liabilities will be brought into the consolidated accounts at the figures at which they stand in the subsidiary's accounts, subject to adjustments authorised or required by the Act, for example, to achieve uniformity of accounting policies or to eliminate intra-group transactions. 1985 4A sch 11(2) (1989 2 sch) SSAP 23:18

89 A difference may arise on consolidation between: 1985 4A sch 11(5) (1989 2 sch) SSAP 23:20

(a) the purchase consideration, being the aggregate of:

(i) the nominal value (together with any minimum premium value under section 132) of any shares issued by the parent company or any subsidiaries as consideration, where merger relief is available (see Chapter 11); and

(ii) the fair value of any other consideration at the date of acquisition;

and

(b) the nominal value of the subsidiary's share capital held by the group.

90 The difference shall be shown, if positive, as a reduction from reserves or, if negative, as a reserve arising on consolidation. 1985 4A sch 11(6) (1989 2 sch)

91 The income and expenditure of the acquired subsidiary should be brought into the consolidated accounts for the entire financial year, including the period before the acquisition. 1985 4A sch 11(3) (1989 2 sch) SSAP 23:19

92 The consolidated accounts should show corresponding amounts for the previous financial year as if the subsidiary had been included in the consolidation throughout the previous period and at the previous balance sheet date. 1985 4A sch 11(4) (1989 2 sch) SSAP 23:19

Disclosure of business combinations

93 The following information must be given in respect of all acquisitions in the financial year: 1985 4A sch 13(2) (1989 2 sch) SSAP 23:21

(a) the name of the undertaking acquired or, where a group was acquired, the name of the parent of that group; and

(b) whether the acquisition has been accounted for by the acquisition or merger method of accounting.

94 Where there have been material additions to the group during the financial year, the consolidated accounts should contain sufficient information to enable shareholders to understand the effect of the changes on the consolidated results. In relation to acquisitions which significantly affect the figures shown in the consolidated accounts, this must include the following information: 1985 4A sch 13(3),(4) (1989 2 sch) SSAP 23:21 SSAP 23:22

(a) the composition and fair value of the consideration given by the parent company and its subsidiaries, including the number and class of any securities issued in respect of the acquisition;

(b) the profit or loss of the undertaking or group acquired:

(i) for the period from the beginning of the financial year of the undertaking or group acquired up to the date of the acquisition; and

(ii) for the previous financial year of that undertaking or group

and the date on which the financial year referred to in (i) began; and

(c) the date from which the results of major acquisitions have been brought into the accounts.

95 As stated in Chapter 6, the post-acquisition results of acquisitions made during the year should be disclosed separately in aggregate as a component of continuing operations. However, it may not always be possible to determine the post acquisition results of an operation to the end of the period, for instance, where the business and assets of the acquired subsidiary were absorbed into the group's existing subsidiaries immediately after the acquisition. Where it is not practicable to determine the post-acquisition results of an operation to the end of the current period, an indication should be given of the contribution of the acquisition to the turnover and operating profit of the continuing operations. If such an indication of the contribution cannot be given, that fact and the reason should be explained. Author; FRS 3:16

96 Where acquisition accounting has been adopted, the following information shall be given in tabular form, in respect of each class of assets and liabilities of the undertaking or group acquired, including the amount of any goodwill or negative consolidation difference: 1985 4A sch 13(5) (1989 2 sch) SSAP 22:48

(a) the book values immediately prior to the acquisition, as recorded in the acquired company's books;

(b) the fair values at the date of acquisition; and

(c) an explanation of any significant adjustments, analysed between:

(ii) provisions for future trading losses;

(iii) other provisions;

(iv) adjustments to achieve uniformity of accounting policies; and

(v) any other major items.

97 Where merger accounting has been adopted the following must be disclosed in respect of all material mergers taking place in the year: 1985 4A sch 13(6) (1989 2 sch) SSAP 23:23

(a) the fair value of the consideration given by the acquiring company;

(b) an explanation of any significant adjustments made in relation to the amounts of the assets and liabilities of the acquired undertaking, and a statement of any resulting adjustment to the consolidated reserves (including the restatement of opening consolidated reserves). (This will normally only result from conforming accounting policies to those of the group.);

(c) an analysis of the current year's attributable profit before extraordinary items between that arising before and that arising after the effective date of the merger;

(d) an analysis of the attributable profit before extraordinary items of the current year up to the effective date of the merger and of the previous year between that of the acquiring group and that of the acquired subsidiary or group. This requirement is similar to that set out in paragraph 93(b) above, but relates to the group's rather than the subsidiary's financial year; and

(e) an analysis of extraordinary items indicating whether each individual extraordinary item relates to pre or post merger events and to which party the item relates.

98 The disclosures required by paragraphs 94 to 97 above and 101 and 102 below should be made separately for each acquisition which significantly affects the figures in the consolidated accounts, and in aggregate for acquisitions which are material in total, but not so individually. 1985 4A sch 13(2) (1989 2 sch) SSAP 22:51

99 Where the disclosures above relate to the acquisition of a group, the profit or loss and book or fair values of assets and liabilities of that group shall be calculated after the set-offs and other adjustments required by the Act in respect of the consolidated accounts of that sub-group. 1985 4A sch 13(7) (1989 2 sch)

100 If a parent company required to prepare consolidated accounts has allotted shares during the year in circumstances in which merger relief was available (section 131), there must be disclosed particulars of the extent to which and the manner in which the group profit or loss for the financial year is affected by any profit or loss of the acquired company which arose before the time of the allotment. 1985 5 sch 29(2)(e) (1989 3 sch) This information need not be given for undertakings established or carrying on business outside the UK if, in the opinion of the directors, and with the consent of the Secretary of State, it would be seriously prejudicial to the business of the company, that subsidiary or any other subsidiary of the parent company. 1985 s 231(3) (1989 s 6) Disclosures required where merger relief is available in respect of shares issued by an individual company within a group are dealt with in Chapters 5 and 6.

Other disclosures

101 Where either the fair value of the assets and liabilities or the consideration can only be determined on a provisional basis at the end of the accounting period in which the acquisition took place, this should be stated and the reasons given. Where there are subsequent material adjustments to such SSAP 22:50

provisional fair values, with a consequent adjustment to goodwill or negative consolidation difference, those adjustments should be disclosed and explained.

102 Movements on provisions related to acquisitions should be disclosed and analysed between the amounts used and the amounts released unused or applied for another purpose. Sufficient details should be given to identify the extent to which the provisions have proved unnecessary. SSAP 22:49

103 There shall also be stated in a note to the accounts the cumulative amount of goodwill resulting from acquisitions in the current and earlier years which has been written off, after deducting any goodwill attributable to subsidiary undertakings disposed of prior to the balance sheet date. 1985 4A sch 14 (1989 2 sch)

104 Where an undertaking has become a subsidiary undertaking other than as a result of a purchase or exchange of shares, the circumstances should be explained in a note to the consolidated accounts. Disclosure of circumstances may be appropriate where a parent gains control without acquiring a further interest in an undertaking, perhaps by virtue of an agreement with another shareholder or by the undertaking purchasing and cancelling its own shares held by third parties. FRS 3:49 Author

105 Particulars of the participation by the parent company in any vendor consideration placing made during the year under review must be set out in the annual accounts. ASL 22

Ceasing to be a subsidiary undertaking

106 When an undertaking ceases to be a subsidiary undertaking during a period following a direct disposal (e.g. sale of shares in a company), a deemed disposal (e.g. exercise of share options by another party) or other event, the consolidated profit and loss account should include: FRS 2:46

(a) the results of the subsidiary up to the date of its ceasing to be a subsidiary; and

(b) the gain or loss arising on that cessation (to the extent that these have not been already provided).

107 The calculation of the gain or loss arising on cessation is the difference between: FRS 2:47

(a) the group's share of the net assets of that subsidiary undertaking before the cessation together with any related goodwill not previously written off through the profit and loss account; and

(b) the group share of its remaining net assets after the cessation together with any proceeds received.

108 In the context of sub-paragraph 107(a) above, the inclusion of the attributable amount of any purchased goodwill, where it has been previously eliminated against reserves as a matter of accounting policy, in the calculation of the profit or loss on disposal of a previously acquired business is also required by UITF Abstract 3. Amortised goodwill that has passed through the profit and loss account is not included. Negative goodwill should be accounted for in a similar manner. Comparative figures should be adjusted where applicable. The principle also applies to closure of businesses and associated undertakings. UITF Abstract 3

109 UITF Abstract 3 also requires disclosure of: UITF Abstract 3

(a) the profit or loss on disposal; and

(b) the amount of purchased goodwill attributable to the business disposed of either on the face of the profit and loss account or in the notes.

Where it is not possible to ascertain the goodwill attributable to the business disposed of, or to make a reasonable apportionment of the goodwill arising in the original acquisition, the fact and the reason should be stated.

110 The UITF has made it clear that although sub-paragraph 109(b) above requires separate disclosure of goodwill, the goodwill component must be included in the sub-paragraph 109(a) calculation of the profit or loss on disposal, and not distanced from it as a separate item. Where the item is presented as two components there should be, in addition, a single sub-total showing the total profit or loss on disposal.

111 Where there have been material disposals from the group, the consolidated accounts should contain sufficient information to enable shareholders to understand the effect of the changes on the consolidated results. In relation to disposals which significantly affect the figures shown in the consolidated accounts, this must include the following: 1985 4A sch 15 (1989 2 sch) FRS 2:48

(a) the name of that undertaking or of the parent of that group;

(b) the extent to which the profit or loss shown in the consolidated accounts is attributable to that undertaking or group;

(c) the name and any ownership interest retained;

(d) details of circumstances where cessation has occurred other than by disposal of at least part of the interest held by the group; and

(e) details of circumstances where cessation has occurred other than as a result of a purchase or exchange of shares. FRS 2:49

Exemption for non-UK subsidiaries

112 The disclosures detailed in sub-paragraphs 111(a) and (b) above, required by the Act, need not be given for an undertaking which is established outside 1985 4A sch 16 (1989 2 sch)

the UK or carries on business outside the UK, if:

(a) in the opinion of the directors of the parent company the disclosure would be seriously prejudicial to the business of the subsidiary or the parent company; and

(b) the Secretary of State agrees that the information should not be disclosed.

Although FRS 2 does not contain a similar exemption, it would seem that it was not the ASB's intention to restrict this exemption and it should therefore be assumed that the exemption also applies to the disclosure required by sub-paragraphs 110(c), (d) and (e) above. Author

Changes in stakes

Acquiring a subsidiary undertaking in stages

113 The Act's provision regarding fair value in the context of acquisition accounting, set out in paragraphs 81 to 84 above, only requires a fair value exercise to be carried out at the date the investment becomes a subsidiary. It does not require retrospective fair value exercises to be performed where the interests in the subsidiary have been purchased at different dates. Consequently, goodwill or negative goodwill is calculated by comparing the group's share of the fair value of the net assets and the total acquisition cost of the group's interest in that subsidiary, even where part of the acquisition cost arises from purchases of interests at earlier dates. 1985 4A sch 9(4) (1989 2 sch)

114 FRS 2 points out that the approach set out in the Act will provide a practical means of applying acquisition accounting in most cases where a subsidiary has been acquired in stages. However, in special circumstances, not using fair values at the dates of earlier purchases, while using an acquisition cost part of which relates to earlier purchases, may result in accounting that is inconsistent with the way the investment has been previously treated in the group's consolidated accounts. It suggests that the inconsistency may lead to the above treatment failing to give a true and fair view. For example, where an associated undertaking subsequently becomes a subsidiary, the group's share of the profits or losses and reserve movements of its associated undertaking becomes reclassified as goodwill (usually negative goodwill). A similar problem may arise where a provision has been made against such an investment which on consolidation will have the effect of increasing reserves and creating goodwill. FRS 2:50,89

115 In the rare cases where calculation of goodwill in accordance with the provisions of the Act would be misleading, goodwill should be calculated as the sum of the goodwill arising from each purchase of an interest in the relevant undertaking adjusted as necessary for any subsequent diminution in value. The goodwill arising on each purchase should be calculated as the difference between the cost of that purchase and the fair value at the date of FRS 2:89

that purchase of the identifiable assets and liabilities attributable to the interest purchased. To adopt this alternative treatment would require the use of the section 227(6) true and fair override. The difference between the goodwill calculated using the true and fair override and that calculated in accordance with the Act's provisions should be shown in reserves.

Increasing an interest held in a subsidiary undertaking

116 Where a group increases its stake in an undertaking that is already its subsidiary undertaking, the identifiable assets and liabilities of a subsidiary undertaking included in the consolidated accounts should be revalued to fair value at the date of the increase in stake, unless the difference between net fair values and carrying amounts of the assets and liabilities attributable to the increase in stake is not material. Goodwill arising on the increase in interest should be calculated by reference to those fair values. The requirement to carry out a fair value exercise whenever a group increases its interest in a subsidiary undertaking has, hitherto, not been carried out in practice. FRS 2:51 Author

Reducing an interest held in a subsidiary undertaking

117 Where a group reduces its interest in a subsidiary undertaking as a result of a partial disposal or a deemed disposal, a gain or loss will normally arise, which should be computed in accordance with paragraph 107 above. However, where the undertaking continues to be a subsidiary after the disposal, the minority interest in that subsidiary undertaking should be increased by the carrying amount of the net identifiable assets that are now attributable to the minority interest because of the decrease in the group's interest. No amount of goodwill that arose on the acquisition of the group's interest should be attributable to the minority interest. FRS 2:52

Associated undertakings

118 An associated undertaking is defined by the Act as any undertaking, apart from a subsidiary of the parent company or a joint venture dealt with by proportional consolidation: 1985 4A sch 20(1) (1989 2 sch)

(a) in which an undertaking included in the consolidation has a participating interest; and

(b) over whose operating and financial policy it exercises a significant influence.

Where an undertaking holds 20 per cent or more of the equity voting rights in another undertaking, it shall be presumed to exercise a significant influence, unless the contrary is shown. 1985 4A sch 20(2) (1989 2 sch) SSAP 1:14 (amended)

119 'Undertaking' and 'participating interest' are defined in paragraphs 9 and 10 above.

120 In determining whether an undertaking holds 20 per cent of the voting rights, there shall be included any rights held by a subsidiary or a nominee of the undertaking. There shall be excluded any rights held on behalf of another person. Voting rights exercisable only in certain circumstances shall be taken into account only when the circumstances have arisen or when the circumstances are within the control of the person having the rights. Where an undertaking does not have a share capital, voting rights means the right to vote at general meetings on all, or substantially all, matters.

1985 4A sch 20(4) (1989 2 sch) SSAP 1:16

1984 4A sch 20(3) (1989 2 sch)

121 Associated companies (including non-corporate undertakings) are also defined by SSAP 1. The definition of associated undertaking in SSAP 1 is not consistent with the definition in the Act as stated in paragraph 118 above. In order to avoid inconsistency in applying SSAP 1 as an accounting standard within the meaning of section 256 of the Act, the ASB amended certain paragraphs of SSAP 1 to bring the statement in line with the Act. The amendments are contained in the ASB's statement on 'Interim Statement: Consolidated Accounts' dated December 1990 (see paragraph 3 above). References in this section to the various paragraphs of SSAP 1 as amended by the interim statement are identified where applicable.

Author

122 SSAP 1 provides additional guidance relevant to determining whether a particular undertaking is an associated undertaking, in particular:

Author

(a) the interest of the investing group or company should be for the long-term;

SSAP 1:13 (amended)

(b) regard should be had to the disposition of other share holdings in determining whether the investing group or company is in a position to exercise a significant influence;

(c) operating and financial policy decisions include dividend policy but significant influence does not necessarily mean control of those policies. Representation on the board of directors is indicative of participation in those decisions, but is not conclusive and is not the only method by which the investing company may participate; and

(d) where an undertaking holds less than 20 per cent of the voting rights it should be presumed that it does not have the ability to exercise significant influence, unless it can clearly demonstrate otherwise. Unless there are exceptional circumstances, this demonstration should include a statement from the company in which the investment is made that it accepts that the undertaking is in a position to exercise significant influence over it.

SSAP 1:15 (amended)

123 Where a group has an interest in one or more associated undertakings, that interest, and the income arising from it, must be stated in the consolidated balance sheet and profit and loss account separately from other participating

1985 4A sch 21,22 (1989 2 sch)

interests. Any material interest in associated undertakings and the profit or loss attributable must be shown by the equity method of accounting, including dealing with any goodwill arising in accordance with the Act and SSAP 22. Where the associated undertaking itself has subsidiary or associated undertakings, the net assets and profits or losses will be based on that undertaking's consolidated accounts.

124 The accounting requirements for the inclusion of interests in associated undertakings following the equity method of accounting are as follows:

(a) the group's interest in associated undertakings should be shown as the total of: SSAP 1:26

(i) the share of net assets other than goodwill; and
(ii) the share of any goodwill in the associated undertaking's own balance sheet; together with
(iii) the premium paid (or discount) on the acquisition of the interest so far as not written off or amortised.

Item (i) should be disclosed separately; items (ii) and (iii) may be aggregated;

(b) there should be separate disclosure in the consolidated profit and loss account of the total of the group's share of associated undertakings': SSAP 1:18 (amended)

(i) profits less losses before taxation; SSAP 1:19 (amended)
(ii) taxation (disclosed separately as part of group tax charge); SSAP 1:20
(iii) extraordinary items in the unlikely event that items are so classified following the criteria set out in FRS 3; and SSAP 1:21
(iv) net profits less losses retained; SSAP 1:22

(c) the group's share of associated undertakings' turnover and depreciation should not be included in group turnover and depreciation respectively in the consolidated accounts. If the results of one or more associated undertakings are so material in the context of the investing group's accounts that more detailed information about these would assist in giving a true and fair view, this information should be given by separate disclosure of the total turnover of the associated undertakings concerned, their total depreciation charge, their total profits less losses before taxation and the amount of such profits attributable to the investing group; and SSAP 1:23

(d) adjustments similar to those required for the purposes of including subsidiaries in the consolidated accounts should be made when the associated undertakings are incorporated into the group's consolidated accounts. Unrealised profits on, for example, stock transferred to or from associated undertakings should be eliminated to the extent of the group's share only and not in full. SSAP 1:39

125 *Disclosure of associated undertakings*
The following information must be given in respect of each associated undertaking, whether or not that undertaking is material to the consolidated accounts: 1985 5 sch 22(2) (1989 3 sch)

(a) the undertaking's name; SSAP 1:49

(b) the country of incorporation (if other than Great Britain), the country of registration (England and Wales or Scotland) if incorporated in Great Britain or the address of its principal place of business if unincorporated;

(c) a description of each class of shares held and the proportion of the nominal value of the allotted shares of that class represented by those shares (distinguishing between shares held by the parent company and those held by the group). The corresponding amount for the previous year need not be stated; and 1985 4 sch 58(3) (1989 1 sch 9) SSAP 1:49

(d) an indication of the nature of its business. SSAP 1:49

126 The disclosures set out in the preceding paragraph are subject to the exceptions set out in paragraphs 53 and 54 of Chapter 5 (information of excessive length or seriously prejudicial to the business). 1985 s 231 (1989 s 6)

127 Loans to and from associated undertakings should be separately disclosed in the consolidated accounts. SSAP 1:27,28

128 Balances arising from unsettled normal trading transactions with associated undertakings should be included under current assets or liabilities as appropriate, with separate disclosure if material. SSAP 1:29

129 More detailed information should be given about the associated undertakings' tangible and intangible assets if the interests in the associated undertakings are so material in the context of the accounts of the investing group that the information would assist in giving a true and fair view. This will entail at least an indication of total assets employed and total borrowings and will usually include a summary balance sheet. SSAP 1:30

130 The investing group's share of the post acquisition accumulated reserves of associated undertakings and any movements therein should be disclosed in the consolidated accounts. This disclosure should include movements in reserves which have not passed through the profit and loss account. If the accumulated reserves of the associated undertakings overseas would be subject to further tax on distribution, this should be made clear. SSAP 1:31

131 If there are significant statutory, contractual or exchange control restrictions on the ability of an associated undertaking to distribute its retained profits (other than those shown as non-distributable), the extent of the restrictions should be indicated. SSAP 1:40

132 If there has been a permanent impairment of the value of any goodwill (including premium paid) attributable to an investment in an associated undertaking, the amount written off in the accounting period should be disclosed. SSAP 1:32

133 If the accounts of an associated undertaking are not coterminous with those of the investing group and the effect is material the facts and the dates of year ends should be disclosed. SSAP 1:37

134 If the investing group holds 20 per cent or more of the equity voting rights in an undertaking which is not a subsidiary or a proportionately consolidated joint venture and the investing group does not account for that undertaking as an associated company, details of the accounting treatment adopted and the reason for doing so should be stated. Where disclosure of the reason would be harmful, the directors may omit that information. The Secretary of State's approval is not required in this case. Conversely if an investing group holds less than 20 per cent of the equity voting rights, but accounts for the undertaking as an associated undertaking, the basis on which significant influence is exercised should also be stated. SSAP 1:38 (amended)

Joint ventures

135 The Act defines a joint venture as an undertaking which is managed by an undertaking included in the consolidation jointly with one or more other undertakings not included in the consolidation. The Act uses 'joint management' to describe something which could in fact more aptly be described as 'joint control'. In order to supplement the Act's definition the ASB in its interim statement included the following definition of a joint venture; "a joint venture is an undertaking by which its participants expect to achieve some common purpose or benefit. It is controlled jointly by two or more venturers. Joint control is the contractually agreed sharing of control". 1985 4A sch 19(1) (1989 2 sch)

136 A non-corporate joint venture may be dealt with in the consolidated accounts by the method of proportional consolidation. Proportional consolidation may not be used for joint venture companies, which would therefore be accounted for as associated undertakings unless this would be inconsistent with the requirement to give a true and fair view. 1985 4A sch 19(1) (1989 2 sch) SSAP 1:18

137 Under the Act, proportional consolidation is an option, but ED 50 'Consolidated accounts' proposed that proportional consolidation should be the basis used for non-corporate joint ventures. The proposals of ED 50 relating to associated undertakings and joint ventures are excluded from the provisions of FRS 2, which is based on the proposals of ED 50 relating to subsidiary undertakings only. The ASB excluded associated undertakings and joint ventures from FRS 2 because they are special types of investment. The ASB will deal with these types of investment in a separate accounting standard. Author

138 Proportional consolidation is not defined in the Act. However, it entails including in the consolidated balance sheet the group's proportionate share of individual assets and liabilities of the joint venture on a line by line basis, together with any premium or discount on acquisition. In the consolidated profit and loss account dividends received or receivable from the joint venture are excluded and instead the group's proportionate share of the joint venture's profit and loss is included, again on a line by line basis. The provisions of part VII of the Act (accounts and audit) relating to consolidated accounts apply to proportional consolidation, with any necessary modifications. These provisions include elimination of unrealised profits on, for example, stock transferred to or from the joint venture. Author SSAP 1:18 1985 4A sch 19(2) (1989 2 sch)

139 The following must be disclosed in respect of any joint venture dealt with in the accounts by proportional consolidation: 1985 5 sch 21 (1989 3 sch)

(a) the name of the undertaking;

(b) the address of its principal place of business;

(c) the factors on which joint management of the undertaking is based;

(d) the proportion of its capital held by undertakings included in the consolidation (the corresponding amount for the previous year need not be stated); and

(e) if the financial year of the joint venture did not end with that of the parent company, the date on which its last financial year before that date ended.

Investment companies

140 Investment companies are exempted from some of the applications of the alternative accounting rules (see Chapter 5). Details are given in part V of schedule 4 to the Act but are outside the scope of this book. Where a parent company is treated as an investment company for those purposes the group shall be similarly treated. 1985 4A sch 1(3) (1989 2 sch)

9 Publication and the Accounting Exemptions

Overview

1 Reference is made in this chapter to companies 'publishing' accounts. A company is regarded as publishing a document if it publishes, issues or circulates it or otherwise makes it available for public inspection in a manner calculated to invite members of the public generally, or any class of members of the public, to read it, for example by publishing a preliminary profits statement.

1985 s 240(4)
(1989 s 10)

2 This chapter explains the various types of published accounts specified in the Act. The Act distinguishes between 'statutory accounts', being those prepared under the Act and delivered to the registrar and 'non-statutory' accounts, being any other profit and loss account or balance sheet (e.g. an employee report). Both are regulated by the Act.

3 In respect of each financial year, copies of the annual accounts (balance sheet, profit and loss account and notes) together with the directors' and auditors' reports must be:

1985 s 226(1), 227(1)
(1989 s 4,5)
1985 s 234(1), 235(1)
(1989 s 8,9)

(a) prepared;

(b) laid before the company in general meeting;

1985 s 241(1)
(1989 s 11)

(c) delivered to the registrar (together with a certified translation into English of any document in any other language); and

1985 s 242(1)
(1989 s 11)

(d) sent to every member, debenture holder and anyone else entitled to receive notice of general meetings, not less than 21 days before the date of the meeting at which the accounts are to be laid.

1985 s 238(1)
(1989 s 10)

4 Exemptions are provided from the requirements of paragraph 3 as follows:

(a) small and medium-sized groups need not *prepare* consolidated accounts (see paragraph 22 below);

(b) small and medium-sized companies may deliver to the registrar an 'abbreviated' form of annual accounts (see paragraphs 26 to 34 below). These exemptions are additional to the exemptions that are available to a small company in the preparation of its annual accounts for shareholders and the information to be given in the notes to the accounts (see chapter 3);

(c) dormant companies need not appoint auditors (see paragraphs 36 to 39 below); and

(d) listed public companies may send 'summary financial statements' to those members who do not wish to receive 'full accounts and reports' (see paragraphs 45 to 47 below).

Revision of defective accounts

5 Before the Companies Act 1989 Act, there was no legal provision for the revision of accounts or directors' reports. The Companies Act 1989 Act amends the 1985 Act by introducing provisions which:

(a) permit directors to prepare revised accounts or a revised directors' report where it appears to them that the annual accounts or the directors' report did not comply with the Act ('voluntary revision'); and 1985 s 245 (1989 s 12)

(b) permit the Secretary of State (in the absence of a satisfactory explanation from the directors of a company as to the question of whether the annual accounts or the directors' report comply with the Act), to apply to the court for an order that revised accounts or directors' report should be prepared. Application may also be made by a person authorised by the Secretary of State. The Financial Reporting Review Panel is such a person ('compulsory revision'). 1985 s 245(A),(B),(C) (1989 s 12)

6 Regulations making detailed provisions for the revision of accounts and their audit are contained in SI 1990 No 2570. These regulations govern the preparation, audit and issuance of revised accounts and directors' reports, where the revision is voluntary. There are no regulations governing the preparation, audit and issuance of accounts and directors' reports that are compulsorily revised, as the court is empowered to give directions as to these and other matters as it thinks fit.

Statutory accounts

7 The accounts, whether individual or consolidated accounts, which are required to be delivered to the registrar are called 'statutory accounts'. When applying the rules relating to publication of accounts the term statutory accounts also includes abbreviated accounts which take advantage of the accounting exemptions for small and medium-sized companies, as explained in paragraphs 26 to 35 below.

1985 s 240(5)
(1989 s 10)
1985 8 sch 26(2)
(1989 6 sch)

8 The provisions explained in paragraphs 8 to 10 below do not apply to summary financial statements issued by listed public companies (see paragraph 45 below).

1985 s 251(7)
(1989 s 15)

9 Where a company which is required to prepare consolidated accounts publishes its statutory individual accounts it must also publish with those accounts its statutory consolidated accounts.

1985 s 240(2)
(1989 s 10)

10 Where a company publishes its statutory accounts it must publish with those accounts the relevant auditors' report. In the case of abbreviated accounts of small or medium-sized companies the relevant report is the special report described in paragraph 35 below.

1985 s 240(1)
(1989 s 10)
1985 8 sch 26(3)
(1989 6 sch)

Non-statutory accounts

11 Where a company publishes non-statutory accounts (i.e. any profit and loss account or balance sheet of the company or group relating to a financial year or purporting to deal with any such financial year, published otherwise than as part of the statutory accounts) it must publish with those accounts a statement indicating:

1985 s 240(5),(3)
(1989 s 10)

(a) that the accounts are not statutory accounts;

(b) whether statutory accounts dealing with the same financial year have been delivered to the registrar;

(c) whether an auditors' report has been given on such statutory accounts; and

(d) whether any such auditors' report was qualified or contained a statement that the accounting records were inadequate or did not agree with the accounts or a statement that there was inadequate information.

Where the auditors' report is qualified, it might be regarded as good practice to outline the nature and extent of the qualification. However, a company publishing non-statutory accounts is not permitted to publish with those accounts the auditors' report on the statutory accounts.

Author

Accounting exemptions for small and medium-sized companies and groups

Eligibility

12 The accounting exemptions are available to certain small and medium-sized companies and groups. To qualify as small or medium-sized a company or group of companies must meet at least two of the following three conditions:

Company	*Small*	*Medium-sized*	
(a) Annual turnover not exceeding	£2,800,000	£11,200,000	1985 s 247(3) (1989 s 13) (amended by SI 1992 No 2452)
(b) Balance sheet total not exceeding	£1,400,000	£5,600,000	
(c) Average number of employees not exceeding	50	250	
Group			
(a) Annual turnover not exceeding (see paragraph 14)	£2,800,000 (net) £3,360,000 (gross)	£11,200,000 (net) £13,440,000 (gross)	1985 s 249(3) (1989 s 13) (amended by SI 1992 No 2452)
(b) Balance sheet total not exceeding	£1,400,000 (net) £1,680,000 (gross)	£5,600,000 (net) £6,720,000 (gross)	
(c) Average number of employees not exceeding	50	250	

13 If the accounts are for a period other than a year the maximum figures for turnover must be proportionately adjusted. 1985 s 247(4) (1989 s 13)

14 The above thresholds have been recently increased by SI 1992 No 2452 and apply for financial years ending on or after 16 November 1992. Transitional provisions allow a company or group to take early advantage of the new thresholds for financial years ending on or after 16 November 1992:

(a) if it qualifies as small or medium-sized under the new thresholds in that year and would have done so in the preceding year; or

(b) even though it does not qualify in that year, if it would have qualified as small or medium-sized in the preceding years ending on or after *9 November 1990* had the new thresholds applied.

15 Balance sheet total is the aggregate of items A to D in format 1 or the aggregate of amounts shown under the general heading 'Assets' in format 2, i.e. it is gross assets and not net assets. 1985 s 247(5) (1989 s 13)

16 In deciding whether a group meets each of the relevant conditions, either the net or gross figures may be used. The net figures are the aggregate turnover and balance sheet totals of the group after making consolidation adjustments, and the gross figures are those without making consolidation adjustments. 1985 s 249(4) (1989 s 13)

17 Except in the first financial year, a company or group only qualifies as small or medium-sized if it meets the conditions for both the current and the preceding accounting periods. 1985 s 247(1), 249(1) (1989 s 13)

18 A company or group will, however, be treated as qualifying as small or medium-sized in any period if: 1985 s 247(2), 249(2) (1989 s 13)

(a) it fails to meet the relevant conditions in the current period, but met the conditions in paragraph 17 in the preceding period; or

(b) it meets the relevant conditions in the current period and was treated as qualifying under (a) above in the preceding period.

A company or group failing to qualify in two successive years will therefore cease to be entitled to the accounting exemptions for the second year in which it fails to meet the relevant conditions.

19 A company will not be entitled to the exemptions, regardless of its size, if it is: 1985 s 246(3) (1989 s 13)

(a) a public company;

(b) a banking or insurance company;

(c) an authorised person under the Financial Services Act 1986; or

(d) a member of an ineligible group (as defined in the following paragraph).

20 A group will not be entitled to the group exemptions, regardless of its size, if it is an ineligible group. A group is ineligible if either the parent undertaking or any of its subsidiary undertakings is: 1985 s 246(4), 248(1) (1989 s 13)

(a) a public company;

(b) a body corporate (other than a company) which has power to offer shares or debentures to the public (including a foreign company with the legal authority and power under its constitution to offer its shares to the public);

(c) a banking or insurance company; or

(d) an authorised person under the Financial Services Act 1986.

21 A parent company will not qualify as a small or medium-sized company unless the group headed by it qualifies as a small or medium-sized group respectively. 1985 s 246(5) (1989 s 13)

Exemptions for small and medium-sized groups

22 The accounting exemptions permit parent companies of small and medium-sized groups not to prepare consolidated accounts. A special auditors' report must be attached to the individual accounts of the parent company stating that in the auditors' opinion the company is entitled to the exemption. 1985 s 248(1),(4) (1989 s 13)

Exemptions for small and medium-sized companies

23 The accounting exemptions permit small and medium-sized companies to file with the registrar of companies an abbreviated form of annual accounts. These accounts are an abbreviated form of the annual accounts which companies are required to prepare and lay before their shareholders. 1985 s 246(1) (1989 s 13)

24 The opportunity to file or publish abbreviated accounts in no way affects the requirement to prepare annual accounts for the shareholders. Consequently, the advantage of filing abbreviated accounts does not provide any significant relief for small or medium-sized companies from preparing annual accounts and, if advantage is taken for delivering abbreviated accounts to the registrar of companies, additional time and expense will be incurred in preparing them. They will also require a special auditors' report. The only advantage to be gained from abbreviated accounts is therefore a degree of confidentiality because certain information which might be of interest to competitors (e.g. profit margin, sales analyses) can be omitted from such accounts. For small companies this advantage is further mitigated because of the wide range of exemptions available to them in the preparation of their annual accounts and directors' report. Author

25 A small or medium-sized company is relieved from the requirement to disclose in its accounts whether accounting standards have been followed and to give particulars of material departures from these standards (see Chapter 4). 1985 s 246(1) (1989 s 13)

Small company exemptions

26 A company qualifying to be treated as small is entitled to the following accounting exemptions:

(a) it may *prepare* its annual accounts and directors' report for shareholders under the new exemptions contained in schedule 8 to the Act (see Chapter 3) and *file* them with the registrar; or 1985 8 sch 1-12,15 (amended by SI 1992 No 2452)

(b) it may take further exemption by delivering abbreviated accounts to the registrar irrespective of whether advantage has been taken of the exemption mentioned in (a) above. 1985 8 sch 17-20 (amended by SI 1992 No 2452)

27 Where a small company takes advantage of the exemption in sub-paragraph 26(b) above:

(a) it need not file a profit and loss account;

(b) it need not file a directors' report;

(c) it may file an abbreviated balance sheet; and

(d) certain information normally required to be given in the notes to the accounts may be omitted.

28 The abbreviated balance sheet need include only those headings in the standard formats marked with Roman numerals (Appendix 1). For debtors and creditors separate totals must be shown, either on the balance sheet or in the notes to the accounts, of aggregate amounts falling due before and after one year.

1985 8 sch 17 (1989 6 sch) (amended by SI 1992 No 2452)

29 The notes to the abbreviated accounts need only include the following information required by the schedule 4 to the Act:

1985 8 sch 19(1) (1989 6 sch) (amended by SI 1992 No 2452)

(a) accounting policies;

(b) share capital;

(c) particulars of allotments;

(d) details of fixed assets, so far as they relate to the fixed asset categories: intangibles, tangibles and investments;

(e) particulars of debts;

(f) basis of translation of foreign currencies; and

(g) corresponding amounts for the previous financial year, so far as they relate to amounts required to be included in the notes.

30 It should be emphasised that these exemptions are confined to the disclosure requirements contained in Part III of schedule 4. Therefore, in general, the other statutory requirements must still be met. However, the notes to the accounts need not include information on:

Author

1985 8 sch 19(2)-(4) (1989 6 sch) (amended by SI 1992 No 2452)

(a) financial years of subsidiaries;

(b) the aggregate amount of investment in subsidiaries stated by the equity method of valuation;

(c) any qualifications in the auditors' reports on any subsidiaries' accounts;

(d) shares and debentures of the company held by its subsidiaries;

(e) arrangements attracting merger relief;

(f) directors' emoluments, as required by Part I of schedule 6 to the Act (see Chapter 6); and

(g) auditors' remuneration.

Because abbreviated accounts are not intended to give a true and fair view, it will not be necessary for such accounts to comply with the disclosure provisions contained in accounting standards. Author

Medium-sized company exemptions

31 A company qualifying to be treated as medium-sized is *not entitled* to prepare its annual accounts for shareholders under the exemptions that are available to small companies, but is entitled to file an abbreviated profit and loss account. The normal requirements for full directors' report, balance sheet and notes to the accounts are not affected, except that details of turnover are not required to be given in the notes to the accounts. 1985 8 sch 21,22 (1989 6 sch) (amended by SI 1992 No 2452)

32 An abbreviated profit and loss account will be as set out in the standard formats except that the following items may be combined as one item, under the heading 'Gross profit or loss': 1985 8 sch 21 (1989 6 sch) (amended by SI 1992 No 2452)

(a) items 1, 2, 3 and 6 in format 1;

(b) items 1 to 5 in format 2;

(c) items A1, B1 and B2 in format 3; and

(d) items A1, A2 and B1 to B4 in format 4.

Directors' responsibilities

33 Where abbreviated accounts of a company are filed, they must be signed on behalf of the board by a director. 1985 8 sch 17(3) (1989 6 sch)

34 Immediately above the signature of the director there must be included a statement that advantage is taken of the exemptions for individual accounts on the grounds that the company is, in the directors' opinion, entitled to do so as a small or a medium-sized company (and stating which). 1985 8 sch 23 (1989 6 sch) (amended by SI 1992 No 2452)

Auditors' responsibility

35 Where abbreviated accounts of a company are filed there must be included a special report by the auditors to the directors stating that in their opinion: 1985 8 sch 24 (1989 6 sch) (amended by SI 1992 No 2452)

(a) the company is entitled to the exemptions; and

(b) the accounts have been properly prepared in accordance with schedule 8;

and reproducing the full text of their report on the accounts prepared for the shareholders including any further material necessary to understand any qualification.

Dormant companies

36 A company is regarded as dormant if during any period there were no accounting transactions required to be entered in the accounting records. Transactions arising from the initial issue of shares to the subscribers to the memorandum may be ignored for this purpose. It would seem that provisions for depreciation would not constitute 'transactions', in which case if they are the only entries in the accounting records the company may still be regarded as dormant. Such items as the receipt or payment of dividends would, however, be classed as 'transactions'.

1985 s 250(3)
(1989 s 14)
Author

37 A dormant company, may by special resolution decide not to appoint auditors (provided it is not prohibited from so doing by its articles of association) either:

1985 s 250(1)
(1989 s 14)

(a) if the company has been dormant since its incorporation; or

(b) if it has been dormant since the end of the previous financial year, and:

   (i) it meets the small company conditions set out in the accounting exemption rules, or would do so but for being a member of an ineligible group; and

   (ii) it is not required to prepare consolidated accounts.

This exemption is not available to a public company, a banking or insurance company, or an authorised person under the Financial Services Act 1986.

1985 s 250(2)
(1989 s 14)

38 There must be included in the unaudited balance sheet of a dormant company filed with the registrar, a statement by the directors to the effect that the company was dormant throughout the period covered by the accounts.

1985 s 250(4)
(1989 s 14)

39 A dormant company is entitled to the accounting exemptions for its individual accounts which are available to small companies even if it is a member of an ineligible group. In addition, a statement by the directors (see paragraph 34 above) or a special auditors' report to the directors (see paragraph 35 above) are not required.

1985 s 250(4)(d)
(1989 s 14)
1985 8 sch 25
(1989 6 sch)
(amended by SI 1992 No 2452)

Delivery and publication of accounts in ECUs

40 Companies are now permitted to publish their accounts in ECUs for financial years ending on or after 16 November 1992. This may be done either by preparing annual accounts in ECUs (in addition to the normal annual accounts) or including equivalent ECU information in the annual

1985 s 242B(1),(3)
(inserted by SI 1992 No 2452)

accounts. However, in both cases, the company must comply with the following conditions:

(a) the amounts shown in ECUs must be translated at the relevant exchange rate prevailing on the balance sheet date; and

(b) the rate must be disclosed in the notes to the accounts.

41 The directors may (when delivering the company's annual accounts, directors' report and auditors' report to the registrar as required by section 242) deliver to him an additional copy of the annual accounts in which the amounts have been translated into ECUs. 1985 s 242B(2) (inserted by SI 1992 No 2452)

42 In addition, if a company wishes to publish, circulate or generally make available to the public copies of its accounts which show the amounts in ECUs and which comply with the above: 1985 s 242B(4) (inserted by SI 1992 No 2452)

(a) it must treat them as its statutory accounts for the purposes of section 240 and the requirements of that section will apply to any publication of those accounts; and

(b) the auditors' report required by that section to accompany them is the auditors' report on the annual accounts of which they are a copy.

43 'ECU' is defined as a unit equal to the value of the unit of account known as the ECU used in the European Monetary System. 'Relevant exchange' rate is defined as the rate used for translating the value of the ECU for the purposes of that system. 1985 s 242B(5) (inserted by SI 1992 No 2452)

44 Although not specifically dealt with in the Act, the registrar of companies will accept annual accounts prepared in a foreign currency, as long as similar disclosure to that required by paragraph 40 has been made. Author

Listed public companies: summary financial statements

45 A listed public company may send a summary financial statement (derived from the annual accounts and directors' report) to those members who do not wish to receive the full accounts and reports. The summary financial statement must: 1985 s 251(1) (1989 s 15)

(a) state that it is only a summary of information in the annual accounts;

(b) contain a statement by the auditors of their opinion as to whether the summary financial statement:

  (i) is consistent with the annual accounts and directors' report;

  (ii) complies with the requirements of the relevant section of the Act and regulations made under it; and

(c) state whether the auditors' report on the annual accounts was qualified or contained a statement regarding inadequate accounting records or information; and if it was qualified, reproduce the full text of that report together with any further material necessary to understand the qualification.

This provision in no way changes the requirement for companies to prepare full accounts and reports, to lay them before members and to file them with the registrar.

A company is regarded as listed for this purpose if any class of its shares is admitted to the Official List of The International Stock Exchange of the United Kingdom and the Republic of Ireland Limited. 1985 s 251(1) (1989 s 15)

The detailed form and content of summary financial statements and the conditions that should be complied with before summary financial statements can be issued to shareholders are set out in SI 1992 No 3075. The regulations will need to be read in conjunction with the requirements of section 251.

10 Company Records and Regulations

Introduction

1 This chapter sets out some important aspects of company law, The Admission of Securities to Listing and other regulations, some of which are not directly concerned with accounts disclosure, but of which the preparers or auditors of accounts should be aware.

Accounting records and statutory books

Nature of records

2 It is the duty of the company to keep accounting records which are sufficient to show and explain the company's transactions and are such as to: 1985 s 221(1) (1989 s 2)

(a) disclose with reasonable accuracy, at any time, the financial position of the company at that time; and 1985 s 221(1)(a) (1989 s 2)

(b) enable the directors to ensure that any balance sheet and profit and loss account prepared by them under Part VII of the Companies Act 1985 complies with the requirements of that Act. 1985 s 221(1)(b) (1989 s 2)

3 The accounting records must in particular contain:

(a) entries from day to day of all sums of money received and expended, and the matters in respect of which the receipt and expenditure takes place; 1985 s 221(2)(a) (1989 s 2)

(b) a record of assets and liabilities; and 1985 s 221(2)(b) (1989 s 2)

(c) if the company's business involves dealing in goods, statements of stock held by the company at the end of each financial year. The company must retain statements of stocktakings from which the statements of stock are prepared and, except in the case of goods sold by way of ordinary retail trade, records of goods sold and purchased identifying the goods and the buyers and sellers. 1985 s 221(3) (1989 s 2)

4 A parent company whose subsidiary undertaking is not governed by the Act, (e.g. a non corporate undertaking or a foreign company), should take reasonable steps to ensure that such accounting records are kept by its subsidiary undertaking as to enable the directors of the parent company to meet the requirement in sub-paragraph 2(b) above. 1985 s 221(4) (1989 s 2)

5 Accounts and returns must be sent to, and kept in, Great Britain in respect of accounting records kept outside Great Britain and must be such as to: 1985 s 222(2),(3) (1989 s 2)

(a) disclose with reasonable accuracy the financial position of the business in question at intervals not exceeding six months; and

(b) enable the directors to prepare accounts which comply with the requirements of the Act.

Retention of records

6 The accounting records described above must be kept, in the case of a private company, for three years from the date on which they are made and, in any other case, for six years. The retention period stated in the Act should be regarded as a minimum. For VAT purposes a period of six years is now required. There are, however, many other regulations that impact on the retention period for accounting records and reference should be made to Accountants Digest No 205, 'Business documents - management and retention', published by the Institute of Chartered Accountants in England and Wales. 1985 s 222(5) (1989 s 2) Author

Form of records

7 A register, index, minute book or accounting record may be kept in a bound book or otherwise. Where any of these items are maintained by recording data otherwise than in a legible form, for example on a computer file, the item does not need to be kept at the location specified below, provided a legible reproduction is available for inspection at that location. 1985 s 722,723 SI 1985 No 724

Statutory books and records and their location

8 The books and records to be kept and, subject to paragraph 7 above, their location are set out below:

Statutory books	*To be kept at*	
(a) Register of directors (including shadow directors) and secretaries. The directors' past directorships are also required to be stated. Every company must have a secretary (a sole director cannot also be a secretary) and, unless a private company, at least two directors. The statement of first directors and secretary and changes thereto is to be notified to the registrar.	Registered office.	1985 s 282,283 1985 s 288-290

(b)	Register of charges and copies of all instruments creating such charges.	Registered office.	1985 s 411 (1989 s 101) 1985 s 703J (1989 15 sch)
(c)	Minute books of general meetings.	Registered office.	1985 s 383
(d)	Minute books of meetings of directors or managers.	No statutory requirement.	1985 s 382
(e)	Register of members and, where required, index thereto.	Registered office or such other place as may be notified to the registrar.	1985 s 352-354
(f)	Register of debenture holders.	Registered office or such other place as may be notified to the registrar.	1985 s 190
(g)	Register of directors', including shadow directors', interests in shares and debentures of group companies, together with index.	Registered office or place at which register of members is kept. Registrar to be notified of place kept if other than registered office.	1985 s 325 1985 13 Sch 25,28
(h)	For public companies, a register of persons, or persons acting together, interested in 3 per cent or more of the share capital of the company and associated index.	Wherever the register of directors' interests is kept.	1985 s 211
(i)	For public companies, reports of investigations into shareholdings made in the last six years.	Registered office.	1985 s 215(7)
	Accounting records		
(j)	The records referred to in paragraphs 2 to 5 above.	Registered office or such other place as directors think fit.	1985 s 222(1) (1989 s 2)

9 A company may change its registered office by giving notice to the registrar of companies and the change will take effect on the notice being registered by him. Documents held at the registered office must be transferred to the new registered office not more than 14 days after the company gives the notice. 1985 s 287(3)(5)

Annual return

10 Every company must submit an annual return (in the prescribed form) each year. It must be made up to a date not later than the anniversary of its incorporation unless the company's last return was made up to a different date, in which case the return must be made up to the anniversary of that date. The annual return must contain the following information: 1985 s 363,364A (1989 s 139)

(a) the address of the registered office;

(b) the type of company and its principal business activities;

(c) the name and address of the company secretary;

(d) details of the company's directors, to include name, any former name, usual residential address, nationality, date of birth, business occupation and other directorships;

(e) the locations of registers of members and debenture holders, if not kept at the registered office;

(f) if the company has elected to dispense with holding annual general meetings or the laying of accounts before general meeting, a statement to that effect;

and, in the case of a company having a share capital:

(g) details of the company's share capital and of each class of share capital; and

(h) the names and addresses of members and their holdings including persons who have ceased to be members since the last return.

A full list of shareholders is required only every third year. In other years, a list of changes in membership and holdings will suffice.

11 The annual return must be delivered to the registrar within 28 days after the date to which it is made up. The return must be signed by a director or the company secretary. 1985 s 363(2) (1989 s 139)

Regulations concerning directors

Directors' service contracts

12 For each director, including a shadow director, of the company who is employed under a service contract with either the company or any of its subsidiaries, there must be kept available for inspection by the members a copy of the contract. If the contract is not in writing, or if the director is required to work wholly or mainly outside the UK, a written memorandum of the terms of the contract will suffice. Also refer to paragraph 40 below. 1985 s 318

13 The location of these documents, which may be the registered office, the principal place of business or the place where the register of members is kept, must be notified to the registrar. 1985 s 318(3),(4)

14 No copy or memorandum of a director's service contract is required to be made available if the contract has less than 12 months to run, or may be terminated by the company within the next 12 months without payment of compensation. 1985 s 318(11)

Directors' qualification shares

15 The number of qualification shares as specified by the articles must be acquired within two months, or such period as is stated by the articles if less. Qualification shares cannot consist of bearer shares. 1985 s 291

Directors' age limit

16 Subject to the exceptions in the following paragraph:

(a) no person may be appointed a director of a company if, at the time of the appointment, he has reached the age of 70; and 1985 s 293(2) 1985 s 293(3)

(b) a director shall vacate office (and shall be ineligible for re-election) at the conclusion of the annual general meeting next after he reaches the age of 70.

17 The above provisions do not apply if:

(a) the appointment is made or approved by the company in general meeting and special notice (section 379), stating the age of the person concerned, has been given; or 1985 s 293(5)

(b) there are provisions to the contrary in the company's articles; or 1985 s 293(7)

(c) the company is a private company, not being the subsidiary of a public company incorporated in the UK. 1985 s 293(1)(b)

18 A person who is proposed or appointed as a director of a company subject to these provisions must give notice of his age to the company, if at that date he has reached the age of 70 or any other retiring age specified by the articles. 1985 s 294

Secretarial matters

19 Business letters, order forms, invoices, and other documents must show:

(a) the company's name; 1985 s 349(1)

(b) the place of registration; 1985 s 351(1)

(c) the company's registered number; and

(d) the address of the registered office.

If such documents refer to the share capital of the company, this must be the paid up capital. The fact that a company is a limited company must also be stated, even if the company is authorised under section 30 of the Act to omit the word 'limited' from its name. 1985 s 351(2) 1985 s 351(1)(d)

20 Business letters on which the company's name appears must not state the name of any of its directors (otherwise than in the text or as a signatory) unless the letter states the names of all individual or corporate directors of the company. 1985 s 305(1)

21 If a company which carries on business uses a name that is not its corporate name, it must state its corporate name legibly on all business letters, orders, invoices, receipts and written demand for payments arising in the course of business. BNA 1985 s 1,4

22 An up to date version of the company's memorandum and articles must be filed with the registrar. Any alterations to either document must be printed. Where the amendments are minor the registrar allows, by concession, amendment slips to be inserted, provided these obscure the amended words. 1985 s 18 Author

Accounts

Duty to prepare accounts

23 The directors must prepare individual accounts for each financial year, which consist of:

(a) a balance sheet as at the last day of the financial year; 1985 s 226(1) (1989 s 4)

(b) a profit and loss account;

(c) a statement of total recognised gains and losses; FRS 3

(d) a statement of cash flows; and FRS 1

(e) additional information to be provided by way of notes.

Where at the end of a financial year a company is a parent company, consolidated accounts must also be prepared. 1985 s 227(1) (1989 s 5)

Financial year and accounting reference date

24 A company's first financial year begins with the date of its incorporation. Subsequent financial years begin with the day immediately following the end of its previous financial year. The financial year ends on a date determined by the directors within seven days either side of the last day of the accounting reference period. 1985 s 223 (1989 s 3)

25 The financial year of an undertaking not formed under the Act is any period in respect of which a profit and loss account is required to be drawn up either by its constitution or by the law under which it is established. 1985 s 223(4) (1989 s 3)

26 A company's accounting reference periods are determined by its accounting reference date. The first accounting reference period of a company is the period of more than six months, but not more than 18 months, from the date of incorporation to its accounting reference date. Subsequent accounting reference periods are periods of 12 months ending with the accounting reference date. — 1985 s 224(1),(4),(5) (1989 s 3)

27 Within nine months of incorporation, a company may notify the registrar of companies of its accounting reference date. If no such notice is given, the accounting reference date will be deemed to be the last day of the month of incorporation (or 31 March in the case of companies incorporated prior to 1 April 1990). — 1985 s 224(2),(3) (1989 s 3)

28 A company may alter its accounting reference date for the current and future periods by giving notice of change at any time during the current accounting reference period. — 1985 s 225(1) (1989 s 3)

29 Notice of change may also be given after the end of the last accounting reference period to apply to that accounting period and future periods, but only if: — 1985 s 225(2) (1989 s 3)

(a) the company is a subsidiary undertaking or parent undertaking of another company and the new accounting reference date coincides with that of the other company; and

(b) the period allowed for laying and delivering accounts relating to that accounting period has not expired. — 1985 s 225(5) (1989 s 3)

30 There is no minimum period for which an accounting reference period may run, because a company can always shorten its current period if proper notice is given. Extending the period is more difficult because, in addition to the restrictions in paragraph 29 above, no accounting reference period may exceed 18 months and also there are restrictions on a company extending its accounting reference period more than once every five years, unless it is a change to coincide with a subsidiary or parent undertaking. — Author; 1985 s 225(6) (1989 s 3); 1985 s 225(4) (1989 s 3)

Approval and signature

31 The annual accounts must be approved by the board and the company's balance sheet must be signed on behalf of the board by a director. The accounts should disclose the date of their approval (see Chapter 5). — 1985 s 233(1),(2) (1989 s 7) SSAP 17:26

32 There is no legal requirement for the consolidated balance sheet to be signed in the same way, but this procedure is regarded as good practice. — Author

33 Every copy of the balance sheet which is laid before the company in general meeting, or which is otherwise circulated, published or issued, shall state the name of the director who signed it. The copy of the balance sheet (whether full or abbreviated, in the case of small companies) which is delivered to the registrar must be signed by a director. — 1985 s 233(3),(4) (1989 s 7) 1985 8 sch 17(3) (1989 6 sch)

34 A company's accounts, together with a copy of the directors' report and auditors' report, must be delivered to the registrar of companies within ten months of the accounting reference date (for private companies) or within seven months of the accounting reference date (for public companies). In either case: 1985 s 242(1) (1989 s 11) 1985 s 244 (1989 s 11)

(a) the period will be reduced for a first accounting period of more than 12 months;

(b) the period can be extended by three months where the company carries on business, or has interests, outside the UK, providing notice is given to the registrar within the normal period allowed for filing accounts; and

(c) the period can be extended in some cases to three months from the date of a notice which shortens the company's accounting reference period.

35 Where a company fails to deliver accounts and reports to the registrar within the period allowed, it is liable to a civil penalty. It should be noted that the registrar is rigorously applying this provision of the Act and imposing late filing penalties even if the company is just one day late. The general rule that the registrar uses to calculate the seven or ten month period is based on the House of Lords decision in *Dodds v Walker (1981)* which determined that the period ends upon the *corresponding* date in the appropriate subsequent month (i.e. not necessarily the end of the month). Consequently, a company with an accounting reference date of 30 September must file its accounts with the registrar by 30 April for a public company or by 30 July (*not 31 July*) for a private company. 1985 s 242A (1989 s 11) Author

General meetings

36 A company must hold its first annual general meeting within 18 months of incorporation, and subsequently once in each calendar year, but not more than 15 months after the date of the previous general meeting. Annual accounts, together with directors' report and auditors' report, are to be laid before the company in general meeting (usually, but not necessarily, at the annual general meeting). 1985 s 366(1)-(3) 1985 s 241(1) (1989 s 11)

37 The accounts and reports must be circulated not less than 21 days before the general meeting at which they are to be laid, to every member and debenture holder and also to any other person who is entitled to receive notice of general meetings. If all members entitled to attend and vote at the meeting agree, notice may be waived. 1985 s 238(1) (1989 s 10) 1985 s 238(4) (1989 s 10)

38 A private company may elect not to lay its accounts and reports before the company in general meeting. However, these documents must be distributed to those entitled to receive accounts not less than 28 days before the end of the period allowed for delivering accounts to the registrar. 1985 s 252, 253 (1989 s 16)

39 Where a private company has elected not to lay its accounts before a meeting, any member or auditor may nevertheless require such a meeting to be held by requesting it in writing within 28 days of the sending out of the annual accounts. 1985 s 252, 253 (1989 s 16)

40 The notice convening the annual general meeting of a listed company is to state that there will be made available for inspection at the registered office, or transfer office, from the date of the notice to the date of the meeting and at the meeting, copies of, or a written memorandum of the terms of, all directors' service contracts with the company or any subsidiary (unless the contract of service is expiring, or determinable by the company without payment of compensation, within one year). If there are no contracts, that fact is to be stated in the notice. However, no company may approve a director's service contract unless a memorandum of the proposed terms under which a director's employment is to continue for a period exceeding five years was available at the general meeting itself, and at the registered office for the 15 preceding days. The Cadbury Committee Report recommends that directors' service contracts should not exceed three years without shareholders' approval. ASL 42 1985 s 319(5)

Listed companies

Half yearly reports and preliminary profits statements

41 For listed companies a half yearly report is to be circulated to holders of listed securities, or inserted as a paid advertisement in two leading daily newspapers, no later than four months after the end of the period to which it relates. In the case of the USM, the report need only be circulated to shareholders or published in one newspaper. ASL 23 USM 8:4

42 The half yearly report or preliminary profits statements for the full year must consist of figures in table form. In the absence of any special circumstances, the following minimum information should be included in preliminary profits statements or in half yearly reports. In the case of a parent company, the information should be given in respect of the group. Figures which are provisional or subject to audit should be so qualified. The particulars required are: ASL 24(a) ASL 24(b)

(a) net turnover;

(b) profit or loss before taxation and extraordinary items;

(c) taxation on profits (UK taxation and, if material, overseas and share of associated undertakings' taxation to be shown separately);

(d) minority interests;

(e) profit or loss attributable to shareholders, before extraordinary items;

(f) extraordinary items (net of taxation);

(g) profit or loss attributable to shareholders;

(h) rates of dividend(s) paid and proposed and amount absorbed thereby;

(i) earnings per share expressed as pence per share (computed on the figures shown for profits after taxation as defined in SSAP 3); and

(j) comparative figures in respect of (a) to (i) inclusive for the corresponding previous period.

43 Preliminary profits statements constitute the publication of non-statutory accounts. The relevant statutory provisions set out in Chapter 9 must be followed. Half yearly reports need not be regarded as non-statutory accounts unless they incorporate corresponding figures dealing with a financial year. Author

44 Half yearly reports also have to contain an explanatory statement relating to the group's activities and profit or loss for the relevant period. The explanatory statement must: ASL 24(a) ASL 24(c)

(a) include any significant information enabling investors to make an informed assessment of the trend of the group's activities and profit or loss together with an indication of any special factor which has influenced those activities and the profit or loss for the year in question;

(b) enable comparison to be made with the corresponding period of the preceding financial year; and

(c) as far as possible, refer to the group's prospects in the current financial year.

45 Where the accounting information given in a half yearly report has not been audited that fact must be stated. If the accounting information contained in a half yearly report has been audited, the audit report thereon including any qualifications must be set out in the half yearly report. ASL 24(d)

Sundry matters - listed companies

46 The Yellow Book requires that listed companies include in the annual report and accounts the identity of independent non-executive directors together with a short biographical note on each. ASL 21(t)

47 It is normal practice for listed companies to disclose in the annual report: Author

(a) a table of relevant comparative figures for at least the past five years; and

(b) a list of principal activities or products.

48 Where companies adopt the provisions of FRS 3 for the first time, the question arises as to whether the figures included in the historical summaries and the five year tables should be restated. Although no guidance is provided in FRS 3, it is recommended that companies should restate the figures as far as reasonably practicable. For example, it is relatively simple to restate items that had been classified as extraordinary in the past as exceptional items under FRS 3. However, where data needed to distinguish between continuing and discontinued activities, and to segregate the effects of acquisitions, are not readily available, there should be an explanation, by way of a note to the summaries, that the figures for the current and the comparative period are fully in compliance with FRS 3 but that figures for the previous years comply in some respects but not others. The note would also need to explain which aspects of FRS 3 had and had not been adopted for those years. Author

Vendor consideration placings

49 Where the company has listed shares in issue, is a subsidiary of another company and has received notification from its parent company of the parent company's proposal to participate in future issues of shares by the company not made on a pro rata basis to existing shareholders, in order that the parent company may maintain its stake in the company, the proposal must be given the authority of a resolution of the company passed at a general meeting. Such authority must be renewed annually and the parent company must abstain from voting. Particulars of the participation by the parent company in any vendor consideration placing made during the year under review must be set out in the annual accounts. ASL 22

Share capital

50 A company may not exercise its power to allot shares, unless it is, in accordance with the provisions of the Act, authorised to do so by: 1985 s 80

(a) the company in general meeting; or 1985 s 80(1)

(b) the company's articles.

A company may not allot shares at a discount. 1985 s 100

Types of company

51 **Public companies**

A public company is one which fulfils the following requirements: 1985 s 1(3)

(a) it must be limited by shares or be limited by guarantee and have a share capital, although no company in the latter category may be newly formed as a public company;

(b) its memorandum of association must state that it is to be a public company;

(c) the provisions in relation to the registration of such a company must be fulfilled;

(d) it must have not less than two members and two directors; 1985 s 1(1) 1985 s 282

(e) its name must end with the words 'public limited company' or 'plc' or, in the case of a company whose registered office is in Wales, those words, or initials or their equivalent in Welsh; and 1985 s 25(1)

(f) it must have a minimum allotted share capital of £50,000, of which at least a quarter of the nominal value plus the whole of any premium must be paid up. 1985 s 11, 118(1) 1985 s 101(1)

Any share offers to the public must comply with the provisions of the Act. 1985 s 82

Private companies

52 A private company is any company which is not a public company. Such companies will therefore include all unlimited companies, and all companies limited by guarantee which do not have a share capital. A private company has the following privileges: 1985 s 1(3)

(a) the minimum number of members is one; SI 1992 No 1699

(a) the minimum number of directors is one, but a sole director cannot also hold the office of secretary; 1985 s 282, 283

(b) the provision regarding the age limit of directors does not apply, provided the company is not a subsidiary of a public company incorporated in the UK; 1985 s 293(1)

(c) when authorised to purchase or redeem its own shares, a private company may do so out of capital, rather than only out of distributable profits; 1985 s 171

(d) it may more readily give financial assistance for the purchase of its own or its holding company's shares; and 1985 s 155

(e) less strict criteria apply in determining distributable profits. 1985 s 263, 264

However, a private company is prohibited from offering its shares or debentures to the public. 1985 s 81

Unlimited companies

53 An unlimited company incorporated under the Act is subject to the same accounting requirements as a limited company. However, an unlimited company is not required to file its accounts, auditors' or directors' reports with the registrar provided that, at no time during the accounting reference period, was it: 1985 s 254 (1989 s 17)

(a) the subsidiary of a limited undertaking; nor

(b) if more than one limited undertaking had rights in it, would it have been a subsidiary if all those rights had been held by a single undertaking; nor was it

(c) the parent company of a limited undertaking; or

(d) carrying on business within the meaning of the Trading Stamps Act 1964.

Oversea companies

General

54 Oversea companies are defined as companies, including any body corporate, incorporated outside Great Britain which have a place of business in Great Britain, which for this purpose means England, Scotland and Wales. 1985 s 691, 744 1985 s 699

55 On 1 January 1993 The Oversea Companies and Credit and Financial Institutions (Branch Disclosure) Regulations 1992 brought into force a new regime for oversea companies - *the branch registration regime* which will run in parallel with the *existing place of business regime*. An oversea company must register under one of these regimes. SI 1992 No 3179

56 Prior to these regulations, an oversea company having a place of business or a branch in Great Britain was regulated by Chapter 1, as to registration, and Chapter 2, as to delivery of accounts and reports, of Part XXIII of the Act. The requirement to introduce new rules for oversea companies that have a branch in Great Britain stems from the Eleventh EC Company Law Directive (Council Directive 89/666/89) on the disclosure requirements (including disclosure of accounting documents) in respect of branches opened by limited companies (whether incorporated within the EC or outside) in an EC Member State and the Bank Branches Directive (Council Directive 89/117/EEC).

57 Any limited company which is incorporated outside the UK (meaning Great Britain and Northern Ireland) and Gibraltar and has a branch in Great Britain must register under the branch registration regime. All other oversea companies that do not qualify to be registered under the branch registration regime must register under the place of business regime. 1985 s 690A (inserted by SI 1992 No 3179)

58 Therefore, the branch registration regime created by the new regulations complements the existing place of business registration scheme set out in Part XXIII of the Act. The regulations make a number of amendments to Part XXIII, including the addition of four new schedules as follows: SI 1992 No 3179

(a) schedule 21A which sets out the particulars to be disclosed by an oversea company registering as a branch;

(b) schedule 21B which provide for certain transitional arrangements where an oversea company moves from the place of business registration regime to the branch registration regime and vice versa;

(c) schedule 21C which sets out the requirement for delivery of reports and accounts of credit and financial institutions to which the Bank Branches Directive applies; and

(d) schedule 21D which sets out the reports and accounts to be delivered by an oversea company subject to branch registration.

59 There is no comprehensive statutory or common law definition of what constitutes 'a place of business'. The term is defined only to include a share transfer or a share registration office. In general, if an oversea company performs functions in Great Britain that are only ancillary or incidental to the company's business as a whole (e.g. warehouse facilities, administrative offices, internal data processing facilities), then the company has established a place of business in Great Britain and will be subject to the registration requirements under the place of business regime. 1985 s 744 Author

60 No precise definition of a 'branch' is given in the Act, but the Department of Trade and Industry has given some guidance. In general, if the functions performed in Great Britain are not ancillary or incidental to the oversea company's business, but are conducted by the branch on behalf of the company, then the oversea company has established a branch and will be subject to the registration requirements under the branch regime. It should be noted that the term 'branch' is not used in the commonly understood sense of a local bank branch or an office branch at a single locality. Rather, it is used more in a sense closer to a subsidiary, although it will not necessarily be a separate body corporate. This means that a person resident in the UK will be able to conduct business directly with the branch, instead of the company in its country of incorporation. Author

61 An oversea company that has established a place of business or a branch in Great Britain must, within one month of establishing that place of business or branch, deliver to the registrar of companies a return in the prescribed form and documents. 1985 s 691,692 1985 21A sch 2-8 (inserted by SI 1992 No 3179)

Accounting requirements

62 The reports and accounts required to be delivered by an overseas company to the registrar of companies also depend upon the manner in which the company in question has been registered.

Oversea companies registered as a place of business

63 Every oversea company that has established a place of business in Great Britain is required to deliver to the registrar of companies, in respect of each financial year of the company, copies of its reports and accounts prepared in 1985 s 700 (1989 10 sch 13) SI 1990 No 440

accordance with the Oversea Companies (accounts) (Modifications and Exemptions) Order 1990. Under this the oversea company must in respect of every financial year prepare accounts substantially in the form that would have been required had the company been incorporated under the Act, although certain exemptions are available. The accounts, subject to the available exemptions set out in paragraph 67 below, have to comply with the requirements of sections 258 and 259 of and schedule 9 (accounts of banking and insurance companies) to the Companies Act 1985 *before it was amended by the Companies Act 1989* as if they were old special category companies in so far as those requirements applied.

64 Oversea companies are not required to refer to the fact that their accounts are drawn up in compliance with section 258 or 259 and schedule 9 to the unamended Companies Act 1985. Oversea companies are not entitled to take advantage of the exemptions available to small, medium-sized or dormant companies. SI 1990 No 440 sch 5; SI 1990 No 440 2(2)

65 There is no requirement that such documents must be circulated to shareholders, but copies must be delivered to the registrar of companies, together with a certified translation thereof where they are not written in the English language. The period allowed for delivery to the registrar is 13 months from the accounting reference date. If the oversea company's first accounting reference period exceeds 12 months, the period allowed for filing accounts is 13 months from the first anniversary of the company establishing a place of business in Great Britain. 1985 s 702 (1989 10 sch 13)

66 These provisions may have the effect that some foreign companies will have to place on public record in the UK more information concerning their accounts than is required by the laws of the country in which they are incorporated. This is because the accounts of oversea companies as defined must be accounts not of the UK operation, but of the legal entity incorporated overseas (containing the transactions of the UK operation as appropriate). Author

67 The exemptions referred to above allow oversea companies to omit the following from their accounts: SI 1990 No 440

(a) auditors' report;

(b) directors' report;

(c) information to be disclosed in respect of UK taxation;

(d) turnover;

(e) details of subsidiaries and investments;

(f) identity and place of incorporation of ultimate parent company;

(g) details of directors' and employees' emoluments; and

(h) particulars of transactions favouring directors and officers.

In addition, such companies should not apply section 130 of the Act (creation of share premium account).

Oversea companies registered as a branch

68 The reports and accounts required to be delivered by an oversea company 1985 s 699A
that has established a branch depend on whether or not the company in (inserted by SI 1990
question is required to prepare, have audited and disclose its reports and No 3179)
accounts under the law of its country of incorporation (parent law).

69 Where an oversea company is required by its parent law to prepare, have 1985 21D sch 1, 2(2)
audited and publicly disclose its accounts it must, within one month of
opening a branch, deliver with the return for registration copies of its latest
accounting documents prepared and disclosed in accordance with that law to
the registrar. In the subsequent years after first registration, accounting 1985 21D sch 4
documents prepared in relation to a financial period of the company must be
delivered within three months of the date when they are first disclosed in
accordance with the parent law. As a general rule the documents must be
filed in respect of each branch. However, it is possible for a principal branch 1985 21D sch 3
to file accounts in respect of other branches provided this is specified in
those branch returns.

70 The accounting documents in relation to the financial period of the company 1985 21D sch 6(2)
referred to in the preceding paragraph consist of the individual accounts of
the company and where it has subsidiaries, its group accounts, the directors'
report for the period if any and auditors' report on the accounts. A certified 1985 21D sch 2(4)
copy must be provided of any document that is not in English. If the parent 1985 21D sch 2(3)
law permits the company to disclose its accounting documents in a modified
form, the oversea company may file these with the registrar.

71 A company incorporated outside the EC and required to file home country 1985 21A sch 2(2)
accounts must notify the registrar on registration of its accounting reference
period and the date by which it is required to file accounts in its home
country.

72 Where an oversea company with a branch is not required to make public 1985 21D sch 7,8
disclosure of its accounts under its parent law, it is required to prepare and
deliver accounts in the same manner as an oversea company subject to the
place of business regime as described in paragraphs 63 to 67 above.

73 If the Secretary of State serves notice on an oversea company that its 1985 s 694
corporate name is undesirable as a business name, such company must, if it
wishes to continue in business in Great Britain, adopt another name,
approved by the Secretary of State, as its business name, and that other name
must be notified to the registrar of companies.

74	Oversea companies incorporated in the Channel Islands or the Isle of Man which have a branch in Great Britain are also subject to the branch registration regime.	1985 s 690A (inserted by SI 1992 No 3179)
75	Oversea companies incorporated in the Channel Islands or the Isle of Man which have a place of business in Great Britain are additionally, for the purpose of the provisions of the Act relating to documents to be forwarded, delivered or filed with the registrar of companies, treated as if they were registered in England or Scotland, subject to certain exceptions.	1985 s 699

11 Provisions Affecting Capital and Distributions

Introduction

1 This chapter sets out certain of the legal requirements concerning capital and distributions which, although not directly related to disclosure, are relevant to the production of annual accounts. The provisions included relate to:

(a) the purchase by a company of its own shares;

(b) financial assistance for acquisition of shares;

(c) share premiums; and

(d) distributions of profits and assets.

2 These particular topics are complex, and this chapter does not set out to be comprehensive. In cases of doubt, reference should always be made to the legislation, and in difficult cases it is recommended that appropriate legal advice is obtained.

The purchase by a company of its own shares

3 A company, if empowered by its articles, may purchase its own shares (whether or not these shares are designated as redeemable) provided that, after any purchase, non-redeemable shares are still in issue. 1985 s 162(1) 1985 s 162(3)

4 A purchase may be made from: 1985 s 160(1),(2)

(a) the proceeds of an issue made for that purpose; and/or

(b) distributable profits.

Any premium payable on purchase must be paid out of distributable profits, except where the purchase is of shares originally issued at a premium when, with certain limits (see below), the premium may be paid out of the proceeds of an issue for that purpose.

5 A public company may only purchase its own shares from the above sources. However, a private company may also make purchases out of capital (see below).

6 Shares purchased are treated as cancelled and the nominal value of the issued share capital is reduced accordingly. Where a purchase is made wholly out of distributable profits an amount equal to the reduction of the issued share capital is required to be transferred to a capital redemption reserve. This reserve may thereafter only be applied for a bonus issue of new capital. 1985 s 160(4),162(2) 1985 s 170(1),(4)

7 If a purchase of shares is made wholly or partly out of a fresh issue of shares and the proceeds of this issue are less than the aggregate nominal value of shares purchased, the difference must be transferred to a capital redemption reserve. 1985 s 170(2)

8 If the shares being purchased were themselves issued at a premium, any premium payable on the purchase may be paid out of the proceeds of a fresh issue made for that purpose and the share premium account reduced accordingly by an amount up to the lower of: 1985 s 160(2),162(2)

(a) the aggregate of the premiums received on the issue of the shares being purchased; and

(b) the current amount of share premium account including the amount of the premium on the new issue transferred to it.

9 The following further provisions apply to purchase of own shares:

(a) the shares to be purchased must be fully paid; 1985 s 159(3),162(2)

(b) the purchase terms must provide for payment on redemption; and 1985 s 159(3),162(2)

(c) the authorised share capital is not reduced by the purchase. If a company is about to purchase its own shares, it can issue new shares up to the nominal amount of the shares to be purchased as if the original shares had never been issued and so not exceed its authorised capital. 1985 s 160(4),(5), 162(2)

Purchase out of capital

10 In addition to being able to purchase its own shares out of distributable profits and the proceeds of a new issue, a private company is allowed to purchase shares out of capital, but only if: 1985 s 171(1)

(a) it provides the safeguards for creditors set out below; and

(b) it is empowered to do so by its articles.

1 The payment which may be made out of capital is referred to as the 'permissible capital payment'. The permissible capital payment is the cost of purchase of the shares less: 1985 s 171(3)

(a) any available profits of the company; and

(b) the proceeds of any fresh issue made for the purpose of the redemption or purchase.

The available profits for this purpose are the profits out of which a distribution could be made under the Act as shown by the 'relevant accounts' prepared as at a date within the three months immediately prior to the statutory declaration of the directors (see below). The 'relevant accounts' are such accounts as are necessary to enable a reasonable judgement to be made of the amounts of the items included. 1985 s 172

2 The effect of these provisions is that the purchase of own shares will result in a depletion of capital only to the extent that the distributable profits and/or the proceeds of a fresh issue are inadequate.

3 If the permissible capital payment, which includes for this purpose the proceeds of any new issue applied in making the purchase:

(a) is less than the nominal value of the shares purchased, the difference must be transferred to the capital redemption reserve; or 1985 s 171(4)-(6)

(b) exceeds the nominal value of the shares purchased, the following may be reduced by the excess: 1985 s 171(5),(6)

(i) the capital redemption reserve or share premium account (if any) or the fully paid share capital; and

(ii) unrealised profits included in the revaluation reserve maintained under paragraph 34 of schedule 4.

The revision of paragraph 34(3) of schedule 4 made by the Companies Act 1989 (see paragraph 46 below) has introduced some doubt as to whether the revaluation reserve may now be used for this purpose. Companies wishing to do so should seek legal advice. Author

4 The safeguards for creditors are as follows:

(a) the directors must make and file with the registrar a statutory declaration, in the prescribed form, that after making full enquiry they are of the opinion that after making the capital payment: 1985 s 173(3),(4)

(i) there will be no grounds on which the company could be found unable to pay its debts; and

(ii) the company will be able to continue as a going concern, paying its debts as they fall due, for the next 12 months;

(b) the statutory declaration must have annexed to it a report by the auditors of the company to the directors stating that they have enquired into the company's state of affairs, the amount of the permissible capital payment has been properly determined and they are not aware of anything to indicate that the directors' opinion is unreasonable in all the circumstances; 1985 s 173(5)

(c) payments out of capital must be approved by special resolution. The members holding shares to which the resolution relates cannot exercise the voting rights carried by those shares if this exercise would be necessary to enable the resolution to be passed; 1985 s 173(2), 174(2),(3),(5)

(d) the special resolution is ineffective unless the statutory declaration and the auditors' report are available for inspection by members at the meeting at which the resolution is passed; 1985 s 173(4)

(e) the special resolution must be passed within a week of the statutory declaration, and the payment out of capital cannot be earlier than five or later than seven weeks after the date of the resolution; 1985 s 174(1)

(f) within a week following the date of the resolution the company must have published a notice giving specified information in the Gazette, and also either published the same notice in an appropriate national newspaper, or sent the information to each of its creditors; 1985 s 175(1)-(3)

(g) the statutory declaration together with the report of the auditors thereon must be filed with the registrar not later than the day on which the first notice under (f) above is published, and must be available for inspection at the registered office; 1985 s 175(5),(6) (1989 s 143(3))

(h) within five weeks of the date of the resolution any creditor or any member of the company who did not consent to or vote in favour of the payment may apply to the court to have the resolution cancelled. The court may make an order on such terms as it thinks fit, either confirming or cancelling the resolution; and 1985 s 176,177

(i) if a company is wound up within a year of making a purchase out of capital, the directors who signed the statutory declaration and the members from whom the shares were purchased may become liable to meet any insufficiency of assets up to the amount paid out of capital on the purchase. Insolvency Act 1986 s 76

Authorisation of purchases by members

15 The purchase of a company's own shares on a recognised stock exchange must be authorised by a resolution in general meeting: 1985 s 166

(a) specifying the maximum number of shares to be acquired;

(b) determining the maximum and minimum prices that may be paid for those shares; and

(c) specifying a date not more than 18 months in advance upon which the authority is to expire.

6 Where a company wishes to purchase its own shares otherwise than on the Stock Exchange it must obtain a special resolution approving the proposed off-market purchase contract. This approval procedure is subject to the following safeguards: 1985 s 164(1),(2)

(a) the members holding shares to which the resolution relates cannot exercise the voting rights carried by those shares if their exercise would be necessary to enable the resolution to be passed; 1985 s 164(5)

(b) the proposed purchase contract must be available for inspection by the members at the registered office for the 15 days preceding the meeting and at the meeting itself; and 1985 s 164(6)

(c) in the case of public companies, the resolution must specify a date, not more than 18 months in advance, by which the authority conferred will expire. 1985 s 164(4)

Filing and inspection requirements

7 Details of every purchase must be filed with the registrar within 28 days. In addition, companies are required to keep available for public inspection at their registered office details of contracts of purchase of own shares for ten years after each purchase. 1985 s 169(1),(4)

Redeemable shares

8 Companies may issue redeemable equity shares provided that non-redeemable shares are also in issue. The rules that govern the redemption of redeemable shares are similar to those for the purchase of own shares. Companies' articles may include any redemption terms that do not conflict with the requirements of the Act. 1985 s 159(1),(2) 1985 s 160(3)

Financial assistance for acquisition of shares

9 Subject to the exemptions set out below companies cannot give, either directly or indirectly, financial assistance for the purpose of the acquisition of their own shares or the shares of their holding company. This applies to financial assistance given: 1985 s 151

(a) both before or at the same time as the acquisition; or 1985 s 151(1)

(b) by means of reducing or discharging after acquisition a liability incurred by any person for the purpose of the acquisition. 1985 s 151(2)

20 The above provisions do not prohibit: 1985 s 153(4) (1989 s 132)

(a) the lending of money by a company in the ordinary course of its business; or

(b) the provision of financial assistance for an employees' share scheme; or

(c) the provision of financial assistance to enable or facilitate transactions in the company's shares by employees, former employees or their families; or

(d) loans to employees (who are not directors) to enable them to acquire beneficial ownership of fully paid shares in the company;

provided in the case of a public company that it has net assets which are not thereby reduced or the reduction is provided out of distributable profits. 1985 s 154

21 Giving financial assistance by these means would result in a reduction in net assets if the resultant debt were not collected. Author

22 The prohibition does not apply if the company's principal purpose in giving financial assistance is not to give it for the purpose of acquisition of shares, or the assistance given is an incidental part of some larger purpose of the company, and the assistance is given in good faith and in the interests of the company. 1985 s 153(1),(2)

23 Under this provision it seems that if, for example, a subsidiary is acquired and that subsidiary proceeds to guarantee the borrowings of the holding company as part of a prior contractual arrangement (e.g. contained in the holding company's debenture stock trust deed) that subsidiary would not be regarded as providing financial assistance for the purpose of the acquisition of its shares. However, care will be needed in interpreting this provision, and legal advice should be obtained where necessary. Author

24 The above provisions do not prohibit the following, although they may effectively represent financial assistance: 1985 s 153(3)

(a) distribution by lawfully paid dividend or in the course of winding up;

(b) allotment of bonus shares;

(c) reduction of capital confirmed by court order;

(d) the redemption or purchase of own shares (see above); and

(e) a scheme of arrangement between the company and members or creditors under section 425 or an arrangement under section 110 or Part I of the Insolvency Act 1986.

Private companies

25 A private company may give financial assistance for the purchase of its own shares or, if its holding company and any intermediate holding companies are all private companies, its holding company's shares, provided that: 1985 s 155(1),(3)

(a) the net assets of the company are not thereby reduced, or the reduction is provided out of distributable profits; 1985 s 155(2)

(b) before the financial assistance is given the directors of the company make a statutory declaration that immediately after the financial assistance has been given there will be no grounds on which the company would be found unable to pay its debts and the company will be able to pay its debts as they fall due during the next 12 months. Where the shares acquired or to be acquired are those of the holding company the directors of that company and of any intermediate holding company must also make an equivalent statutory declaration; 1985 s 155(6), 156(1)-(3)

(c) the statutory declaration has annexed to it a report by the auditors of the company to the directors stating that they have enquired into the company's state of affairs and that they are not aware of anything to indicate that the directors' opinion is unreasonable in all the circumstances; 1985 s 156(4)

(d) the giving of financial assistance is approved by special resolution in general meeting, passed within one week of the statutory declaration. No special resolution is required where the company is a wholly-owned subsidiary. Where the shares to be acquired are those of the holding company, approval by that company (and any partly owned intermediate holding company) by special resolution in general meeting is also required. The statutory declaration and auditors' report thereon must be available for inspection at the meeting at which the resolution is passed; and 1985 s 155(4),(5) 1985 s 157(1) 1985 s 157(4)

(e) the financial assistance is not given before four weeks after the special resolution (if required) is passed or after eight weeks from the date of the statutory declaration. 1985 s 158

26 The statutory declaration, the auditors' report thereon, and a copy of the special resolution passed (if applicable) must be delivered to the registrar within 15 days after the passing of the resolution or, if no resolution is necessary, after the making of the statutory declaration. 1985 s 156(5)

27 The holders of not less than ten per cent of the company's issued shares or any class thereof who had either not consented to, or not voted in favour of, the special resolution may apply to the court for the resolution to be cancelled. The court may make an order on such terms as it thinks fit either confirming or cancelling the resolution. 1985 s 157(2)

Share premiums

28 Where a company issues shares at a premium (whether for cash or otherwise) the amount or value of the premium must be transferred to a share premium account, except as set out below. 1985 s 130

29 The premium on the allotment of shares shall not be transferred to a share premium account where: 1985 s 130(4)

(a) a company has secured at least a 90 per cent equity holding in another company in an arrangement which provides for the allotment of equity shares by the issuing company to the shareholders in the other company. If the arrangement also provides for the allotment of any shares by the company in return for non-equity shares acquired from the other company, or for the cancellation of any such shares not held by the issuing company, the relief extends to those shares; 1985 s 131

(b) in a group reconstruction, a wholly-owned subsidiary allots shares to its holding company or another wholly-owned subsidiary in consideration for the transfer to it of any non-cash assets, which may include shares, owned by another wholly-owned subsidiary. However, in this case a 'minimum premium value', which is the lesser of the cost or book value of the net assets transferred to the transferor over the nominal value of the shares issued, must be transferred to the share premium account of the issuing company. 1985 s 132

30 However, care is required in interpreting the Act, in particular as to what is meant by 'has secured' and what constitutes 'an arrangement providing for the allotment of equity shares'. Author

31 The Act explicitly provides that where merger relief is available (in accordance with sub-paragraph 29(a) or (b) above), the value of the premium not credited to share premium account may also be disregarded in determining the cost of investment to be carried in the balance sheet. The investment may therefore be included in the investing company's accounts either at the nominal value (together with any minimum premium value under sub-paragraph 29(b) above) of the shares issued plus the fair value of any other consideration, or at its fair value. 1985 s 133(1)

32 If fair value is adopted the difference is usually credited to a merger reserve. There is some uncertainty as to whether that reserve is distributable. It is thought that the reserve becomes distributable only as the investment is sold or as a result of dividends paid out of pre-acquisition profits. A merger reserve will also arise in group accounts when acquisition accounting is used with merger relief. The question of distributability does not arise as dividends are paid by individual companies not by groups. Author SSAP 23:Appendix:2,4

33 The accounting treatment for business combinations is dealt with in Chapter 8.

34 The Secretary of State is empowered to give further relief from the requirements of section 130 or to restrict or modify any relief given by sections 130 to 133. 1985 s 134

Distributable profits

Profits available for distribution

35 No company may make a distribution except out of profits available for the purpose. The definition of profits available for distribution is more restrictive for a public company than for a private company. 1985 s 263(1) Author

Meaning of distribution

36 A distribution means any distribution of the company's assets to its members other than by way of: 1985 s 263(2)

(a) an issue of shares as fully or partly paid bonus shares;

(b) the redemption or purchase of any of the company's own shares out of capital (including the proceeds of a fresh issue) or out of unrealised profits;

(c) a reduction of share capital; or

(d) a distribution on winding up.

Private companies

37 For private companies, profits available for distribution are a company's accumulated realised profits, so far as not previously utilised by distribution or capitalisation, less its accumulated realised losses so far as not previously written off in a reduction or reorganisation of capital. 1985 s 263(3)

38 Taking account of the prudence concept embodied in SSAP 2, the amount of profits legally distributable should, *prima facie*, be the accumulated balance of retained profits shown in the accounts. However, this balance may be subject to adjustment in determining the amount of profits legally distributable in the circumstances described below. Author

Public companies

39 A public company is bound by the rules for private companies but in addition can make a distribution only if at that time its net assets after making the distribution are at least equal to the aggregate of its called up share capital and undistributable reserves (as defined below). The effect of this is that a public company must deduct net unrealised losses (i.e. unrealised losses less unrealised profits) from net realised profits (i.e. realised profits less realised losses) before making a distribution. 1985 s 264(1) Author

40 Undistributable reserves for this purpose are: 1985 s 264(3)

(a) the share premium account;

(b) the capital redemption reserve;

(c) the excess of accumulated unrealised profits (where not previously capitalised, i.e. all forms of capitalisation except transfers to a capital redemption reserve) over accumulated unrealised losses (where not previously written off in a reduction or reorganisation of capital); and

(d) any other reserve which is not distributable (e.g. because of provisions in the memorandum or articles).

Realised profits and losses

41 The Act states that only profits 'realised' at the balance sheet date can be included in the profit and loss account. 'Realised profits' and 'realised losses' are stated to be profits or losses determined in accordance with accounting principles generally accepted for the determination of realised profits or losses. Thus profits or losses included in the profit and loss account in accordance with accounting standards will generally be realised profits or losses. 1985 4 sch 12 1985 s 262(3) (1989 s 22) Author

42 The recognition of profit only when realised, either in the form of cash or other assets the ultimate cash realisation of which can be assessed with reasonable certainty, is embodied in the prudence concept in SSAP 2. Particular care is required in determining whether an intra-group sale of an asset results in a realised profit. SSAP 2:14(d)

43 For the purpose of calculating realised profits, where a company makes a distribution of, or the distribution includes, any non-cash asset and any part of the book value of that asset represents an unrealised profit, the act of distribution will be regarded as an act of realisation and that profit must be treated as a realised profit. 1985 s 276

44 A provision must be treated as a realised loss unless it is in respect of a diminution in value of a fixed asset appearing on a revaluation of all the fixed assets or of all the fixed assets other than goodwill (see below). A provision is defined in schedule 4 and comprises provisions for depreciation and diminution in value of assets and provisions for liabilities or losses. 1985 s 275(1) 1985 4 sch 88,89

45 Development costs, even if carried forward as an asset must be treated as a realised loss. This does not apply if: 1985 s 269

(a) there are special circumstances justifying the directors in deciding that the amount should not be treated as a realised loss (see Chapter 5): and

(b) the note to the accounts giving reasons for including development costs as an asset (required by paragraph 20 of schedule 4) states that the asset is not to be treated as a realised loss and explains the circumstances relied upon to justify the decision of the directors to that effect.

Revaluation of fixed assets

Revaluation reserve

46 The Act requires any profit or loss arising on the revaluation of an asset to be accounted for in a revaluation reserve, to be disclosed separately in the accounts. The revaluation reserve must be reduced to the extent that the amounts transferred to it are no longer necessary for the purposes of the valuation method used (e.g. if major fixed assets are disposed of or if for any reason current cost or market value declines, perhaps as a result of technological advance). However, an amount may only be transferred from the revaluation reserve: 1985 4 sch 34 (1989 1 sch 6) Author 1985 4 sch 34(3) (1989 1 sch 6)

(a) to the profit and loss account if the amount was previously charged to that account or if it represents a realised profit; or

(c) on capitalisation, i.e. applying it in wholly or partly paying up unissued shares in the company to be allotted to members as fully or partly paid shares.

The revaluation reserve may not be used for any other purpose. In particular, goodwill may not be written off against it. Author

Deficits on revaluation of fixed assets

47 Where certain fixed assets or a class or classes of fixed assets are revalued it would seem that under section 275(1) individual deficits are provisions, and therefore realised losses (unless offsetting a previous unrealised surplus on the same asset) and individual surpluses would be unrealised profits. However, as noted above this is not the case when a revaluation of all the fixed assets (or all the fixed assets except goodwill) has taken place. In these circumstances individual deficits should be treated as unrealised in the same way as individual surpluses against which they can be set off. As noted above, a private company does not have to make good net unrealised losses before making distribution, and it would therefore seem to be the intention of the Act to treat private companies more liberally than public companies. The above comments are, however, subject to the following two provisos: Author 1985 s 275(1) Author

(a) where on a revaluation of all the fixed assets there are surpluses and deficits leading to a net deficit, the law as outlined above would appear to provide that such a deficit is unrealised, whether or not charged in the profit and loss account, and on that basis (for a private company) would not restrict the ability to pay dividends. However,

   (i) the net deficit should be charged in the profit and loss account (to the extent that it is not covered by revaluation surpluses previously recognised on any of the assets concerned); and

   (ii) it would be commercially imprudent to disregard the net deficit in determining dividend policy;

(b) a provision for permanent diminution in the value of fixed assets required by paragraph 19(2) of schedule 4 will not normally arise merely as a result of the revaluation of fixed assets. As such it should be regarded as a realised loss and charged to the profit and loss account. Such treatment is in any event regarded as desirable on the grounds of accounting prudence.

48 A revaluation of all the fixed assets is deemed to have taken place in this context if the directors give consideration to the value of all fixed assets not actually revalued provided: 1985 s 275(4)-(6)

(a) they are satisfied that the aggregate value of those fixed assets is not less than their aggregate book value in the accounts; and

(b) the relevant accounts refer to the directors' valuation in the notes.

49 This provision that the directors may consider the value of all of those fixed assets which are not included in the accounts at a valuation is significant. Individual valuation deficits recognised in the accounts will be treated as unrealised in these circumstances. For private companies this will ensure that the amount of distributable profits is not thereby reduced and for public companies that distributable profits will only be reduced if unrealised losses exceed unrealised profits. Thus, where the inclusion of certain fixed assets in the accounts at a valuation is proposed it would seem advantageous for the directors to consider the value of all fixed assets and make the necessary disclosure. Author

Depreciation on revalued fixed assets

50 If a fixed asset is revalued, written up in the balance sheet and subsequently depreciated, the depreciation charge relating to the revaluation surplus element will not be taken to reduce distributable profits. This may require companies to keep memorandum records of the accumulated depreciation on the revaluation element or to transfer corresponding amounts from the revaluation reserve to the profit and loss account as a movement on reserves. The difference between historical cost depreciation and depreciation calculated on the revalued amount will need to be shown in the note of historical cost profits and losses (see Chapter 3). 1985 s 275(2) Author

Uncertainty as to profits available

51 Where there is no record of the original cost of an asset, the earliest record of 'value' can be assumed to be 'cost' and the calculation of the surplus may be based on that figure. 1985 s 275(3)

Foreign currency translation

52 Exchange gains and losses arising on settled transactions and on unsettled short-term monetary transactions taken to profit and loss account are realised profits and losses. Exchange gains on unsettled long-term monetary items are unrealised profits and thus not available for distribution. Schedule 4 permits SSAP 20:65 Author

departures from the accounting principle only to include realised profits in the profit and loss account if it appears to the directors that there are special reasons for doing so, provided certain disclosures are made. The need to give a true and fair view of the results by including both gains and losses on long-term monetary items constitutes a special reason for departure from an accounting principle, although it should be noted that in the case of gains it is necessary to consider on the grounds of prudence whether the amount of gains to be recognised in the profit and loss account should be restricted. Companies that prepare accounts in accordance with schedule 4 which include unrealised exchange gains in the profit and loss account, must disclose the particulars, the reasons and the effects of the departure in a note to the accounts (see Chapter 3). 1985 4 sch 15

53 Where a company has used foreign currency borrowings to finance, or provide a hedge against, its foreign equity investments, SSAP 20 permits, subject to certain conditions, the equity investments to be denominated in the appropriate foreign currencies with exchange differences taken to reserves, against which the exchange gains or losses on the foreign currency borrowings should be offset as a reserve movement. Doubts have been expressed as to whether losses on foreign currency borrowings taken to reserves are realised losses which should be taken into account in determining the amount of profits available for distribution. It has been suggested that such losses come within the definition of a provision contained in the Act and these would be realised losses. However, the reality is that the hedging is designed to avoid the creation of a loss and therefore the exchange losses taken to reserves merely offset exchange profits on the investment and should not be regarded as a provision (nor a realised loss). As the matter is not free from doubt companies may have to take legal advice where it is necessary to take account of losses on hedges in determining whether a distribution is permitted. SSAP 20:51 Author

Goodwill

54 Distributions are made from profits of individual companies, not by groups, and hence the elimination of goodwill arising on consolidation has no effect on the distributable profits of the company. If however a provision is made by the holding company against the investment in the subsidiary company this would constitute a realised loss, unless the provision is not for a permanent diminution in value and it arises on a revaluation of all fixed assets (see paragraphs 47 to 49). SSAP 22: Appendix 2:1

55 If goodwill arises in the accounts of an individual company the requirement of paragraph 21 of schedule 4 to the Act means that elimination of the goodwill from the balance sheet over a period not exceeding its useful economic life constitutes a realised loss. If the goodwill is eliminated immediately on acquisition as a matter of accounting policy in accordance with SSAP 22, rather than because of an actual diminution in value, realised reserves need not be reduced immediately. If the elimination is made against SSAP 22: Appendix 2:2

an unrealised reserve a transfer should be made each year to realised reserves so as to reduce realised reserves on a systematic basis in the same way as if goodwill is amortised. If goodwill is eliminated immediately on acquisition because it is considered to have suffered an actual diminution in value, this will constitute a realised loss. If goodwill is amortised over its useful economic life each annual charge to profit and loss account will constitute a realised loss.

56 When negative goodwill arises in the accounts of an individual company it should be credited initially to an unrealised reserve, from which it may be transferred to realised reserves in line with the depreciation or realisation of the assets acquired in the business combination that gave rise to the negative goodwill in question. SSAP 22: Appendix 2:3

Paying up issued shares

57 An unrealised profit of a company must not be applied in paying up debentures or unpaid amounts on its issued shares. 1985 s 263(4)

Relevant accounts

58 In order to calculate whether a company can make a distribution, the relevant accounts must be referred to. These are: 1985 s 270

(a) the latest accounts laid before a general meeting; or

(b) if basing the calculation only on (a) above would lead to a contravention of the Act, interim accounts 'to enable reasonable judgement to be made as to the amounts of the relevant items'; or

(c) during a company's first accounting period, initial accounts to enable reasonable judgement to be made as to the amounts of the relevant items. There are further requirements in relation to the interim and initial accounts of a public company (see paragraphs 60 and 61 below).

59 Where the accounts used are the latest annual accounts, they must have been properly prepared (i.e. to give a true and fair view) or have been so prepared subject only to matters which are not material to the question of whether the distribution can be made, and must have been audited. If the audit report was qualified, the auditor must have stated in writing (either at the time or subsequently) whether the subject of the qualification is material for the purposes of determining whether the distribution proposed or to be proposed would contravene the Act. A copy of such a statement must have been laid before the company in general meeting. 1985 s 271

60 For a public company only, the interim accounts referred to above must also be 'properly prepared' or have been so prepared subject only to matters which are not material to the question of whether the distribution can be made. They must be in the English language and a copy should be delivered to the registrar. They do not have to be audited. 1985 s 272

61 The initial accounts of a public company must also have been properly prepared or have been so prepared subject only to matters which are not material to the question of whether the distribution can be made. The auditors must have reported on whether the initial accounts were properly prepared and, if their report was qualified, state whether the qualification is material for determining whether the distribution would contravene the Act. The accounts and auditors' report must also be translated into English if necessary and be delivered to the registrar. 1985 s 273

Memorandum and Articles

62 Where a company's memorandum or articles of association contain distribution restrictions more rigorous than those in the Act, such further restrictions still stand. 1985 s 281

Investment companies

63 An 'investment company', which must be a public company, may in addition to the requirements described above make a distribution out of its accumulated retained revenue profits less its accumulated revenue losses. The effect is that an investment company does not have to make good its realised or unrealised capital losses before making a distribution, provided that at the time of the further distribution its assets at least equal one and a half times its aggregate liabilities and the distribution does not reduce the assets below this amount. 1985 s 265,266

Appendix 1

Balance Sheet and Profit and Loss Account Formats

This appendix reproduces the balance sheet and profit and loss account formats set out in the schedule 4 to the Companies Act 1985. The formats apply, with certain amendments to group accounts (Chapter 8) as well as to the accounts of individual companies. Small companies (as defined in Chapter 9) may apply all or any of the modifications to the balance sheet formats, permitted in the way as indicated in italics below (SI 1992 No 2452). The modifications also apply to the group accounts where a small company prepares them. The notes provided at the end of the balance sheet and profit and loss account formats explain the further amendments required for consolidated accounts and are referred to from each format. The rules relating to the selection and modification of these formats are explained in Chapter 3.

Balance Sheet Format I

A Called up share capital not paid

B Fixed assets

I Intangible assets
1 Development costs
2 Concessions, patents, licences, trade marks and similar rights and assets
3 Goodwill
4 Payments on account

(Small companies may show goodwill as item B I 1 and combine items 1, 2 and 4 under a new item B I 2 'Other intangible assets'.)

II Tangible assets
1 Land and buildings
2 Plant and machinery
3 Fixtures, fittings, tools and equipment
4 Payments on account and assets in course of construction

(Small companies may combine items 2, 3 and 4 under a new item B II 2 'Plant and machinery etc'.)

III Investment
1 Shares in group undertakings
2 Loans to group undertakings
3 Participating interests (excluding group undertakings) **(see note 1)**
4 Loans to undertakings in which the company has a participating interest
5 Other investments other than loans
6 Other loans
7 Own shares

(Small companies may combine:
items 1 and 3 under a new item B III 1 'Shares in group undertakings and participating interests' **(see note 2)**;
items 2 and 4 under a new item B III 2 'Loans to group undertakings and undertakings in which the company has a participating interest'; and
items 6 and 7 under a new item B III 4 'Others', to be shown after new item B III 3 (item 5 above).)

C Current assets

I Stocks
1 Raw materials and consumables
2 Work in progress
3 Finished goods and goods for resale
4 Payments on account

(Small companies may combine items 1, 2 and 3 under a new item C I 1 'Stocks', to be shown before new item C I 2 (item 4 above).)

II Debtors
1 Trade debtors
2 Amounts owed by group undertakings
3 Amounts owed by undertakings in which the company has a participating interest
4 Other debtors
5 Called up share capital not paid
6 Prepayments and accrued income

(Small companies may combine:
items 2 and 3 under a new item C II 2 'Amounts owed by group undertakings and undertakings in which the company has a participating interest'; and
items 4, 5 and 6 under a new item C II 3 'Others'.) **(see note 3).**

III Investments
1 Shares in group undertakings
2 Own shares
3 Other investments

(Small companies may combine items 2 and 3 under a new item C III 2 'Other investments'.)

IV Cash at bank and in hand

D Prepayments and accrued income

E **Creditors: amounts falling due within one year**

1 Debenture loans
2 Bank loans and overdrafts
3 Payments received on account
4 Trade creditors
5 Bills of exchange payable
6 Amounts owed to group undertakings
7 Amounts owed to undertakings in which the company has a participating interest
8 Other creditors including taxation and social security
9 Accruals and deferred income

(Small companies may combine:
items 6 and 7 under a new item E 3 'Amounts owed to group undertakings and undertakings in which the company has a participating interest', to be shown after new item E 1 (item 2 above) and new item E 2 (item 4 above); and
items 1, 3, 5, 8 and 9 under a new item E 4 'Other creditors'.) **(see note 4).**

F **Net current assets (liabilities)**

G **Total assets less current liabilities**

H **Creditors: amounts falling due after more than one year**

1 Debenture loans
2 Bank loans and overdrafts
3 Payments received on account
4 Trade creditors
5 Bills of exchange payable
6 Amounts owed to group undertakings
7 Amounts owed to undertakings in which the company has a participating interest
8 Other creditors including taxation and social security
9 Accruals and deferred income

(Small companies may combine:
items 6 and 7 under a new item H 3 'Amounts owed to group undertakings and undertakings in which the company has a participating interest', to be shown after new item H 1 (item 2 above) and new item H 2 (item 4 above); and
items 1, 3, 5, 8 and 9 under a new item H 4 'Other creditors'.) **(see note 4).**

I **Provisions for liabilities and charges**

1 Pensions and similar obligations
2 Taxation, including deferred taxation
3 Other provisions

(Small companies need not show items 1, 2 and 3 as sub-items of item I.)

J **Accruals and deferred income**

Minority interests (see note 5)

K Capital and reserves

I Called up share capital

II Share premium account

III Revaluation reserve

IV Other reserves
1 Capital redemption reserve
2 Reserve for own shares
3 Reserves provided for by the articles of association
4 Other reserves

(Small companies need not show items IV (1 to 4) as sub-items of item K IV.)

V Profit and loss account

Minority interests (see note 5)

Balance Sheet Format 2

ASSETS

A Called up share capital not paid

B Fixed assets

I Intangible assets
  1 Development costs
  2 Concessions, patents, licences, trade marks and similar rights and assets
  3 Goodwill
  4 Payments on account

(Small companies may show goodwill as item B I 1 and combine items 1, 2 and 4 under a new item B I 2 'Other intangible assets'.)

II Tangible assets
  1 Land and buildings
  2 Plant and machinery
  3 Fixtures, fittings, tools and equipment
  4 Payments on account and assets in course of construction

(Small companies may combine items 2, 3 and 4 under a new item B II 2 'Plant and machinery etc'.)

III Investments
  1 Shares in group undertakings
  2 Loans to group undertakings
  3 Participating interests (excluding group undertakings) (1)
  4 Loans to undertakings in which the company has a participating interest
  5 Other investments other than loans
  6 Other loans
  7 Own shares

(Small companies may combine:
items 1 and 3 under a new item B III 1 'Shares in group undertakings and participating interests' **(see note 2)**;
items 2 and 4 under a new item B III 2 'Loans to group undertakings and undertakings in which the company has a participating interest'; and
items 6 and 7 under a new item B III 4 'Others', to be shown after new item B III 3 (item 5 above).)

C Current assets

I Stocks
  1 Raw materials and consumables
  2 Work in progress
  3 Finished goods and goods for resale
  4 Payments on account

(Small companies may combine items 1, 2 and 3 under a new item C I 1 'Stocks', to be shown before new item C I 2 (item 4 above).)

II Debtors
1 Trade debtors
2 Amounts owed by group undertakings
3 Amounts owed by undertakings in which the company has a participating interest
4 Other debtors
5 Called up share capital not paid
6 Prepayments and accrued income

(Small companies may combine:
items 2 and 3 under a new item C II 2 'Amounts owed by group undertakings and undertakings in which the company has a participating interest'; and
items 4, 5 and 6 under a new item C II 3 'Others'.) **(see note 3).**

III Investments
1 Share in group undertakings
2 Own shares
3 Other investments

(Small companies may combine items 2 and 3 under a new item C III 2 'Other investments'.)

IV Cash at bank and in hand

Prepayments and accrued income

LIABILITIES

Capital and reserves

I Called up share capital

II Share premium account

III Revaluation reserve

IV Other reserves
1 Capital redemption reserve
2 Reserve for own shares
3 Reserves provided for by the articles of association
4 Other reserves

(Small companies need not show items IV (1 to 4) as sub-items of item A IV.)

V Profit and loss account

Minority interests (see note 5)

B Provisions for liabilities and charges

1 Pensions and similar obligations
2 Taxation including deferred taxation
3 Other provisions

(Small companies need not show items 1, 2 and 3 as sub-items of item B.)

C Creditors

1 Debenture loans
2 Bank loans and overdraft
3 Payments received on account
4 Trade creditors
5 Bills of exchange payable
6 Amounts owed to group undertakings
7 Amounts owed to undertakings in which the company has a participating interest
8 Other creditors including taxation and social security
9 Accruals and deferred income

(Small companies may combine:
items 6 and 7 under a new item C 3 'Amounts owed to group undertakings and undertakings in which the company has a participating interest', to be shown after new item C 1 (item 2 above) and new item C 2 (item 4 above); and
items 1, 3, 5, 8 and 9 under a new item C 4 'Other creditors'.) **(see note 4).**

D Accruals and deferred income

Notes

(1) In consolidated accounts, this item to be replaced by two items:
Interests in associated undertakings;
Other participating interests.

(2) In consolidated accounts, small companies cannot combine shares in group undertakings (item B III 1) with participating interests (item B III 3). In consolidated accounts, item B III 3 is replaced by the two items mentioned in note 1 above.

(3) In the case of both Formats 1 and 2, small companies need not comply with the requirements to show the amount falling due after more than one year separately for each item included under debtors (see 4 Sch formats, Note 5) if it discloses in the notes to the accounts the aggregate amount included under 'Debtors' (items CII 1 to 6) falling due after more than one year.

(4) In the case of Format 2, small companies need not comply with the requirements to show separately the amounts falling due within one year and after one year for each of the items C 1 to 9 above (see 4 sch formats, Note 13) if it discloses in the notes to the accounts the aggregate amount included under 'Creditors' (Item C under Liabilities) falling due within one year and the aggregate amount falling due after one year.

(5) In consolidated accounts, this item is to be treated as one to which a letter is assigned.

Profit and Loss Account Format 1

1 Turnover
2 Cost of sales
3 Gross profit or loss
4 Distribution costs
5 Administration costs
6 Other operating income
7 Income from shares in group undertakings
8 Income from participating interests (excluding group undertakings) **(see note 1)**
9 Income from other fixed asset investments
10 Other interest receivable and similar income
11 Amounts written off investments
12 Interest payable and similar charges
13 Tax on profit or loss on ordinary activities
14 Profit or loss on ordinary activities after taxation
Minority interests **(see note 2)**
15 Extraordinary income
16 Extraordinary charges
17 Extraordinary profit or loss
18 Tax on extraordinary profit or loss
Minority interests **(see note 2)**
19 Other taxes not shown under the above items
20 Profit or loss for the financial year

Profit and Loss Account Format 2

1 Turnover
2 Change in stocks of finished goods and work in progress
3 Own work capitalised
4 Other operating income
5 (a) Raw materials and consumables
(b) Other external charges
6 Staff costs:
7 (a) Deprecation and other amounts written off tangible and intangible fixed assets
(b) Exceptional amounts written off current assets
8 Other operating charges
9 Income from shares in group undertakings
10 Income from participating interests (excluding group undertakings) **(see note 1)**
11 Income from other fixed asset investments
12 Other interest receivable and similar income
13 Amounts written off investments
14 Interest payable and similar charges
15 Tax on profit or loss on ordinary activities
16 Profit or loss on ordinary activities after taxation
Minority interests **(see note 2)**
17 Extraordinary income
18 Extraordinary charges
19 Extraordinary profit or loss
Minority interests **(see note 2)**
21 Other taxes not shown under the above items
22 Profit or loss for the financial year

Profit and Loss Account Format 3

A Charges

1 Cost of sales
2 Distribution costs
3 Administrative expenses
4 Amounts written off investments
5 Interest payable and similar charges
6 Tax on profit or loss on ordinary activities
7 Profit or loss on ordinary activities
Minority interests **(see note 2)**
8 Extraordinary charges
9 Tax on extraordinary profit or loss
10 Other taxes not shown under the above items
11 Profit for the financial year

B Income

1 Turnover
2 Other operating income
3 Income from shares in group undertakings
4 Income from participating interests (excluding group undertakings) **(see note 1)**
5 Income from other fixed asset investments
6 Other interest receivable and similar income
7 Profit or loss on ordinary activities after taxation
8 Extraordinary income
Minority interests **(see note 2)**
9 Loss for the financial year

Profit and Loss Format 4

A Charges

1 Reduction in stock of finished goods and in work in progress
2 (a) Raw materials and consumables
(b) Other external charges
3 Staff costs:
(a) Wages and Salaries
(b) Social security costs
(c) Other pension costs
4 (a) Depreciation and other amounts written off tangible and intangible fixed assets
(b) Exceptional amounts written off current assets
5 Other operating charges
6 Amounts written off investments
7 Interest payable and similar charges
8 Tax on profit or loss on ordinary activities
9 Profit or loss on ordinary activities after taxation
Minority interests **(see note 2)**
10 Extraordinary charges
11 Tax on extraordinary profit or loss
Minority interests **(see note 2)**
12 Other taxes not shown under the above items
13 Profit for the financial year

B Income

1 Turnover
2 Increase in stocks of finished goods and in work in progress
3 Own work capitalised
4 Other operating income
5 Income from shares in group undertakings
6 Income from participating interests (excluding group undertakings) **(see note 1)**
7 Income from other fixed asset investments
8 Other interest receivable and similar income
9 Profit or loss on ordinary activities after taxation
Minority interests **(see note 2)**
10 Extraordinary income
Minority interests **(see note 2)**
11 Loss for the financial year

Notes

(1) In consolidated accounts, this item to be replaced by two items:
Income from interests in associated undertakings
Income from other participating interests

(2) In consolidated accounts, this item is to be treated as one to which an Arabic number is assigned.

ppendix 2

cimen annual report

specimen annual report that follows includes the consolidated financial statements of the GAAP UK plc group of panies. The annual report has been prepared for illustrative purposes only and shows the disclosures and formats that ht be expected for a group of this size which prepares its financial statements in accordance with Schedule 4 and edule 4A to the Companies Act 1985 as amended by the Companies Act 1989.

AP UK plc is a fictitious listed UK company. It has a number of UK and overseas investments including subsidiaries, ciates and a joint venture.

intention is not to show all conceivable disclosures in this annual report and it should not, therefore, be used as a cklist. The financial statements include many of the disclosure requirements contained in current Financial Reporting dards, Statements of Standard Accounting Practice, Urgent Issues Task Force Abstracts and The International Stock hange's Continuing Obligations for listed companies (the Yellow Book). Proposals included in exposure drafts are not standard practice and have therefore not been reflected in these financial statements. FRS 3 'Reporting financial ormance' applies to accounting periods ending on or after 22 June 1993 and the Accounting Standards Board mmended it's early adoption. GAAP UK plc includes the provisions of FRS 3.

AP UK plc also includes certain provisions from the Cadbury code. That code will apply from July 1993, but before many companies will opt to comply with the code as far as possible. GAAP UK plc complies where possible with code, but does not include examples of, or deal with, the statement by the directors of compliance with the code, the ctiveness of internal controls and the statement on going concern. Nor does it include a more general statement on orate governance which is encouraged by Cadbury, but would be outside the scope of the audited financial statements. dance on these aspects of the Cadbury code is still awaited from the Accountancy Profession and representatives of arers of accounts.

suggested disclosure throughout is intended for guidance only and would not necessarily be applicable to all groups all companies. The names of the undertakings included in the annual reports are used for illustration only and any mblance to any existing undertaking is not intended.

reviations used

bury code	=	The Cadbury committee's code of best practice
bury para	=	Paragraph of the report of the Cadbury committee on the financial aspects of corporate governance
	=	The International Stock Exchange's Continuing Obligations for listed companies
P date	=	Financial Reporting Review Panel press release

Appendix 2

FRS	=	Financial Reporting Standards
SSAP	=	Statements of Standard Accounting Practice
s	=	Section of the Companies Act 1985 (as amended by the Companies Act 1989)
Sch	=	Schedule to the Companies Act 1985 (as amended by the Companies Act 1989) (4 Sch 85 Schedule 4, paragraph 85)
UITF Abs	=	Urgent Issues Task Force Abstract

GAAP UK plc

Specimen annual report

for the year ended 31 December 1992

Registered no: xxyyzz

Annual report for the year ended 31 December 1992

* Not reproduced as there are no statutory or other requirements governing the contents.

Directors and advisers

Executive directors

R Graham OBE, MBA *
Chairman

P Jones MA
Managing Director

G Wallace BSc
Marketing

F James BA, FCA
Finance

A Edwards
Distribution

Non-executive directors

Lord Callender † *

N Jagger OBE, LLB † *

A Cartwright FCA † *

Secretary and registered office

R Brian FCIS
GAAP Towers
2 The Square
LONDON
EC4Y 2DE

Registrars

Bank plc
Registrar's Department
5 The Promenade
WESTBURY-ON-SEA
Wessex
WE5 2NU

Registered Auditors

Coopers & Lybrand
1 Embankment Place
LONDON
WC2N 6NN

Solicitors

Campbell & Co
59 Temple Place
LONDON
WC1N 3PR

Bankers

Bank plc

Stockbrokers

Brokers & Co

Cadbury paras 4.35(b), 4.42, code 3.3, 4.3

† member of audit committee
* member of remuneration committee

Financial highlights

Results	1992 £'000	1991 as restated £'000
Turnover (continuing operations)	**63,590**	50,704
Operating profit (continuing operations)	**3,408**	3,176
Profit/(loss) for the financial year	**2,232**	(5,439)
Dividends	**1,043**	939
Total recognised gains and losses	**2,911**	(5,357)
Key ratios		
Operating margin (continuing operations)	**5.4%**	6.3%
Return on capital employed*	**9.8%**	(12.1)%
Earnings/(loss) per share	**5.46p**	(14.21)p
Adjusted earnings per share	**4.95p**	4.06p
Dividends per share	**2.46p**	2.25p

* Calculated as profit before interest and tax divided by net operating assets as defined in note 2 to the financial statements.

Directors' report
for the year ended 31 December 1992

s 234(1) The directors present their report and the audited financial statements for the year ended 31 December 1992.

Principal activities

The consolidated profit and loss account for the year is set out on page [9].

s 234(2) The principal activities of the group are unchanged from last year, and are the manufacture of solid state electronics for the television, radio and medical equipment industries, moulded plastics for packing materials, prefabricated building sections, and domestic appliances. The group is also involved in the construction industry.

Review of business

s 234(1)(a),(3)
7 Sch 6(b) Both the level of business and the year end financial position remain satisfactory, and the directors expect that the present level of activity will be sustained for the foreseeable future.

On 1 March 1992 the company acquired the whole of the issued share capital of Dickens Limited, manufacturers of building materials. This has been accounted for as an acquisition in accordance with Statement of Standard Accounting Practice No 23. Details of the net assets acquired and consideration paid are set out in note 31 to the financial statements.

FRS 3

Changes in presentation of the financial statements

Following the introduction of Financial Reporting Standard No 3, 'Reporting Financial Performance', the following changes in the presentation of the financial statements have been made to conform with the new requirements.

(a) Turnover and operating profit have been analysed between continuing and discontinued operations, with results from additions during the year shown separately under continuing operations.

(b) Items previously treated as extraordinary have been reclassified as exceptional.

(c) A statement of total recognised gains and losses has been presented together with a reconciliation of movements in shareholders' funds.

(d) A note of historical cost profits and losses has been presented immediately following the statement of total recognised gains and losses in order to show the profits calculated on a pure historical cost basis.

Dividends and transfers to reserves

The directors have declared or now recommend the following dividends in respect of the year ended 31 December 1992:

		£'000	£'000
s 234(1)(b)	Preference dividends paid		67
	Ordinary dividends:		
	Interim paid	299	
	Final proposed	677	
		—	976
			1,043

s 234(1)(b) After payment of the above dividends £1,189,000 of the profit for the financial year will be transferred to the group's reserves.

Post balance sheet events

s 234(3) 7 Sch 6(a) SSAP 17 paras 23, 24 In line with the group's policy of long-term expansion and diversification through the acquisition of soundly based companies, the board made an offer of £5 million on 26 February 1993 for the whole of the issued share capital of Hardy Limited. The offer is to be financed by a long-term secured loan.

Hardy Limited supplies high technology equipment to the offshore oil and gas industries, and in the year to 31 December 1992 made a profit before taxation of £370,000 on a turnover of £6 million.

On 1 February 1993, a subsidiary's factory was badly damaged by fire. The costs of repair are not expected to exceed insurance proceeds.

Group research and development activities

s 234(3) 7 Sch 6(3) The group is committed to research and development activities in order to secure its position as market leader in sectors of the electronic components and domestic appliance markets. In addition to the expenditure set out in note 18 to the financial statements, £147,000 (1991: £207,000) of costs attributable to pure and applied research have been written off in the year.

Directors

s 234(2) The directors of the company at 31 December 1992, all of whom have been directors for the whole of the year ended on that date, are listed on page [1].

Mr D Scott, who was a director at 1 January 1992, resigned on 30 June 1992 on his retirement from the business.

CO 21(t)

Biographical details of the independent non-executive directors are shown below:

Lord Callender was for many years a Member of Parliament before being created a life peer in 1988. He has served on many parliamentary committees covering matters concerning the electronics industry.

Cadbury para 4.12 (not part of code)

Mrs N Jagger was a partner in Campbell & Co who are the company's solicitors. Before her retirement in 1989 she specialised in consumer law. She has written an authoritative book on health and safety regulations in the work place.

Mr A Cartwright was, until his recent retirement, a senior partner in a merchant bank. In 1989 he left the bank to form his own consulting firm. He holds a number of other non-executive directorships.

Custom CO 42 (c)

In accordance with the articles of association, Mr G Wallace retires by rotation and, being eligible, offers himself for re-election. Mr G Wallace has a service contract with the company that expires on 31 July 1994.

CO 21 (k)

There were no contracts of significance subsisting during or at the end of the financial year in which a director of the company was materially interested.

Directors' interests

s 234(3) 7 Sch 2,2A, 2B CO 21(h)

The interests of the directors in the shares of the company and other group companies at 31 December 1992, together with their interests at 1 January 1992 and movements in their share options in the year were:

	Shares		**Share options**			
	1 January	**31 December**	1 January	Granted	Exercised	**31 December**
The company						
(ordinary shares 25p each)						
R Graham	*86,000	***86,000**	5,000	10,000	-	**15,000**
P Jones	87,000	**95,700**	-	-	-	-
G Wallace	-	-	-	5,000	-	**5,000**
F James	750	**3,000**	-	-	-	-
A Edwards	-	**2,000**	-	-	-	-
Lord Callender	5,000	**5,000**	-	-	-	-
Austen Limited						
(ordinary shares £1 each)						
F James	10,000	**10,000**	-	-	-	-
Trollope plc						
(preference shares 50p each)						
A Cartwright	-	**5,000**	-	-	-	-

CO 21 (h)

* Includes 20,000 shares in which R Graham has a non-beneficial interest.

s 234(3)
7 Sch 2A

Mrs N Jagger was interested in £500,000 of the company's debenture loan stock at 31 December 1992 and 1 January 1992.

Apart from the interests disclosed above no directors were interested at any time in the year in the share capital or loan stock of the company or other group companies.

CO 21 (h)

There has been no change in the interests set out above between 31 December 1992 and 1 March 1993.

Changes in fixed assets

s 243(3)
7 Sch 1(1)(2)

The movements in fixed assets during the year, including the revaluation of properties, are set out in notes 18 to 20 to the financial statements. An extensive programme of plant replacement has been undertaken during the year. Land and buildings in Derby, no longer required, have been sold. In view of the policy of revaluing properties annually, in the opinion of the directors there was no significant difference between market and book values of property at 31 December 1992.

Substantial shareholdings

CO 21(i)

With the exception of the interest of Trollope plc (see note 42 to the financial statements), the directors have not been advised of any individual interest, or group of interests, held by persons acting together, which at 1 March 1993 exceeds 3% of the company's issue share capital.

Contracts of significance with corporate substantial shareholders

CO 21(l)

GAAP UK plc has a contract with Trollope plc for the supply of the group's research and development. During 1992 the total amounts payable to Trollope plc in this respect amounted to £382,000 (1991: £430,000). The contract is renewable annually.

Charitable and political contributions

s 234(3)
7 Sch 3-5

The contributions made by the group during the year for political and charitable purposes were:

	£
For political purposes - Warmwind Party	250
For charitable purposes	4,320
	£4,570

Employees

7 Sch 11 The group's policy is to consult and discuss with employees, through unions, staff councils and at meetings, matters likely to affect employees' interests.

Information on matters of concern to employees is given through information bulletins and reports (including an annual Employee Report) which seek to achieve a common awareness on the part of all employees of the financial and economic factors affecting the group's performance.

There is no employee share scheme at present, but the directors are considering the introduction of such a scheme as a means of further encouraging the involvement of employees in the group's performance.

7 Sch 9 The group's policy is to recruit disabled workers for those vacancies that they are able to fill. All necessary assistance with initial training courses is given. Once employed, a career plan is developed so as to ensure suitable opportunities for each disabled person. Arrangements are made, wherever possible, for retraining employees who become disabled, to enable them to perform work identified as appropriate to their aptitudes and abilities.

Insurance of directors

7 Sch 5A
s 310(3)(a) The group maintains insurance for GAAP UK plc's directors in respect of their duties as directors of the group.

Taxation status

CO 21(j) The company was not a close company within the provisions of the Income and Corporation Taxes Act 1988 and this position has not changed since the end of the financial year.

Auditors

Custom A resolution to reappoint the auditors, Coopers & Lybrand, will be proposed at the annual general meeting.

s 234 A **By order of the board**

s 234A(2) **R Brian**
Company secretary
6 March 1993

Cadbury para 4.28, code 4.4

Directors' responsibility

The directors are required by UK company law to prepare financial statements for each financial year which give a true and fair view of the state of affairs of the group as at the end of the financial year and of the profit or loss for that period. In preparing the financial statements, appropriate accounting policies have been used and applied consistently, and reasonable and prudent judgements and estimates have been made. Applicable accounting standards have been followed with the exception of the material departure disclosed and explained in note 1 to the accounts. The directors are responsible for maintaining adequate accounting records, for safeguarding the assets of the group, and for preventing and detecting fraud and other irregularities.

By order of the board

R Brian
Company secretary
6 March 1993

Report of the auditors to the members of GAAP UK plc

We have audited the financial statements on pages [9] to [48] in accordance with Auditing Standards.

In our opinion the financial statements give a true and fair view of the state of affairs of the company and the group at 31 December 1992 and of the profit, total recognised gains and cash flows of the group for the year then ended and have been properly prepared in accordance with the Companies Act 1985.

Coopers & Lybrand
Chartered Accountants and Registered Auditors
London
6 March 1993

Consolidated profit and loss account for the year ended 31 December 1992

		Notes	1992 £'000	1991 as restated £'000
s 227(2)(b) 4 Sch Format 1				
	Turnover	2,3		
FRS 3 para 14, 30	Continuing operations		**60,046**	50,704
FRS 3 para 16	Acquisitions		**3,544**	-
			63,590	50,704
FRS 3 para 17	Discontinued operations		**2,130**	3,120
			65,720	53,824
4 Sch Note 14	Cost of sales	4	**(45,083)**	(37,293)
FRS 3 para 19	Exceptional cost of sales	5	**(1,550)**	-
	Gross profit	4	**19,087**	16,531
4 Sch 3(4)	**Operating profit**			
FRS 3 para 14,30	Continuing operations		**3,247**	3,176
FRS 3 para 16	Acquisitions		**161**	-
			3,408	3,176
FRS 3 para 17	Discontinued operations		**192**	(25)
		4	**3,600**	3,151
FRS 3 para 20	Profit/(loss) on sale/termination of operations - discontinued operations	8	**265**	(7,988)
4A Sch 21(3),	Income from interests in associated undertakings		**77**	62
SSAP 1 para 19	Investment income	9	**111**	41
	Amounts written off investments	10	**-**	(6)
	Profit/(loss) on ordinary activities before interest		**4,053**	(4,740)
	Interest payable and similar charges	11	**(734)**	(639)
4 Sch 3(6)	**Profit/(loss) on ordinary activities before taxation**	2,3,12	**3,319**	(5,379)
	Tax on ordinary activities	13	**(650)**	(806)
	Profit/(loss) on ordinary activities after taxation		**2,669**	(6,185)
4A Sch 17(3)	Minority interests		**(437)**	746
FRS 2 para 35				
4 Sch 3(7)(b)	**Profit/(loss) for the financial year**	14	**2,232**	(5,439)
SSAP 6 para 34	Dividends	15	**(1,043)**	(939)
4 Sch 3(7)(a)	**Retained profit/(loss) for the year**	33	**1,189**	(6,378)
SSAP 3 para 14	**Earnings/(loss) per ordinary share**	16	**5.46p**	(14.21)p
FRS 3 para 25	Adjustment for disposal of discontinued operation		**(0.51)p**	-
	Adjustment for confiscation of subsidiary assets		**-**	18.27p
FRS 3 para 25	Adjusted earnings per share	16	**4.95p**	4.06p

FRS 3 para 27

Statement of total recognised gains and losses

		Notes	1992 £'000	1991 as restated £'000
	Profit for the financial year		**2,232**	(5,439)
	Unrealised surplus on revaluation of properties		**612**	272
	Currency translation differences on foreign currency net investments		**177**	(94)
SSAP 15 para 39	Taxation on realisation of property revaluation gains of previous years	13	**(110)**	(96)
		34	**679**	82
	Total recognised gains and losses relating to the year		**2,911**	(5,357)
FRS 3 para 29	Prior year adjustment	19	**(124)**	
	Total gains recognised since last annual report		**2,787**	

FRS 3 para 26

Note of historical cost profits and losses

	1992 £'000	1991 as restated £'000
Reported profit/(loss) on ordinary activities before taxation	**3,319**	(5,379)
Realisation of property revaluation gains of previous years	**762**	512
Difference between historical cost depreciation charge and the actual depreciation charge of the year calculated on the revalued amount	**312**	238
Historical cost profit/(loss) on ordinary activities before taxation	**4,393**	(4,629)
Historical cost profit/(loss) for the year retained after taxation, minority interests, extraordinary items and dividends	**2,153**	(5,724)

Balance sheets at 31 December 1992

			Group		Company	
s226(3) s227(2)(a) 4 Sch Format 1			**1992**	1991 as restated	**1992**	1991 as restated
		Notes	**£'000**	£'000	**£'000**	£'000
	Fixed assets					
	Intangible assets	18	**898**	969	**-**	-
	Tangible assets	19	**30,958**	30,492	**9,518**	9,401
	Investments	20	**1,024**	833	**7,842**	7,785
			32,880	32,294	**17,360**	17,186
	Current assets					
	Stocks	21	**7,821**	8,004	**3,269**	3,586
UITF Abs 4	Debtors: amounts falling due after one year	22	**510**	509	**510**	509
	Debtors: amounts falling due within one year	22	**8,029**	8,217	**4,165**	3,909
	Investments	23	**166**	247	**166**	247
	Cash at bank and in hand		**1,600**	86	**1,490**	323
			18,126	17,063	**9,600**	8,574
	Creditors: amounts falling due within one year	24	**8,419**	9,529	**4,825**	5,520
4 Sch Note 11	**Net current assets**		**9,707**	7,534	**4,775**	3,054
	Total assets less current liabilities		**42,587**	39,828	**22,135**	20,240
	Creditors: amounts falling due after more than one year	25	**6,575**	5,880	**3,000**	2,000
	Provisions for liabilities and charges	26	**8,858**	8,577	**3,856**	3,955
	Accruals and deferred income	27	**1,000**	2,000	**-**	-
			16,433	16,457	**6,856**	5,955
	Net assets	2,3	**26,154**	23,371	**15,279**	14,285
	Capital and reserves					
	Called up share capital	29	**11,161**	10,886	**11,161**	10,886
	Share premium account	33	**1,512**	1,523	**1,512**	1,523
	Revaluation reserve	33	**5,426**	5,865	**-**	-
	Merger reserve	33	**373**	-	**-**	-
	Profit and loss account	33	**5,587**	3,191	**2,606**	1,876
	Shareholders' funds	34	**24,059**	21,465	**15,279**	14,285
4A Sch 17(2) FRS 2 para 35	**Minority interests**		**2,095**	1,906	**-**	-
			26,154	23,371	**15,279**	14,285

s 233 (1)(4)
SSAP 17 para 26

The financial statements on pages [9] to [48] were approved by the board of directors on 6 March 1993 and were signed on its behalf by:

s 233(3)
Cadbury para 4.22
(not part of code)

F James
Finance Director

Consolidated cash flow statement for the year ended 31 December 1992

FRS 1 paras 7, 9,12		Notes	1992 £'000	1991 £'000
Good practice	**Operating activities**			
	Net cash inflow from continuing operating activities		**6,445**	7,033
	Net cash inflow/(outflow) from discontinued operating activities		**210**	(15)
	(reconciliation to operating profits on page [13])			
	Net cash inflow from operating activities		**6,655**	7,018
	Returns on investments and servicing of finance			
FRS 1 para 19(a)	Interest received		**68**	7
FRS 1 para 20(a)	Interest paid		**(842)**	(691)
FRS 1 para 20(c)	Interest paid on finance leases		**(9)**	(8)
FRS 1 para 19(b)	Dividend received from associated companies		**10**	8
	Dividends received from other investments		**41**	34
FRS 1 para 20(b)	Dividends paid		**(1,044)**	(935)
FRS 1 para 38	Dividends paid to minorities		**(248)**	(98)
	Net cash outflow from returns on investments and servicing of finance		**(2,024)**	(1,683)
	Taxation			
FRS 1 para 23	UK corporation tax paid		**(646)**	(446)
	Overseas tax paid		**(282)**	(235)
	Tax paid		**(928)**	(681)
	Investing activities			
	Development expenditure capitalised		**(235)**	(84)
	Purchase of tangible fixed assets		**(5,516)**	(4,662)
FRS 1 para 26(a)	Sale of tangible fixed assets		**2,156**	623
FRS 1 para 25(c)	Purchase of fixed asset investments		**(151)**	(103)
FRS 1 para 26(c),	Purchase of subsidiary (net of cash acquired)	31	**(86)**	(1,013)
(b), 40	Sale of subsidiary	32	**854**	-
FRS 1 para 25(b), 40	Subsidiary no longer consolidated (cash confiscated)	20	**-**	(372)
			(2,978)	(5,611)
FRS 1 para 25(a)	Sale of current asset investments		**103**	87
	Net cash outflow from investing activities		**(2,875)**	(5,524)
	Net cash inflow/(outflow) before financing		**828**	(870)
FRS 1 para 12				
	Financing			
	Issue of debentures		**1,000**	2,000
FRS 1 para 28(b)	Repayment of loan		**(100)**	-
FRS 1 para 29(a)	Expenses paid in connection with share issue		**(11)**	-
FRS 1 para 29(d)	Repayment of principal under finance leases		**(136)**	(117)
FRS 1 para 29(b)				
	Net cash inflow from financing		**753**	1,883
	Increase in cash and cash equivalents	35	**1,581**	1,013

Reconciliation of operating profit to net cash inflow from operating activities

		1992 £'000	1991 £'000
FRS 1 para 17	**Continuing activities**		
	Operating profit	**3,408**	3,176
	Amortisation of intangible fixed assets	**306**	335
	Depreciation on tangible fixed assets	**5,175**	4,101
	Gain on sale of tangible fixed assets	**(23)**	(54)
	Gain on sale of current asset investments	**(22)**	(25)
	Amounts written off investments	**-**	6
	(Increase)/decrease in stocks	**132**	(142)
	(Increase)/decrease in trade debtors	**(619)**	78
	Decrease in prepayments and accrued income	**548**	110
	Increase/(decrease) in trade creditors	**(2,021)**	398
	Increase/(decrease) in amounts owed to parent and fellow subsidiaries	**88**	(42)
	Increase/(decrease) in amounts owed to associated companies	**16**	(8)
	Increase in other taxation and social security	**53**	24
	Increase in payments on account	**25**	15
	Decrease in accruals and deferred income	**(1,079)**	(1,021)
	Increase in pension provisions	**458**	82
	Net cash inflow from continuing operating activities	**6,445**	7,033
FRS 1 example 2	**Discontinued activities**		
	Operating profit/(loss)	**192**	(25)
	Decrease in stock	**36**	21
	(Increase) in debtors	**(28)**	(26)
	Increase in creditors	**10**	15
	Net cash inflow/(outflow) from discontinued operating activities	**210**	(15)
	Net cash inflow from operating activities	**6,655**	7,018

Notes to the financial statements for the year ended 31 December 1992

1 Principal accounting policies

4 Sch 36,36A
SSAP 2 para 18
UITF Abs 7

The financial statements have been prepared in accordance with applicable Accounting Standards in the United Kingdom. However, compliance with SSAP 19 'Accounting for investment properties', requires departure from the requirements of the Companies Act 1985 relating to depreciation and an explanation of the result of the departure is given in the note relating to tangible fixed assets and other intangible fixed assets below. A summary of the more important group accounting policies, which have been applied consistently, except for the policy on depreciation of freehold property as explained under tangible fixed assets, is set out below.

Changes in accounting policies

FRS 3

The new accounting standard, FRS 3, requires the adoption of accounting policies which differ from those previously adopted by the company. Accordingly, the following changes have been made. Comparative figures have been amended where necessary for the changes.

(a) In previous years profits and losses on the sale of fixed assets carried at valuation have been included in the profit and loss account based on the difference between proceeds and depreciated historical cost. This policy has now been changed and such profits and losses are now included based on the difference between proceeds and net carrying amount, whether at valuation or at depreciated historical cost.

(b) In previous years certain profits and losses were treated as extraordinary items in accordance with standard accounting practice at that time. Such profits or losses are now treated as exceptional items and shown after operating profit, but before interest, in accordance with the new accounting standard.

(c) In previous years earnings per share has been calculated on the figure for profit after taxation, minority interests and preference dividends, but before extraordinary items. Under the new accounting standard earnings per share is based on profit after taxation, minority interests, preference dividends and extraordinary items.

FRRP 10/8/92

In prior years depreciation was not provided on freehold buildings as it is the group's policy to maintain its properties in a sound state of repair and accordingly the directors had considered that the lives of the properties were so long and residual values at such a level that depreciation was immaterial. However, given the current economic difficulties the directors believe that a greater level of prudence is required and such properties are now depreciated at 2% per annum.

The effects of these changes in accounting policies are disclosed in note 17.

Basis of accounting

The financial statements are prepared in accordance with the historical cost convention modified by the revaluation of certain fixed assets.

Basis of consolidation

FRS 2 para 20
SSAP 23 para 21
4A Sch 1(1),2,3

The consolidated profit and loss account and balance sheet include the financial statements of the company and its subsidiary undertakings made up to 31 December 1992 except where standard accounting practice requires that a subsidiary should be excluded from consolidation. The results of subsidiaries sold or acquired are included in the consolidated profit and loss account up to, or from the date control passes. Intra-group sales and profits are eliminated fully on consolidation.

Associated undertakings

SSAP 1 para 18,26

The group's share of profits less losses of associated undertakings is included in the consolidated profit and loss account, and the group's share of their net assets is included in the consolidated balance sheet. These amounts are taken from the latest audited financial statements of the undertakings concerned, which all have the same accounting reference date, except in the case of Collins Limited where management accounts have been used. Audited financial statements for Collins Limited were drawn up to 30 September 1992, being a requirement by other shareholders in Collins Limited. Because the accounting policies of associated undertakings do not necessarily conform in all respects to those of the group, adjustments are made on consolidation where the amounts involved are material to the group.

Goodwill

SSAP 22 para 43

Goodwill arising on consolidation represents the excess of the fair value of the consideration given over the fair value of the identifiable net assets acquired. Goodwill arising on the acquisition of subsidiaries and associates is written off immediately against reserves. Other purchased goodwill is eliminated by amortisation through the profit and loss account over its useful economic life.

Tangible fixed assets and other intangible fixed assets

4 Sch 17,26(3)

The cost of fixed assets is their purchase cost, together with any incidental costs of acquisition. The cost of land and buildings includes interest paid on funds specifically taken out to finance assets in the course of construction.

SSAP 19, UITF Abs 7

In accordance with SSAP 19, (i) investment properties are revalued annually and the aggregate surplus or deficit is transferred to a revaluation reserve, and (ii) no depreciation or amortisation is provided in respect of freehold investment properties and leasehold investment properties with over 20 years to run. The requirement of the Companies Act 1985 is to depreciate all properties, but that requirement conflicts with the generally accepted accounting principle set out in SSAP 19. The directors consider that to depreciate such properties would not give a true and fair view, but that a true and fair view is given by following SSAP 19 as described above. If this departure had not been made the profit for the financial year would have been reduced by depreciation on the revalued properties of £9,000 (1991: £8,000) and this charge would have been reduced by £5,000 (1991: £4,000) if the historical cost accounting rules had been used.

4 Sch 31(2)

Other interests in land and buildings are also stated at valuation.

SSAP 19

Full valuations are made by independent professionally qualified valuers every five years and in the intervening years these valuations are updated by directors with the assistance of independent professional advice as required. The basis of valuation is explained in note 19.

4 Sch 17

The cost of other tangible and intangible fixed assets is their purchase cost, together with any incidental expenses of acquisition.

4 Sch 36

Depreciation is calculated so as to write off the cost, or valuation, of tangible fixed assets (excluding investment properties) and intangible fixed assets, less their estimated residual values, on a straight line basis over the expected useful economic lives of the assets concerned. The principal annual rates used for this purpose are:

	%
Freehold buildings	2
Precision plant	25
Other plant	10
Motor vehicles	25
Fixtures and fittings	15
Patents	20

Leasehold land and buildings are amortised over 50 years or, if shorter, the period of the lease. Freehold land is not depreciated.

Development expenditure

4 Sch 20(2) SSAP 13 para 30

Development expenditure relating to specific projects intended for commercial exploitation is carried forward. Such expenditure is amortised over the period expected to benefit. Expenditure on pure and applied research is written off as incurred.

Finance and operating leases

SSAP 21 para 57 Costs in respect of operating leases are charged on a straight line basis over the lease term. Leasing agreements which transfer to the group substantially all the benefits and risks of ownership of an asset are treated as if the asset had been purchased outright. The assets are included in fixed assets and the capital element of the leasing commitments is shown as obligations under finance leases. The lease rentals are treated as consisting of capital and interest elements. The capital element is applied to reduce the outstanding obligations and the interest element is charged against profit in proportion to the reducing capital element outstanding. Assets held under finance leases are depreciated over the shorter of the lease terms and the useful lives of equivalent owned assets.

Investment income

Income from investments, other than from associated undertakings, is included, together with the related tax credit, in the consolidated profit and loss account on an accruals basis.

Stocks and work in progress, excluding long-term contracts

SSAP 9 para 32 Stocks and work in progress are stated at the lower of cost and net realisable value. In general, cost is determined on a first in first out basis and includes transport and handling costs. In the case of manufactured products, cost includes all direct expenditure and production overheads based on the normal level of activity. Where necessary, provision is made for obsolete, slow moving and defective stocks.

Long-term contracts

SSAP 9 para 32 Turnover on long-term contracts is recognised according to the stage reached in the contract by reference to the value of work done. A prudent estimate of the profit attributable to work completed is recognised once the outcome of the contract can be assessed with reasonable certainty. The amount by which the turnover exceeds payments on account is shown under debtors as amounts recoverable on contracts. The costs on long-term contracts not yet taken to the profit and loss account less related foreseeable losses and payments on account are shown in stocks as long-term contract balances.

Government grants

SSAP 4 para 28 Grants that relate to specific capital expenditure are treated as deferred income which is then credited to the profit and loss account over the related asset's useful life. Other grants are credited to the profit and loss account when received.

Foreign currencies

4 Sch 58(1)
SSAP 20 para 59

Assets and liabilities of subsidiaries in foreign currencies are translated into sterling at rates of exchange ruling at the end of the financial year and the results of foreign subsidiaries are translated at the average rate of exchange for the year. Differences on exchange arising from the retranslation of the opening net investment in subsidiary companies, and from the translation of the results of those companies at average rate, are taken to reserves and are reported in the statement of total recognised gains and losses. All other foreign exchange differences are taken to the profit and loss account in the year in which they arise.

Turnover

s 262 (1)
SSAP 5 para 8

Turnover, which excludes value added tax, sales between group companies and trade discounts, represents the invoiced value of goods and services supplied and the value of long-term contract work done.

Deferred taxation

SSAP 15

Provision is made for deferred taxation, using the liability method, on all material timing differences to the extent that it is probable that a liability or asset will crystallise. Full provision is made for deferred taxation on timing differences arising from the provision of employee pensions.

Pension costs and other post retirement benefits

SSAP 24 para 88

Most of the companies in the group operate defined benefit pension schemes which are contracted out of the state scheme. The funds are valued every three years by a professionally qualified independent actuary, the rates of contribution payable being determined by the actuary. In the intervening years the actuary reviews the continuing appropriateness of the rates. Pension costs are accounted for on the basis of charging the expected cost of providing pensions over the period during which the company benefits from the employees' services. The effects of variations from regular cost are spread over the expected average remaining service lives of members of the scheme.

UITF Abs 6

The cost of providing other post retirement benefits is recognised in the year in which payments are made. No provision is made for future benefits.

2 Segmental analysis by class of business

The analysis by class of business of the group's turnover, profit before taxation and net assets is set out below:

Turnover

		1992			1991	
	Total sales £ million	**Inter-segment sales £ million**	**External sales £ million**	Total sales £ million	Inter-segment sales £ million	External sales £ million
Class of business						
Electronic components	**19.5**	**(2.1)**	**17.4**	16.0	(1.5)	14.5
Moulded plastics	**10.1**	**(0.2)**	**9.9**	9.8	(0.1)	9.7
Domestic appliances	**16.5**	**(1.3)**	**15.2**	13.9	(0.8)	13.1
Building - materials	**17.0**	**(-)**	**17.0**	11.8	(-)	11.8
Building - contracting	**6.2**	**(-)**	**6.2**	4.7	(-)	4.7
	69.3	**(3.6)**	**65.7**	56.2	(2.4)	53.8

4 Sch 55(1)(3)(4) SSAP 25 paras 34, 35

Profit before taxation

		1992			1991 as restated	
	Group under-takings £ million	**Associated under-takings £ million**	**Total £ million**	Group under-takings £ million	Associated under-takings £ million	Total £ million
Class of business						
Electronic components	**1.6**	**0.1**	**1.7**	1.3	0.1	1.4
Moulded plastics	**0.7**	**-**	**0.7**	0.7	-	0.7
Domestic appliances	**0.7**	**-**	**0.7**	(7.5)	-	(7.5)
Building - materials	**1.0**	**-**	**1.0**	0.9	-	0.9
Building - contracting	**0.5**	**-**	**0.5**	0.2	-	0.2
	4.5	**0.1**	**4.6**	(4.4)	0.1	(4.3)
Common costs	**(0.6)**	**-**	**(0.6)**	(0.5)	-	(0.5)
Profit/(loss) before interest	**3.9**	**0.1**	**4.0**	(4.9)	0.1	(4.8)
Net interest payable	**(0.7)**	**-**	**(0.7)**	(0.6)	-	(0.6)
	3.2	**0.1**	**3.3**	(5.5)	0.1	(5.4)

4 Sch 55 (1)(3)(4) SSAP 25 paras 34, 35,36

FRS 3 para 53

The above analysis includes the results from the sale and termination of operations (see note 8) as follows: domestic appliances £nil (1991: £(8.0)m), building - contracting £0.3m (1991: £nil).

Net assets

		1992			1991		
		Group undertakings £ million	**Associated undertakings £ million**	**Total £ million**	Group undertakings £ million	Associated undertakings £ million	Total £ million
SSAP 25 paras 34, 35,36	**Class of business**						
	Electronic components	**20.1**	**0.2**	**20.3**	18.6	0.2	18.8
	Moulded plastics	**2.3**	**-**	**2.3**	2.2	-	2.2
	Domestic appliances	**3.9**	**-**	**3.9**	2.8	-	2.8
	Building - materials	**13.1**	**0.2**	**13.3**	13.6	0.2	13.8
	Building - contracting	**1.6**	**-**	**1.6**	1.5	-	1.5
	Net operating assets	**41.0**	**0.4**	**41.4**	38.7	0.4	39.1
SSAP 25 para 37	Unallocated net liabilities						
	Other fixed asset investments	**0.3**	**-**	**0.3**	0.2	-	0.2
	Loans and debentures	**(5.5)**	**-**	**(5.5)**	(5.7)	-	(5.7)
	Current and deferred tax	**(9.3)**	**-**	**(9.3)**	(9.5)	-	(9.5)
	Dividend payable	**(0.7)**	**-**	**(0.7)**	(0.7)	-	(0.7)
		25.8	**0.4**	**26.2**	23.0	0.4	23.4

Net operating assets includes intangible and tangible fixed assets, stocks, and debtors and creditors arising on operating activities.

Associated undertakings' profits are shown after interest and the group's share of associates' net assets has been shown as net operating assets.

3 Analysis by geographical area

The analysis by geographical area of the group's turnover, profit before taxation and net assets is set out below:

Turnover

		1992		1991	
		Sales by destination £ million	**Sales by origin £ million**	Sales by destination £ million	Sales by origin £ million
4 Sch 55 (2)(3)(4)	**Geographical segment**				
SSAP 25 paras 34,	United Kingdom	**37.7**	**47.6**	29.4	39.0
35	Rest of Europe	**11.1**	**12.5**	9.8	10.5
CO 21 (c)	North America	**10.3**	**9.6**	8.8	7.0
	Africa	**6.6**	**-**	5.8	-
		65.7	**69.7**	53.8	56.5
	Inter-area sales	**-**	**(4.0)**	-	(2.7)
		65.7	**65.7**	53.8	53.8

Profit before taxation

	1992			1991 as restated		
	Group under-takings £ million	**Associated under-takings £ million**	**Total £ million**	Group under-takings £ million	Associated under-takings £ million	Total £ million
SSAP 25 paras 34, 35 **Geographical segment**						
CU 21(c) United Kingdom	**3.4**	**0.1**	**3.5**	2.6	0.1	2.7
Rest of Europe	**0.7**	**-**	**0.7**	(7.5)	-	(7.5)
North America	**0.4**	**-**	**0.4**	0.5	-	0.5
	4.5	**0.1**	**4.6**	(4.4)	0.1	(4.3)
Common costs	**(0.6)**	**-**	**(0.6)**	(0.5)	-	(0.5)
Profit/(loss) before interest	**3.9**	**0.1**	**4.0**	(4.9)	0.1	(4.8)
Net interest payable	**(0.7)**	**-**	**(0.7)**	(0.6)	-	(0.6)
	3.2	**0.1**	**3.3**	(5.5)	0.1	(5.4)

FRS 3 para 53

The above analysis includes the results of sale and termination of operations (see note 8) as follows: United Kingdom £0.3m (1991: £nil), Rest of Europe £nil (1991: £(8.0)m).

Net Assets	1992			1991		
	Group under-takings £ million	**Associated under-takings £ million**	**Total £ million**	Group under-takings £ million	Associated under-takings £ million	Total £ million
SSAP 25 paras 34, 35 **Geographical segment**						
United Kingdom	**23.4**	**0.4**	**23.8**	21.9	0.4	22.3
Rest of Europe	**9.8**	**-**	**9.8**	10.0	-	10.0
North America	**7.8**	**-**	**7.8**	6.8	-	6.8
Net operating assets	**41.0**	**0.4**	**41.4**	38.7	0.4	39.1
SSAP 25 para 37 Unallocated net liabilities						
Other fixed asset investments	**0.3**	**-**	**0.3**	0.2	-	0.2
Loans and debentures	**(5.5)**	**-**	**(5.5)**	(5.7)	-	(5.7)
Current and deferred tax	**(9.3)**	**-**	**(9.3)**	(9.5)	-	(9.5)
Dividend payable	**(0.7)**	**-**	**(0.7)**	(0.7)	-	(0.7)
	25.8	**0.4**	**26.2**	23.0	0.4	23.4

4 Cost of sales and other operating income and expenses

FRS 3 para 14

	1992 Continuing £'000	1992 Discontinued £'000	1992 Total £'000	1991 as restated Continuing £'000	1991 as restated Discontinued £'000	1991 as restated Total £'000
Cost of sales	**43,892**	**1,191**	**45,083**	34,990	2,303	37,293
Exceptional cost of sales	**1,550**	**-**	**1,550**	-	-	-
Gross profit	**18,148**	**939**	**19,087**	15,714	817	16,531
Distribution costs	**5,809**	**320**	**6,129**	5,120	373	5,493
Administrative expenses	**9,167**	**427**	**9,594**	7,616	469	8,085
	14,976	**747**	**15,723**	12,736	842	13,578
Less: other operating income - royalties	**(236)**	**-**	**(236)**	(198)	-	(198)
Net operating expenses	**14,740**	**747**	**15,487**	12,538	842	13,380
Operating profit	**3,408**	**192**	**3,600**	3,176	(25)	3,151

4 Sch Format 1

The total figures for continuing operations in 1992 include the following amounts relating to acquisitions: cost of sales £2,780,000 and net operating expenses £603,000 (namely distribution costs £290,000 and administration costs £313,000).

5 Exceptional cost of sales

4 Sch 57(3)
FRS 3 para 19

During the year one of the group's product lines was found to be defective. The exceptional charge represents the cost of correcting the defect, replacing the withdrawn product and meeting product liability claims to the extent that they are not covered by the group's insurance.

6 Directors' emoluments

		1992 £	1991 £
6 Sch 1	Fees	**6,150**	6,150
	Salary payments (including benefits in kind)	**158,302**	152,884
Cadbury para 4.40, code 3.2	Pension contributions	**24,726**	22,699
	Annual incentive payments	**41,225**	32,192
		230,403	213,925
6 Sch 7	Pension paid to a former director	**3,792**	3,792
6 Sch 8	Compensation for loss of office*	**20,000**	10,000
6 Sch 9, 9(2)	Consideration paid in cash to third party for services of director	**7,903**	6,234
		£262,098	£233,951

6 Sch 8(3)
(good practice)

* Includes the monetary value of a car retained by the director and a contribution to his pension plan (1991 compensation included a car).

Cadbury para 4.40, code 3.2 The remuneration of the executive directors is decided by the non-executive directors through the Remuneration Committee. The committee introduced a performance related incentive plan in 1989. Payments under the plan are related to the growth in operating profit and share price up to a maximum of 40% of annual salary. Where a director has responsibility for a business group, part of his bonus relates to the performance of that business and part to the company's consolidated results.

Fees and other emoluments include amounts paid to:

		1992		1991	
		Chairman	**Highest paid director**	Chairman	Highest paid director
		£	**£**	£	£
	Salary payments	**7,715**	**42,000**	6,520	40,000
Cadbury para 4.40, code 3.2	Annual incentive payments	**-**	**8,124**	-	5,649
6 Sch 3, 4(3)	Fees and other emoluments before pensions	**7,715**	**50,124**	6,520	45,649
	Pension contributions	**-**	**1,470**	-	1,299
		7,715	**51,594**	6,520	46,948

6 Sch 4(2)
6 Sch 5

The number of directors (including the chairman and the highest-paid director) who received fees and other emoluments (excluding pension contributions) in the following ranges was:

	1992 Number	1991 Number
£5,001 to £10,000	**3**	3
£20,001 to £25,000	**2**	2
£25,001 to £30,000	**2**	2
£30,001 to £35,000	**1**	1
£45,001 to £50,000	**-**	1
£50,001 to £55,000	**1**	-

6 Sch 6
CO 21(n)

No director waived emoluments in respect of the year ended 31 December 1992. In the year ended 31 December 1991 one director waived emoluments of £2,000.

7 Employee information

4 Sch 56(1)(2) The average weekly number of persons (including executive directors) employed by the group during the year was:

4 Sch 56(5)

	1992 Number	1991 Number
By product group		
Electronic components	**690**	649
Moulded plastics	**89**	103
Building materials	**494**	517
Domestic appliances	**371**	360
Building - contracting	**116**	62
Corporate	**23**	22
	1,783	1,713

		1992 £'000	1991 £'000
4 Sch 56(4),94	**Staff costs (for the above persons)**		
	Wages and salaries	**20,750**	18,689
	Social security costs	**2,050**	1,795
	Other pension costs (see note 28)	**552**	851
		23,352	21,335

8 Profit/(loss) on sale/termination of operations

		1992 £'000	1991 £'000
	Discontinued operations		
4 Sch Format 1	Profit on disposal of subsidiary	**265**	-
FRS 3 para 20	Loss on confiscation of subsidiary's assets	**-**	(7,988)
4 Sch 54(3)	Taxation	**(37)**	-
FRS 3 para 24			
4A Sch 17(4)	Minority interests	**(26)**	908
FRS 3 para 20			
FRS 2 para 36		**202**	(7,080)

4 Sch 57(2) On 1 February 1992 the group sold Shakespeare Limited, an 82% subsidiary, for £854,000. The profit on sale includes £89,000 of goodwill previously written off to reserves (see note 32).

4 Sch 57(2) During 1991 the newly formed government of Newland confiscated the group's subsidiary in that country.

9 Investment income

		1992 £'000	1991 £'000
4 Sch Format 1	Income from fixed asset investments (excluding associates)	**41**	34
	Other interest receivable	**70**	7
		111	41

4 Sch 53(4)
SSAP 8 para 25 Income from investments includes £28,000 (1991: £23,000) from listed investments.

10 Amounts written off investments

		1992 £'000	1991 £'000
4 Sch 19(2) SSAP 12 para 19	Amounts written off fixed asset investments as a result of a permanent diminution in value	**-**	6

11 Interest payable and similar charges

		1992 £'000	1991 £'000
4 Sch 53(2)	On bank loans, overdrafts and other loans:		
	Repayable within 5 years, not by instalments	**701**	480
	Repayable within 5 years, by instalments	**66**	-
	Repayable wholly or partly in more than 5 years	**85**	218
		852	698
SSAP 21 para 53	On finance leases	**9**	8
		861	706
4 Sch 26(3)(b) CO 21(g)	Less: interest capitalised	**(127)**	(67)
		734	639

12 Profit on ordinary activities before taxation

		1992 £'000	1991 £'000
4 Sch 53(5)	Profit on ordinary activities before taxation is stated after crediting:		
	Rent receivable (net of outgoings)	**30**	28
SSAP 4 para 28(b)	Amortisation of government grant	**1,000**	1,000
	Profit on disposal of tangible fixed assets (1991 as restated in note 17)	**23**	54
SSAP 22 para 45(a)	And after charging:		
	Goodwill amortisation	**100**	100
4 Sch Format Note 17	Depreciation charge for the year:		
	Intangible fixed assets	**28**	40
SSAP 12 para 25	Tangible owned fixed assets	**5,067**	4,016
SSAP 21 para 50	Tangible fixed assets held under finance leases	**108**	85
SSAP 13 para 22, 31	Research and development expenditure:		
	Deferred expenditure amortised	**178**	195
	Current year expenditure	**147**	207
390 A (3)(4)	Auditors' remuneration for audit (company £21,000; 1991: £20,000)	**110**	100
4 Sch 53(6)	Hire of plant and machinery - operating leases	**212**	216
SSAP 21 para 55	Hire of other assets - operating leases	**76**	66

SI 1991/2128

Remuneration of the company's auditors for provision of non-audit services to the company and its UK subsidiary undertakings, where also audited by the company's auditors, was £148,000. This includes taxation compliance and advisory fees of £85,000 and non-statutory audit services to provide greater assurance on control systems. It also includes management consultancy fees which are small in relation to the company's total expenditure on external advisory fees.

13 Tax on profit on ordinary activities and recognised gains and losses

		1992 £'000	1991 £'000
4 Sch 54	**Tax on profit on ordinary activities**		
SSAP 8 para 28, 29	United Kingdom corporation tax at 33% (1991: 33.25%):		
	Current	**441**	413
SSAP 15 para 33	Deferred	**77**	80
	Double taxation relief	**(25)**	(17)
	Overseas taxation	**248**	299
	Tax credits on franked investment income	**10**	9
	Under/(over) provision in respect of prior years:		
	Current	**126**	-
	Deferred	**(254)**	-
		623	784
SSAP 1 para 20	Associated undertakings	**27**	22
		650	806
	Tax on recognised gains and losses		
	United Kingdom corporation tax at 33% (1991: 33.25%):		
	Current	**110**	96

SSAP 15 para 35
FRS 3 para 23

The taxation charge for the year has been reduced by £323,000 (1991: £45,000) in respect of the excess of tax allowances over depreciation and other timing differences on which, in accordance with the group's accounting policy, no deferred taxation has been provided.

14 Profit/(loss) for the financial year

s 230

As permitted by section 230 of the Companies Act 1985, the holding company's profit and loss account has not been included in these financial statements. The profit for the financial year is made up as follows:

		1992 £'000	1991 £'000
s 230	Holding company's profit for the financial year	**1,773**	1,306
SSAP 1 para 22	Share of net profits retained by associated undertakings	**40**	23

15 Dividends

		1992 £'000	1991 £'000
4 Sch 3(7)(b)	Preference 5.6% paid	**67**	67
	Ordinary:		
	Interim paid of 0.75p per share (1991: 0.5p per share)	**299**	194
	Final proposed of 1.7p per share (1991: 1.75p per share)	**677**	678
		976	872
4 Sch 51(3)		**1,043**	939

16 Earnings per ordinary share

SSAP 3 para 15

The calculation of earnings per share on the net basis is based on the profit on ordinary activities after taxation and after deduction of preference dividends and minorities, namely £2,165,000 (1991: £(5,506,000)) and on 39,659,278 (1991: 38,744,000) ordinary shares, being the weighted average number of ordinary shares in issue and ranking for dividend during the year.

An alternative figure for earnings per share is disclosed based on the results of operations excluding the profits or losses on sale or termination of discontinued operations. This alternative figure is intended to demonstrate recurring elements of the results of the company after eliminating certain exceptional items arising in the year which are not expected to recur regularly. The adjustment is based on the net result attributable to shareholders as disclosed in note 8 of £202,000 (1991: £(7,080,000)).

17 Changes in accounting policies

(a) The effect of the changes in the accounting policies discussed on page [14] on the comparative profit and loss account figures is as follows:

	1991 £'000
Profit before tax as previously stated	3,245
Adjustment to restate profits on disposal of fixed assets	(512)
Loss on confiscation of subsidiary assets previously treated as an extraordinary item now classified as exceptional	(7,988)
Depreciation on freehold properties	(124)
Loss before tax as restated	(5,379)

(b) The earnings per share figure has been restated from 5.46p to (14.21)p in accordance with the revised basis described on page [14].

18 Intangible fixed assets

The company has no intangible fixed assets. Details of those relating to the group are as follows:

		Development costs £'000	Patents £'000	Goodwill £'000	Total £'000
4 Sch Notes 2,3	**Cost**				
4 Sch 42(1)	At 1 January 1992	528	497	800	1,825
SSAP 13 para 32	Additions	235	-	-	235
SSAP 22 para 45(a)					
	At 31 December 1992	**763**	**497**	**800**	**2,060**
4 Sch 42(3)	**Depreciation**				
SSAP 13 para 28	At 1 January 1992	305	351	200	856
SSAP 22 para 45(a)	Charge for year	178	28	100	306
	At 31 December 1992	**483**	**379**	**300**	**1,162**
	Net book value				
SSAP 22 para 45(a)	**At 31 December 1992**	**280**	**118**	**500**	**898**
	Net book value				
SSAP 22 para 45(a)	At 31 December 1991	223	146	600	969

4 Sch 20(2) Development costs relates to specific projects undertaken by the electronic components and domestic appliance subsidiaries. The production of the electronic components concerned commenced this year and the related development expenditure is being written off over the production life of the products. The domestic appliances subsidiary started marketing the product to which its development costs relates in 1990. The production run lasts for three years and the deferred cost is being written off over the same period.

s 269(2) In the directors opinion the above circumstances justify their decision to defer the costs and not to treat them as a realised revenue loss.

4 Sch 21(4) SSAP 22 para 45(b) Goodwill arose on the purchase by Kipling Limited, a subsidiary, of an unincorporated business manufacturing electronic components. The manufacturing process is protected by a patent, which has five years left to run. Both the patents and the goodwill are being written off over that period.

19 Tangible fixed assets

Group

Ref		Land and buildings £'000	Investment properties £'000	Plant and machinery £'000	Fixtures and fittings £'000	Total £'000
4 Sch 42(1)	**Cost or valuation**					
	At 1 January 1992	10,506	398	30,861	5,749	47,514
	Exchange differences	315	-	247	54	616
	In respect of new subsidiary	458	-	426	188	1,072
	Additions *	1,561	-	3,613	582	5,756
	Surplus on revaluation	130	40	-	-	170
	Disposals	(1,799)	-	(3,355)	(192)	(5,346)
SSAP 12 para 25(d)	**At 31 December 1992**	**11,171**	**438**	**31,792**	**6,381**	**49,782**
4 Sch 42(3)	**Depreciation**					
	At 1 January 1992	-	-	15,186	1,712	16,898
	Prior year adjustment **	124	-	-	-	124
	At 1 January 1992 as restated	124	-	15,186	1,712	17,022
	Exchange differences	3	-	222	57	282
SSAP 12 25(c)	Charge for year	320	-	3,952	903	5,175
	Revaluation	(442)	-	-	-	(442)
	Eliminated in respect of disposals	(5)	-	(3,028)	(180)	(3,213)
SSAP 12 para 25(d)	**At 31 December 1992**	**-**	**-**	**16,332**	**2,492**	**18,824**
	Net book value					
	At 31 December 1992	**11,171**	**438**	**15,460**	**3,889**	**30,958**
	Net book value					
	At 31 December 1991 as restated	10,382	398	15,675	4,037	30,492
4 Sch 43	**Cost or valuation at 31 December 1992 is represented by**					
	Valuation in year	11,171	438	-	-	11,609
	Cost	-	-	31,792	6,381	38,173
		11,171	**438**	**31,792**	**6,381**	**49,782**

4 Sch 26(3)(b) CO 21(g) * Includes £83,000 (1991: £44,000) in respect of interest capitalised net of tax relief of £44,000 (1991: £23,000). Accumulated interest capitalised net of tax relief, included in the total cost or valuation above, amounts to £132,000 (1991: £53,000).

** Prior year adjustment following a change of accounting policy (see accounting policy on page [14]).

SSAP 21 para 50 The net book value of tangible fixed assets includes an amount of £556,000 (1991: £494,000) in respect of assets held under finance leases.

4 Sch 33(2)
4 Sch 43
SSAP 19 para 12

Non-specialised land and buildings, including investment properties, were valued for the purpose of the 1991 financial statements at open market valuation for existing use. Specialised buildings were valued at the same date at depreciated replacement cost. These valuations were made in the United Kingdom by Robert Louis & Stevenson, a firm of independent Chartered Surveyors, and overseas by valuers having equivalent professional qualifications. For the 1992 financial statements these valuations have been updated by the directors with the assistance of independent professional advice.

4 Sch 33(3)(4)

If investment properties and land and buildings had not been revalued they would have been included at the following amounts:

		Investment properties		Land and buildings	
		1992	1991	**1992**	1991
		£'000	£'000	**£'000**	£'000
	Cost	**181**	181	**7,134**	6,605
	Aggregate depreciation based on cost	**24**	20	**1,879**	1,871
4 Sch 33(3)(4)	Net book value based on cost	**157**	161	**5,255**	4,734
4 Sch 44	Investment properties and land and buildings at net book value comprise:				
	Freeholds	**438**	398	**9,770**	8,117
	Long leaseholds	**-**	-	**1,195**	2,011
	Short leaseholds	**-**	-	**206**	254
		438	398	**11,171**	10,382

Depreciation has not been charged on freehold land, which is stated at its revalued amount of £2,200,000 (1991: £1,950,000).

Company

The tangible fixed assets of GAAP UK plc consisted entirely of plant and machinery.

		Plant and machinery £'000
4 Sch 42(1)	**Cost**	
	At 1 January 1992	14,612
	Additions	1,996
	At 31 December 1992	**16,608**
4 Sch 42(3)	**Depreciation**	
	At 1 January 1992	5,211
	Charge for year	1,879
	At 31 December 1992	**7,090**
	Net book value	
	At 31 December 1992	**9,518**
	Net book value	
	At 31 December 1991	9,401

20 Fixed asset investments

Group

		Associated undertakings £'000	Subsidiary excluded from consolidation £'000	Loans £'000	Other investments £'000	Total £'000
4 Sch 42(1)	**Cost or valuation**					
4 Sch 42(2)	At 1 January 1992	367	679	120	352	1,518
	Additions	-	-	-	151	151
	Share of retained profit	40	-	-	-	40
	At 31 December 1992	**407**	**679**	**120**	**503**	**1,709**
4A Sch 21(3)	**Amounts written off**					
	At 1 January and 31 December 1992	-	679	-	6	685
	Net book value					
	At 31 December 1992	**407**	**-**	**120**	**497**	**1,024**
	Net book value					
	At 31 December 1991	367	-	120	346	833

4 Sch 45(1) Investments at net book value include:

	Associated undertakings 1992 £'000	1991 £'000	Other investments 1992 £'000	1991 £'000
Investments listed on a recognised investment exchange	**158**	144	**403**	255
Other listed investments	**-**	-	**72**	69
	158	144	**475**	324
4 Sch 45(2) Aggregate market value of listed investments	**190**	173	**566**	377
SSAP 1 para 26 Interests in associated undertakings:				
Share of associated undertakings' net assets (excluding goodwill)	**370**	325		
Share of associated undertakings' goodwill	**37**	42		
	407	367		

Company

	Interests in group undertakings £'000	Joint venture £'000	Associated undertakings £'000	Other investments £'000	Total £'000
4 Sch 42(1) **Cost or valuation**					
At 1 January 1992	7,991	148	182	149	8,470
Additions	275	-	-	73	348
Disposals	(291)	-	-	-	(291)
At 31 December 1992	**7,975**	**148**	**182**	**222**	**8,527**
4 Sch 42(3) **Amounts written off**					
At 1 January and 31 December 1992	**679**	**-**	**-**	**6**	**685**
Net book value					
At 31 December 1992	**7,296**	**148**	**182**	**216**	**7,842**
Net book value					
At 31 December 1991	7,312	148	182	143	7,785

4 Sch 45(1) Investments at net book value include:

	Participating interests		Other investments	
	1992	1991	**1992**	1991
	£'000	£'000	**£'000**	£'000
Investments listed on a recognised investment exchange	**158**	144	**119**	92
Other listed investments	**-**	-	**31**	13
	158	144	**150**	105
4 Sch 45(2) Aggregate market value of listed investments	**190**	173	**176**	127

Interests in group undertakings

s 231(2),(5) The directors consider that to give full particulars of all subsidiary undertakings would lead to a statement of excessive length. The following information relates to those subsidiary undertakings whose results or financial position, in the opinion of the directors, principally affected the figures of the group:

5 Sch 15,16
FRS 2 para 33(a)

Name of undertaking	Country of incorporation or registration	Description of shares held	Proportion of nominal value of issued shares held by: Group %	Company %
Chaucer Limited	Scotland	Ordinary £1 shares	100	-
Kipling Limited	England and Wales	Ordinary 25p shares	100	-
Austen Inc	USA	Common stock $1	90	60
Dickens Limited	Scotland	Ordinary £1 shares	100	-
Wilde SA	France	Shares of no par value	70	-
Thackeray GmbH	Germany	Shares of DM200	65	-
Swift Inc	Newland	Ordinary £1 shares	100	100

CO 21(d) All the above companies operated principally in their country of incorporation or registration.

On 1 March the company acquired the whole of the share capital of Dickens Limited (see note 31).

On 1 February 1992 the company sold Shakespeare Limited for £854,000 (see note 32). Shakespeare Limited's principal activity is building and contracting.

5 Sch 15(4), 17 FRS 2 paras 25(a), 26, 27

The financial statements of Swift Inc, the group's subsidiary in Newland, have not been consolidated as the group's control over the management of the company is subject to severe long-term restrictions following the confiscation of its assets during 1991. Full provision has been made against the investments in, and amounts due from, that company. Unaudited financial statements have been prepared up to 31 December 1991 and show capital and reserves amounting to £7,988,000. The effect of deconsolidating Swift Inc on the group's cash and cash equivalents was a reduction of £372,000 in 1991. The company has not traded since.

FRS 2 para 31

All intercompany balances between Swift Inc and the rest of the group have been written off.

FRS 2 para 33(b) CO 21(d)

The principal business activities and country of operation of these subsidiaries are:

(i) Chaucer Limited and Kipling Limited - manufacturers of precision electronic components in the UK.
(ii) Austen Inc - pressers of moulded plastics in North America.
(iii) Dickens Limited and Wilde SA - manufacturers of building materials and prefabricated sections, and contracting. Dickins Limited operates in the UK with branches across Europe. Wilde SA operates predominantly in France.
(iv) Thackeray GmbH and Swift Inc - manufacturers of domestic appliances in Europe and in the US respectively.

Unincorporated joint venture

5 Sch 21

The company directly owns 40% of the business of an unincorporated joint venture, Byron, which is included in the consolidation on a proportional basis. Its principal business activity is the manufacture of commercial ceilings in the UK. Its principal place of business is at Groveside Industrial Estate, Westbury-on-Sea, Wessex, UK.

Associated undertakings

5 Sch 22 SSAP 1 para 37, 49

Name of undertaking	**Description of shares held where applicable**	**Proportion of nominal value of ordinary shares held/share of undertaking**	**Accounting year end**
Burns Limited	Ordinary shares of 10p	32%	30 September
Graves Limited	Ordinary shares of 25p	37%	31 December
Tennyson	Unincorporated	25%	31 December

CO 21(e)

The interests are held directly by GAAP UK plc, except in the case of Graves Limited, where the interest is held by a wholly-owned subsidiary. The principal country of operation of the above undertakings is the United Kingdom. Both the companies are registered in Scotland. The principal place of business of Tennyson is 28-34 North End Road, Derby.

SSAP 1 para 49(b)

Burns Limited and Graves Limited manufacture electronic components. Tennyson manufactures domestic appliances.

Other significant interests

5 Sch 26,27 The group had a 19% interest in the £1 ordinary shares of Carroll Limited, a company registered in England and Wales.

21 Stocks

		Group 1992 £'000	Group 1991 £'000	Company 1992 £'000	Company 1991 £'000
4 Sch Formats	Raw materials and consumables	**1,636**	1,820	**1,027**	1,001
SSAP 9 para 27	Work in progress	**3,876**	3,979	**1,266**	1,634
	Finished goods and goods for resale	**2,309**	2,205	**976**	951
		7,821	8,004	**3,269**	3,586
SSAP 9 para 30(c)	**Long-term contracts (included in work in progress)**				
	Net cost less foreseeable losses	**1,300**	1,250	**850**	975
4 Sch Note 8	Less: applicable payments on account	**550**	600	**300**	325
		750	650	**550**	650
4 Sch 27(3)(4)	The replacement cost of raw materials and consumables exceeds the balance sheet value of raw materials and consumables by	**235**	327	**136**	104

22 Debtors

		Group 1992 £'000	Group 1991 £'000	Company 1992 £'000	Company 1991 £'000
SSAP 9 para 30(a)					
4 Sch Note 5	**Amounts falling due after more than one year**				
4 Sch 59(a)	Amounts owed by fellow subsidiary undertakings	**500**	500	**500**	500
	Other debtors (see (a) below)	**10**	9	**10**	9
		510	509	**510**	509
	Amounts falling due within one year				
	Trade debtors	**6,271**	5,699	**2,341**	2,205
4 Sch Formats	Amounts recoverable on contracts	**480**	675	**320**	450
4 Sch 59(b)	Amounts owed by subsidiary undertakings	**-**	-	**1,092**	873
SSAP 1 para 29	Amounts owed by associated undertakings	**23**	42	**-**	-
	Other debtors-loan to a director (see (b) below)	**6**	6	**6**	6
4 Sch Note 6	Prepayments and accrued income	**1,249**	1,795	**406**	375
		8,029	8,217	**4,165**	3,909
		8,539	8,726	**4,675**	4,418

6 Sch 28,29 (a) Other debtors at 31 December 1992 include £7,000 in respect of loans to two officers of the company.

6 Sch 15,22 (b) The loan to a director is a bridging loan to Mr G Wallace, the marketing director. The loan was made prior to his appointment as a director and is unsecured, does not carry interest, and is repayable on demand. The loan started and ended the year at £6,000.

23 Current asset investments

4 Sch 45(1)(2) Current asset investments, which are stated at cost, relate to a holding of British Government Securities, with a market value of £183,000 (1991: £270,000). These securities are listed on The International Stock Exchange.

24 Creditors: amounts falling due within one year

		Group		**Company**	
		1992	1991	**1992**	1991
		£'000	£'000	**£'000**	£'000
4 Sch Formats					
	Debenture loans	**300**	-	**300**	-
	Bank loans and overdrafts	**336**	420	**95**	42
SSAP 21 para 51	Obligations under finance leases	**102**	76	**-**	-
4 Sch Note 8,	Payments received on account	**50**	25	**50**	25
SSAP 9 para 30(b)	Trade creditors	**4,106**	5,552	**1,639**	2,974
	Amounts owed to group undertakings:				
4 Sch 59(a)	Parent company and fellow subsidiary undertakings	**725**	637	**297**	186
4 Sch 59(b)	Subsidiary undertakings	**-**	-	**339**	325
SSAP 1 para 29	Amounts owed to associated undertakings	**193**	177	**98**	142
	Corporation tax:				
	Payable 30 September 1993	**715**	733	**386**	379
SSAP 8 para 26	Advance corporation tax	**246**	246	**244**	244
4 Sch Note 9	Other taxation and social security	**239**	186	**121**	117
	Other creditors	**-**	-	**-**	-
4 Sch Note 10	Accruals	**730**	799	**579**	408
4 Sch 51(3)	Dividends payable	**677**	678	**677**	678
SSAP 8 para 26					
		8,419	9,529	**4,825**	5,520

Debenture loans represents 6½% unsecured loan stock which is redeemable at par on 1 July 1993.

4 Sch 48(4) The bank loans and overdrafts are secured by floating charges over the assets of GAAP UK plc, Chaucer Limited, Dickens Limited and Austen Inc.

Payments received on account include payments in relation to long-term contracts insofar as they are not offset against long-term contract balances (see note 21).

25 Creditors: amounts falling due after more than one year

		Group		Company	
		1992	1991	**1992**	1991
		£'000	£'000	**£'000**	£'000
4 Sch Formats					
	Debenture loans	**4,900**	4,200	**1,200**	200
	Bank loans	**1,200**	1,200	**800**	800
SSAP 21 para 51	Obligations under finance leases	**475**	480	**-**	-
4 Sch 59(b)	Amounts owed to subsidiary undertakings	**-**	-	**1,000**	1,000
		6,575	5,880	**3,000**	2,000
	Debenture loans				
Co 21 (f)	Debenture loans are repayable as follows:				
	In one year or less	**300**	-	**300**	-
	Between one and two years	**-**	300	**-**	-
	Between two and five years	**4,700**	3,000	**1,000**	-
	In five years or more	**200**	900	**200**	200
		5,200	4,200	**1,500**	200
4 Sch 48(1)	Repayable otherwise than by instalments in more than five years:				
4 Sch 48(2)	11¾% unsecured loan stock 1997	**-**	700	**-**	-
4 Sch 48(1)	Repayable by instalments wholly or partly in more than five years:				
4 Sch Note 7	14% convertible unsecured loan stock 1998/2005 (see below)	**200**	200	**200**	200

4 Sch 41(1) During the year the company issued £1,000,000 12% unsecured loan stock 1995, at par, in order to finance medium term working capital requirements.

4 Sch 48(2) Each holder of the 14% convertible unsecured loan stock 1998/2005 has the right, on the dates and at the rates set out below, on giving notice in writing during the month of August in each year, to convert loan stock (being £1 stock or a multiple thereof) into ordinary shares of 25p each, fully paid of GAAP UK plc:

	Number of ordinary shares of 25p each receivable for every £100 loan stock
28 August 1998	200
28 August 1999	190
28 August 2000	180

Bank loans and overdrafts

		Group		Company	
		1992	1991	**1992**	1991
		£'000	£'000	**£'000**	£'000
CO 21(f)	Bank loans and overdrafts are repayable as follows:				
	In one year or less	**336**	420	**95**	42
	Between one and two years	**200**	-	**200**	-
	Between two and five years	**680**	640	**600**	600
	In five years or more	**320**	560	**-**	200
4 Sch 48(1)		**1,536**	1,620	**895**	842
	Repayable by instalments wholly or partly in more than five years:				
	7% unsecured loan repayable by annual instalments of £200,000 commencing in February 1995	**-**	800	**-**	800
	Mortgages at 5¾% and 12% repayable by instalments falling due for payment between 1 January 1997 and 30 June 2010, secured on the freehold properties of the companies concerned	**400**	400	**-**	-
		400	1,200	**-**	800

Finance leases

The net finance lease obligations to which the group is committed are:

		1992	1991
		£'000	£'000
SSAP 21 para 52	In one year or less	**102**	76
	Between one and two years	**102**	76
	Between two and five years	**286**	298
	Over five years	**87**	106
		577	556

4 Sch 48(1)(b) The total value of leases repayable by instalments, any part of which falls due after more than five years, is £492,000 (1991: £378,000).

26 Provisions for liabilities and charges

Group

		Pensions and similar obligations (see note 28) £'000	Deferred taxation (see below) £'000	Total £'000
4 Sch 50(4)	At 1 January 1992	103	8,474	8,577
4 Sch 46,47	Profit and loss account	552	(177)	375
	Contributions paid to pension schemes	(94)	-	(94)
	At 31 December 1992	**561**	**8,297**	**8,858**

Company

		Pensions and similar obligations £'000	Deferred taxation £'000	Total £'000
4 Sch 46	At 1 January 1992	-	3,955	3,955
	Profit and loss account	-	(99)	(99)
	At 31 December 1992	**-**	**3,856**	**3,856**

Deferred taxation

Deferred taxation provided in the financial statements, and the amount unprovided of the total potential liability, are as follows:

Group

		Amount provided		Amount unprovided	
		1992 £'000	1991 £'000	**1992 £'000**	1991 £'000
SSAP 15 paras 37, 42	Tax effect of timing differences because of:				
	Excess of tax allowances over depreciation	**8,600**	8,746	**1,379**	697
	Other	**(57)**	(26)	**-**	-
		8,543	8,720	**1,379**	697
SSAP 8 para 27	Less: advance corporation tax	**(246)**	(246)	**-**	-
		8,297	8,474	**1,379**	697

The group's medium-term plans show that the amount of tax allowances in respect of eligible new plant and machinery to be acquired will fall short of the charge for depreciation on existing and new assets. Accordingly deferred tax is provided in respect of the estimated amount of this deficiency.

FRS 2 para 54 No provision is made for taxation liabilities which would arise on the distribution of profits retained by overseas subsidiaries because there is no intention in the foreseeable future that such profits will be remitted.

SSAP 15 para 41 If any of the properties were realised at the amounts included in the balance sheet, in view of the group's policy of expansion and continued ownership of its assets it would be necessary to replace them by purchasing similar property; rollover relief would therefore be available. Accordingly, the revalued amounts do not constitute timing differences as defined by Statement of Standard Accounting Practice 15, and the potential amount of deferred tax if they were to be disposed of has not therefore been quantified.

Company

		Amount provided		Amount unprovided	
		1992	1991	**1992**	1991
		£'000	£'000	**£'000**	£'000
SSAP 15 paras 37 to 42	Tax effect of timing differences because of: Excess of tax allowances over depreciation	**4,106**	4,187	**1,532**	432
	Other	**(6)**	12	**-**	-
		4,100	4,199	**1,532**	432
SSAP 8 para 27	Less: advance corporation tax	**(244)**	(244)	**-**	-
		3,856	3,955	**1,532**	432

27 Accruals and deferred income

		£'000
SSAP 4 para 25, 28(b)	**Government grants**	
	At 1 January 1992	2,000
	Amortisation in year	(1,000)
	At 31 December 1992	**1,000**

A regional development grant of £4,000,000 in 1990 was received as a contribution towards the cost of purchasing certain plant and machinery for the electronics factory in Newcastle. The grant is being amortised over four years, the estimated useful life of the plant.

28 Pension and similar obligations

SSAP 24 para 88

The group operates a number of pension schemes in the United Kingdom and overseas. The major schemes, which cover 85% of scheme members, are of the defined benefit type. With the exception of the main scheme in Germany, the assets of the schemes are held in separate trustee administered funds.

The total pension cost for the group was £552,000 (1991: £851,000) of which £140,000 (1991: £135,000) relates to the overseas schemes. The pension cost relating to the United Kingdom schemes is assessed in accordance with the advice of an independent qualified actuary using the attained age method. The latest actuarial valuation of those schemes was at 31 December 1991. The assumptions that have the most significant effect on the valuation are those relating to the rate of return on investments, rate of increase in dividends and the rates of increase in salaries and pensions. It was assumed that the investment return would be 6% per annum, dividend increases would be 5% per annum, that salary increases would average 4% per annum and that present and future pensions would increase at the rate of 3% per annum. The cost has fallen as a result of the amortisation of an experience surplus shown by the latest valuation. The surplus is being amortised over 10 years (the expected average remaining service lives of the employees).

At the date of the latest actuarial valuation, the market value of the assets of the United Kingdom schemes was £20.1 million and the actuarial value of the assets was sufficient to cover 120% of the benefits which had accrued to members, after allowing for expected future increases in earnings. This surplus will be eliminated by 1994 as a result of a pensions holiday taken by the group on the recommendation of the actuary.

The element of the total pension cost relating to overseas schemes includes £28,000 (1991: £25,000) where the charge has been determined in accordance with local best practice and regulations.

An amount of £561,000 (1991: £103,000) is included in provisions, which represents the excess of the accumulated pension cost over the payment of contributions to pension funds.

UITF Abs 6

In addition to pension benefits, all of the 162 full-time US employees become eligible for healthcare and life insurance benefits upon retirement. The cost of providing these benefits is recognised as an expense in the year payments are made. The introduction of UITF 6 requires the present value of such benefits to be accrued over the working life of the employee. This requirement must be implemented in the accounts for 1994 onwards. No provision for future benefits has been included in these accounts as the company is currently renegotiating the extant schemes and an actuarial valuation of the present value of the benefits will need to be determined. Current estimates lie between £1m and £1.8m. The full amount of these benefits would attract tax relief. The amount charged to the profit and loss account in the year was £34,000 (1991: £32,000).

29 Called up share capital

		1992 £'000	1991 £'000
4 Sch 38(1)(a)	**Authorised**		
	56,000,000 ordinary shares of 25p each	**14,000**	14,000
	1,200,000 5.6% cumulative redeemable preference shares of £1 each	**1,200**	1,200
		15,200	15,200
4 Sch 38(1)(b)	**Allotted, called up and fully paid**		
4 Sch Note 12	39,842,333 (1991: 38,744,000) ordinary shares of 25p each	**9,961**	9,686
	1,200,000 (1991: 1,200,000) 5.6% cumulative redeemable preference shares of £1 each	**1,200**	1,200
		11,161	10,886

4 Sch 38(2) The preference shares may be redeemed, at the shareholders' option, between 1 July 1999 and 30 June 2000 at a premium of 10p per share or, if still outstanding on 30 June 2000, must then be redeemed at par.

4 Sch 39 Details of the company's share issue to acquire Dickens Limited are set out in note 31.

30 Options in shares of GAAP UK plc

4 Sch 40 Options have been granted for 25p ordinary shares as follows:

Number of shares	Subscription price per share	Period within which options exercisable
45,000	63p	Before 1 March 1995
15,000	65p	Before 1 June 1995

31 Acquisitions

4A Sch 13
5 Sch 29(2)
SSAP 23 paras 21, 22
SSAP 22 para 47

On 1 March 1992 the company acquired the whole of the issued share capital of Dickens Limited for a total consideration of £859,000. The consideration was satisfied by the issue of 1,098,333 ordinary shares of 25p each having a value of 60p each and cash amounting to £200,000. The company has taken merger relief on the issue of its shares and the group has used acquisition accounting to account for the purchase.

FRS 3 para 14
SSAP 23 para 22

As a result of the acquisition of Dickens Limited turnover increased by £3,544,000 and on operating profit of £161,000 (also see note 4).

4A Sch 13(4) The subsidiary made a profit on ordinary activities before taxation of £29,000 from 1 January 1992, the beginning of the subsidiary's financial year, to the date of acquisition and made a profit of £87,000 for the previous financial year.

4A Sch 13(5)
SSAP 22 para 48

The assets and liabilities of Dickens Limited acquired are set out below:

	Book value £'000	Revaluation £'000	Accounting policy alignment £'000	Fair value to the group £'000
Tangible fixed assets	872	200	-	1,072
Current assets				
Stock	216	-	(10)	206
Debtors	107	-	-	107
Cash at bank and in hand	137	-	-	137
Total assets	**1,332**	**200**	**(10)**	**1,522**
Liabilities				
Creditors	651	-	-	651
Bank overdraft	23	-	-	23
Net assets	**658**	**200**	**(10)**	**848**
Goodwill				11
				859
Satisfied by				
Shares allotted				659
Cash				200
				859

SSAP 22 para 48

Freehold properties acquired were revalued as at 1 March 1992 producing an increase in book value of £200,000.

SSAP 22 para 48
SSAP 23 para 21

The basis of stock valuation was changed from weighted average cost to first in first out, the basis used by the group.

FRS 1 para 42

Dickens Limited contributed £156,000 to the group's net operating cash flows, paid £87,000 in respect of net returns on investments and servicing of finance, paid £18,000 in respect of taxation and utilised £43,000 for investing activities.

Analysis of the net outflow of cash and cash equivalents in respect of the purchase of Dickens Limited

FRS 1 para 40

	£'000
Cash consideration	200
Cash at hand and in bank acquired	(137)
Bank overdrafts acquired	23
Net outflow of cash and cash equivalents in respect of the purchase of Dickens Limited	86

Goodwill

4A Sch 14 The cumulative amount of goodwill resulting from acquisitions which has been written off, after deducting goodwill attributable to subsidiary undertakings disposed of, is set out below:

		£'000
	Net goodwill written off	
	At 1 January 1992	448
SSAP 22 para 52	Eliminated on disposal	(89)
	Charged to profit and loss account in year (see note 12)	100
	Written off to reserves in year	11
	At 31 December 1992	**470**

SSAP 22 para 47 In accordance with the group's accounting policy, the goodwill arising on consolidation of £11,000 has been written off against the merger reserve arising on consolidation. Goodwill eliminated on disposal of £89,000 and included in the profit on sale represents the purchased goodwill attributable to Shakespeare Limited which was written off to reserves in 1988 (see note 32). UITF Abs 3

32 Disposals

4A Sch 15 During the year the group sold Shakespeare Limited.

		£'000
	Net assets disposed of	
	Stocks	197
	Debtors	303
UITF Abs 3	Goodwill previously written off to reserves	89
		589
SSAP 22 para 52	Profit on disposal	265
FRS 1 para 40	**Satisfied by cash**	**854**

FRS 1 para 42 Shakespeare Limited contributed £210,000 to the net operating cash flows, paid £40,000 in respect of net returns on investments and servicing of finance and £71,000 in respect of taxation.

33 Share premium account and reserves

	Group	Share premium account £'000	Revaluation reserve £'000	Merger reserve £'000	Profit and loss account £'000
4 Sch 46	At 1 January 1992 as previously stated	1,523	5,865	-	3,315
FRS 3 para 29	Prior year adjustment (see note 17)	-	-	-	(124)
4 Sch 46	At 1 January 1992 as restated	1,523	5,865	-	3,191
SSAP 20 para 60	Exchange difference	-	23	-	154
s 130	Expenses of share issue	(11)	-	-	-
	Arising on acquisition in year	-	-	384	-
	Goodwill written off (see note 31)	-	-	(11)	-
	Goodwill on disposal	-	-	-	89
	Surplus arising on revaluation of investment properties and land and buildings	-	612	-	-
	Transfer from revaluation reserve to profit and loss account	-	(1,074)	-	1,074
	Tax on realisation of revaluation surpluses	-	-	-	(110)
	Retained profit for the year	-	-	-	1,189
	At 31 December 1992	**1,512**	**5,426**	**373**	**5,587**

SSAP 1 para 31	**Group's share of post acquisition reserves of associated undertakings included above**				
	At 1 January 1992	-	-	-	59
	Retained profit for the year	-	-	-	40
	At 31 December 1992	-	-	-	**99**

	Company	Share premium account £'000	Profit and loss account £'000
4 Sch 46	At 1 January 1992	1,523	1,876
	Expenses of share issue	(11)	-
	Retained profit for the year	-	730
	At 31 December 1992	**1,512**	**2,606**

SSAP 19 para 13 The revaluation reserve includes £40,000 (1991: £50,000) in respect of surpluses on the annual revaluation of investment properties.

The merger reserve was created on the issue of shares in GAAP UK plc to acquire Dickens Limited.

Not statutory

The amount of the reserves of GAAP UK plc that may legally be distributed under section 264 of the Companies Act 1985 is £2,589,000 (1991: £1,812,000).

34 Reconciliation of movements in shareholders' funds

	1992 £'000	1991 as restated £'000
Profit for the financial year	**2,232**	(5,379)
Dividends	**(1,043)**	(939)
	1,189	(6,378)
Other recognised gains and losses relating to the year (net)	**679**	82
New share capital issued	**275**	102
Expenses of share issue	**(11)**	-
Goodwill acquired during the year	**(11)**	(35)
Merger reserve arising on acquisition	**384**	-
Goodwill transferred to the profit and loss account in respect of disposals of business	**89**	-
Net addition to shareholders' funds	**2,594**	(6,229)
Opening shareholders' funds (originally £21,589,000 before deducting prior year adjustments of £124,000)	**21,465**	27,694
Closing shareholders' funds	**24,059**	21,465

35 Cash and cash equivalents

FRS 1 para 44

	1992 £'000	1991 £'000
Changes during the year		
At 1 January	**(234)**	(1,269)
Net cash inflow before adjustments for the effects of foreign exchange rates	**1,581**	1,013
Effect of foreign exchange rates	**(83)**	22
At 31 December	**1,264**	(234)

FRS 1 para 44

	1992 £'000	1991 £'000	1992 Change in year £'000	1991 £'000	1990 £'000	1991 Change in year £'000
Analysis of balances						
Cash at bank and in hand	**1,600**	86	**1,514**	86	259	(173)
Bank overdrafts	**(336)**	(320)	**(16)**	(320)	(1,528)	1,208
At 31 December	**1,264**	(234)	**1,498**	(234)	(1,269)	1,035

36 Analysis of changes in financing during the year

		1992 Share capital (including premium) £'000	1992 Loans and finance lease obligations £'000	1991 Share capital (including premium) £'000	1991 Loans and finance lease obligations £'000
FRS 1 para 44	At 1 January	**12,409**	**6,056**	12,307	4,097
	Expenses of share issue	**(11)**	**-**	-	-
	Cash inflows from financing	**-**	**1,000**	-	2,000
	Shares issued for non-cash consideration	**275**	**-**	102	-
	Loan repayment	**-**	**(100)**	-	-
	Inception of finance lease contracts	**-**	**157**	-	76
	Repayments of principal on finance leases	**-**	**(136)**	-	(117)
	At 31 December	**12,673**	**6,977**	12,409	6,056

37 Major non-cash transactions

FRS 1 para 43 During the year the group entered into finance lease arrangements in respect of fixed assets with a total capital value at the inception of the leases of £157,000.

Part of the consideration for the purchase of Dickens Limited comprised shares. Further details of the acquisition are set out in note 31.

38 Post balance sheet events

Details of post balance sheet events are given in the directors' report.

39 Capital commitments

		Group 1992 £'000	Group 1991 £'000	Company 1992 £'000	Company 1991 £'000
4 Sch 50(3)	Capital expenditure that has been contracted for but has not been provided for in the financial statements	**600**	2,280	**250**	530
4 Sch 50(3)	Capital expenditure that has been authorised by the directors but has not yet been contracted for	**290**	1,580	**170**	590
SSAP 21 para 54	Commitments under finance leases entered into, but not yet provided for in the financial statements	**94**	-	**20**	-

40 Contingent liabilities

		Group		Company	
		1992	1991	**1992**	1991
		£'000	£'000	**£'000**	£'000
4 Sch 50(2)	Amount of guarantees in respect of bank overdrafts of associated undertakings	**400**	550	**200**	350

41 Financial commitments

SSAP 21 para 56 At 31 December 1992 the group had annual commitments under non-cancellable operating leases as follows:

	1992		1991	
	Land and Buildings	**Other**	Land and Buildings	Other
	£'000	**£'000**	£'000	£'000
Expiring within one year	**10**	**42**	8	36
Expiring between two and five years inclusive	**26**	**163**	28	138
Expiring in over five years	**32**	**11**	34	18
	68	**216**	70	192

42 Ultimate parent company

5 Sch 30,31 The directors regard Trollope plc, a company registered in England and Wales, as the ultimate parent company. According to the register kept by the company, Trollope plc has a 55% interest in the equity capital of GAAP UK plc at 2 March 1993. Copies of the parent's consolidated financial statements may be obtained from The Secretary, Trollope plc, 3 Large Square, London EC1Z 4EP.

Summary of accounts for the five years ended 31 December 1992

	1988 £'000	1989 £'000	1990 £'000	1991 £'000	**1992 £'000**
	as restated				
Sales and results					
Turnover					
Continuing operations	41,772	43,235	50,629	50,704	**63,590**
Discontinued operations	-	2,077	-	3,120	**2,130**
	41,772	45,312	50,629	53,824	**65,720**
Operating profit					
Continuing operations	2,332	2,323	3,016	3,176	**3,408**
Discontinued operations	-	157	-	(25)	**192**
	2,332	2,480	3,016	3,151	**3,600**
Profit/(loss) on sale/termination of operations	-	-	-	(7,988)	**265**
Provisions for fundamental restructuring	-	(202)	-	-	**-**
Other income and expenses	50	31	29	97	**188**
Profit/(loss) on ordinary activities before interest	2,382	2,309	3,045	(4,740)	**4,053**
Interest payable and similar charges	(503)	(498)	(531)	(639)	**(734)**
Profit before taxation	1,879	1,811	2,514	(5,379)	**3,319**
Taxation	(752)	(657)	(761)	(806)	**(650)**
Profit after taxation	1,127	1,154	1,753	(6,185)	**2,669**
Minority interests	(87)	(83)	(151)	746	**(437)**
Attributable profit/(loss)	1,040	1,071	1,602	(5,439)	**2,232**
Dividends	(483)	(466)	(722)	(939)	**(1,043)**
Retained profit/(loss)	557	605	880	(6,378)	**1,189**
Net assets employed					
Fixed assets	29,501	30,776	37,582	32,294	**32,880**
Net current assets	5,436	7,803	6,959	7,534	**9,707**
	34,937	38,579	44,541	39,828	**42,587**
Non-current liabilities	(1,986)	(6,358)	(5,235)	(5,880)	**(6,575)**
Provisions for liabilities and charges including deferred tax and pensions	(6,655)	(6,747)	(8,612)	(8,577)	**(8,858)**
Deferred income	-	-	(3,000)	(2,000)	**(1,000)**
	26,296	25,474	27,694	23,371	**26,154**
Ratios					
Operating margin (continuing operations)	5.6%	5.4%	6.0%	6.3%	**5.4%**
Return on capital employed	6.1%	5.8%	7.1%	(12.1)%	**9.8%**
Earnings per ordinary share	2.51p	2.71p	3.96p	(14.21)p	**5.46p**
Adjusted earnings per ordinary share	2.51p	3.11p	3.96p	4.06p	**4.95p**
Dividends per ordinary share	1.07p	1.03p	1.69p	2.25p	**2.46p**

The restated figures fully comply with the requirements of FRS 3, except in respect of discontinued operations in 1988, where best estimates have been used.

Index